Actuality and Provisionality

Eternity and Election in the Theology of Karl Barth

John Colwell

WIPF & STOCK · Eugene, Oregon

Wipf and Stock Publishers
199 W 8th Ave, Suite 3
Eugene, OR 97401

Actuality and Provisionality
Eternity and Election in the Theology of Karl Bart
By Colwell, John

ISBN 13: 978-1-61097-125-6
Publication date 5/1/2011
Previously published by Rutherford House Books, 1989

FOREWORD

Readers of Dr Colwell's book will be reminded, if ever they had been in danger of forgetting, what a remarkable theological achievement is that of Karl Barth. Barth's continuing claim for attention rests in large part upon his achievement in rethinking and reordering many of the central topics of Christian dogmatics. At the very heart of his work is an enterprise which has caused, and will continue to cause, great controversy, alike on what we have misleadingly come to call the 'left' and the 'right'. He has not only centred on Jesus Christ the weight of the eternal God's relations with his world, and particularly his human world, but by means of that centring has forged new conceptions of who is the God whom Christians worship.

The reconceiving led to one of the most remarkable transformation in the history of theology. At the heart of it is the way in which the old 'Calvinist' (but, in fact, Augustinian) doctrine of predestination is changed from what we all know so well – at least in parody – into the eternal choice which God makes in eternity to elect his Son, and with him all humankind, into covenant relation.

Similarly, Barth's concentration on the sheer *actuality* of God's gracious and dynamic action led to changes in both the method and the content of theology. His single-minded achievement inevitably brought in its train both acclaim and criticism. On the negative side it has been contended both that the logic if not the actual content of the theology tends towards a determinist universalism, according to which we are all hurried willy-nilly to heaven; and that Barth's theology of eternity repeats the traditional western inability to guarantee the full reality of time, freedom and history. On the positive side, Barth's theology has been celebrated as a real move towards overcoming the heart of the difficulty.

John Colwell's achievement is a scholarly and illuminating investigation of some of the central areas of contention. The author is particularly careful to discover what Barth means, and picks his way with great skill through conceptual minefields like that concerning the relation of economic and immanent Trinity. His scholarship provides him with the basis for some sharp observations about the more sweeping criticisms of Barth, and shows that this supposedly 'extreme' theologian produces a far more nuanced and subtle account of such topics as the relations of incarnation and atonement, creation and redemption, grace and freedom, than do those who have read and moved rapidly on to provide their own one-sided 'improvements'. Moltmann and Pannenberg, in particular, come in for interesting and pointed questioning.

Here is not, however, an uncritical celebration of Barth. The near scholarly consensus that Barth's chief weakness lies in pneumatology is shared, though whether the cause is, as suggested, a 'hesitance' or 'reticence' about the Spirit, caused by proper caution about subjectivist excesses in Barth's (and our) past and present; or whether the roots go far deeper in the Christian tradition, is a question that will long occupy theology. However that may be, the publication of this work is to be much welcomed both as a valuable contribution to Barth scholarship and as an encouragement to future work – to that 'theology after Barth', which Dr Colwell commends in his concluding comments.

Colin Gunton
King's College, London

Table of Contents

Actuality and Provisionality

Preface to the 2011 Reprint Edition

It would be an understatement to say that I was surprised, albeit pleasantly surprised, to discover a research student at St Andrew's University referring to this dissertation over twenty years after it was written and almost twenty years since it was first published. I was therefore even more surprised to be approached by a publisher wanting to re-print the work. Much can happen in twenty years and I am grateful for the opportunity to pen a preface to what otherwise remains unchanged.

My interests have developed and broadened in these twenty years, I certainly do not consider myself a Barth scholar, and I wouldn't be tempted to re-write the dissertation. Nor, even if I had the time and the desire, would I consider that much needed to be changed. Though (I hope) my style of writing has improved with the years and though I remain embarrassed that this was ever published in unrevised dissertation format, my basic analysis of Barth remains unchanged: I continue to hold that his rejection of universalism is coherent and persuasive once his distinctive account of divine election is understood in the light of his similarly distinctive account of eternity. The eternal decree that is Jesus Christ himself cannot be left behind by time; eternity cannot be reduced to mere everlastingness and an eternal decision cannot be relegated as solely a past event. For Karl Barth divine election is the living event of the Holy Trinity, the defining event of God's being and nature, the eternal decision of the Father which is the true deity and true humanity of the Son made present and future to us by the Spirit. That Barth's account of the Spirit begs for greater definition is, I think, undeniable, but that the contours of his account are evident enough, despite their too common misrepresentation, should similarly be acknowledged.

Beyond the embarrassments of style there are a couple of respects in which I believe I was mistaken in my work. In chapter six and again in the conclusion of the dissertation I believe I may be guilty of confusing, or at least blurring, the distinction between that work of the Spirit that renders us Christians, witnesses to Christ, and that work of the Spirit that renders us ontically elect: the confusion may be understandable but, for Barth, these two dynamics are not the same. This misapprehension is related to another and perhaps deeper failing of the thesis (and where it may be as well that I was not my own examiner) namely the failure to take significant account of the development of Barth's thinking within the *Church Dogmatics*; my concern to hear Barth across the *Dogmatics* obscured the degree to which his ideas were modified and revised over the years of writing. Having admitted the failing, I do not think his understanding of these particular themes of eternity and election were subject to much revision (at least from *CD* II/1 onwards) but my analysis is weakened by my failure to raise the question and by the uncritical ease with which I move between the volumes of the *Dogmatics*.

Discussion of development in Barth, together with subsequent debate concerning the doctrine of election and the humanity of Christ, principally through the work of Bruce McCormack and of those responding to him, probably constitute the most significant questions concerning Barth's contribution since *Actuality and Provisionality* was first published.[1] A short Preface

---

1 See especially Bruce L. McCormack, *Karl Barth's Critical Realistic Dialectical Theology: its genesis and development 1909-1936* (Oxford: Clarendon Press, 1995) and also his essay 'Grace and Being: The Role of God's Gracious Election in Karl Barth's Theological Ontology' in John Webster (ed.), *The Cambridge Companion to Karl Barth* (Cambridge: Cambridge University Press, 2000), 92-110; also Paul D. Molnar, *Divine Freedom and the Doctrine of the Immanent Trinity: in Dialogue with Karl Barth and Contemporary Theology* (London: T & T Clark, 2002).

of this kind is inadequate even to outline these debates, less still to respond to them in anything other than cursory manner. However his critics may view its significance, Barth himself seemed to view his work on Anselm as a turning point (or at least a focal point) in his development[2] - but this is not to deny the significance of a marked turning point between the Prolegomena to the *Church Dogmatics* (I/1) and his treatment of the Doctrine of God (II/1), a turning point perhaps more significant than that between the *Christlichen Dogmatik* and the *Kirchliche Dogmatik.* Nor is it to deny the significance of developments later within the *Church Dogmatics,* for instance in his understanding of sacramentality. It is in this latter respect that I now find myself an ardent critic of the later Barth: my concern now would not so much be to defend him from the charge of universalism as to regret the degree to which the promise of God's presence to us in Holy Baptism and Holy Communion are undermined by the time we arrive at the end of volume four of the *Dogmatics.* The focus on prayer in the projected fourth part of this fourth volume is perceptive and a welcome enhancement of sacramental understanding, but this seems to be achieved at the expense of any genuinely sacramental expectation of a promised presence: as the *Dogmatics* proceeds Barth increasingly reduces Christian expectation to that of an unmediated (and arbitrary) immediacy.[3] In this respect, sadly, Barth falls to precisely the insightful criticism levelled

---

2 Karl Barth, *Anselm: Fides Quaerens Intellectum – Anselm's Proof of the Existence of God in the Context of his Theological Scheme,* trans. Ian W. Robertson (London: SCM Press, 1960)

3 For an elaboration of this criticism see my *Promise and Presence: an exploration of sacramental theology* (Milton Keynes: Paternoster, 2005).

by Robert Jenson against Jonathan Edwards,[4] a criticism that can be levelled against so much of the Pietism and Liberalism from which, in so many other respects, Barth distances himself. In his gradual rejection of any ecclessially and sacramentally mediated presence Barth, as much as the tradition he repudiates, effectively privatises Christian faith and experience and, to this degree, his *Dogmatics* reverts to being more *Christlichen* than *Kirchlichen*. That which is forfeited by the end of volume four of the *Dogmatics* is precisely that ecclesial rootedness that Barth previously had been so concerned to embrace. Finally the question to be posed to Barth is not that of a presumptuous and universal assurance but rather the question of whether there can be any embodied token of assurance at all.

John E. Colwell
Trinity 2010.

4 Robert W. Jenson, *America's Theologian: A Recommendation of Jonathan Edwards* (Oxford: OUP, 1988).

Preface

In declaring this dissertation to be entirely the outcome of my own reflection and study rather than the result of any form of collaboration I am glad, nonetheless, to express my gratitude to those who have encouraged, stimulated and supported me during the process of research. Firstly, I am indebted to my supervisor, Dr. Colin E. Gunton, for his patience, encouragement, advice and criticism throughout the years of preparation. I have also benefitted greatly from correspondence and conversations with Professor T. F. Torrance, Dr. R. H. Roberts, Dr. John B. Webster and Dr. D. Bruce Milne. Particularly I thank Dr. David F. Ford and Dr. Richard H. Roberts for making available to me unpublished theses at the initial stage of my study. I am grateful to the Council of Spurgeon's College, the Grants Committee of the Baptist Union, the Trustees of Dr. Williams's Trust and the members of Maldon Baptist Church without whose financial and practical support this project would have been impossible. I am indebted to Mrs Beryl Glanville for the present typescript (and to my wife for its predecessors) but above all I am grateful to my wife, family and friends for their patience, toleration and practical assistance.

John E Colwell Easter 1985.

List of Abbreviations

C.D. — Church Dogmatics, vols. I - IV, Eng. trans. eds. G. W. Bromiley and T. F. Torrance (Edinburgh, 1956-1975).

J.T.S. — The Journal of Theological Studies (Clarendon Press, Oxford).

Rel.St. — Religious Studies (Cambridge University Press, Cambridge).

S.J.T. — Scottish Journal of Theology (Scottish Academic Press, Edinburgh).

Introduction

It is the habit of some when reading a novel to turn at once to the final chapter to see how the matter will end. This thesis is certainly no novel (though there are those, regretfully, who would view Barth's theology as fiction), but, even if it were, the practice would be unproductive since the conclusion of this thesis is given, not so much to summarize the preceding interpretation as to reflect upon the requirements for doing the work of theology 'after' Barth in the light of the preceding interpretation. It is therefore all the more apposite that this Introduction should give some indication of the direction which the following discussion is intended to take.

How ought Barth's theology to be interpreted? Initially there were those who enthusiastically and uncritically embraced his teaching, were dubbed 'Barthians', and were promptly and prudently disowned by their namesake. Conversely there have been and still are those who presume to dismiss Barth and his thought as an irrelevant albeit lengthy footnote in the historical development of theology. Such unqualified approval or dismissal usually springs from an over-hasty and simplistic reading of Barth, or perhaps no direct reading of Barth at all. As the conclusion of this thesis suggests, its aim is neither to ignore Barth nor simply to repeat him but to attempt to understand him and to develop the work of theology in the light of his massive contribution.

There have been several attempts (of which some are referred to in the course of this thesis) to reduce Barth's thought to a single, all-pervading theme. Confronted by such a vast edifice it is certainly tempting to do so. Yet this approach involves the liability of imposing such a theme upon Barth instead of attentively listening to him. Moreover, the flaw of this approach is that Barth's theology plainly cannot be reduced in this way, its dialectic roots are constantly betrayed by irresolvable tensions, tensions which many of his critics insist upon resolving in one way or another.

It may appear that this thesis has adopted this latter approach but that is certainly not its intention. There has been no conscious attempt to reduce Barth's theology to any all-pervading theme or to impose upon it any pre-conceived structure. Rather this thesis attempts critically to consider two key and interrelated aspects of Barth's thought, not as themes to which his whole theology can be reduced but as a framework through which it can be reviewed.

Barth's concept of eternity and his doctrine of Election lead to the very centre of his understanding of the being, will and action of God. Barth's doctrine of Election, more than any other word that can be said, recounts to us who this God is and what

He does. Barth's concept of eternity informs us where this being, will and action of God is to be temporally located. It is the aim of this thesis not only to interpret these two aspects of Barth's thought but particularly to clarify the manner in which the latter informs the former. Indeed, it is the contention of this thesis that Barth's distinctive understanding of the doctrine of Election is determined as much by his concept of eternity as it is by his concern for Christocentricity.

Moreover, while Barth's theology may not be reduced to a single theme, the exposition of these interrelated aspects of his thought will expose the common and recurring theme of his more perceptive critics:

> "I suspect that it is in wrestling with the problems of presence and completion that one faces the deepest theological problems in the Dogmatics......
> They arise in his anthropology......
> They arise in his orientation of all world history to the one history of Jesus Christ.....
> They arise in the questioning of commentators such as W. Pannenberg, J. Moltmann, and R. Jenson......"[1]

It is hoped that this thesis may contribute in some way to relieving this common sense of unease, not by means of any innovation but by making explicit that which is at least implicit within the structure of Barth's own dogmatic thought; by indicating

---

1) David Ford, 'Barth's interpretation of the Bible' in Karl Barth: Studies of his Theological Method, ed. S. W. Sykes (Oxford, 1979), pp.55-87 (pp.84f.).

a direction through the impasse of any apparent ambiguity in Barth's thought, a direction already pursued in some respects by some of Barth's critics, notably Eberhard Jüngel.

I The Concept of Eternity and the Doctrine of God

a) Concepts of Eternity and theological method:

The central themes of Karl Barth's mature theological thought derive in essence from his adoption of a theological method radically distinct from the Liberalism which dominated the theology of the 19th century. In a postscript to a celebratory collection of Schleiermacher texts within which, with characteristic humour, he surveys his uneasy but compelling relationship with this "Father of the 19th (and also the 20th!?) century Church", Barth traces the developments which influenced his change of mind and initiated this new theological direction.[1] During his period of study at Berlin Barth had already been introduced to the thought of Schleiermacher alongside a study of Wilhelm Herrmann's Ethics, but the opportunity to pursue this approach to systematic theology under Herrmann's supervision at Marburg confirmed Barth as an enthusiastic heir of the German Liberal tradition.[2] Karl Barth's father, Johann Friedrich ("Fritz") Barth, who had encouraged his son's studies at Berne, accepted their continuation at Berlin as a compromise arrangement and insistently advised a semester in the "positive" atmosphere of Tübingen, strongly resisted this move to Marburg and a theological

---

1) Karl Barth, 'Nachwort' in Schleiermacher - Auswahl mit einem Nachwort von Karl Barth, ed. Heinz Bolli (München u. Hamburg, 1968), pp.290-312

2) ibid., p.291

approach so contrary to his own "positive" stance.[3] The death of Fritz Barth within a year of his son's commencement of pastoral duties at Safenwil may have had a more profound psychological effect on Karl Barth than he realized at the time, initiating a questioning of the theological liberalism which he had so fervently embraced and of which his father was so deeply suspicious.[4] Certainly the horrific discovery of the names of almost all of his German teachers among the "93 German Intellectual" signatories identifying with the Kaiser's war policy compounded Barth's disillusionment:

> "With this and with the other material which one received from German theologians at that time a whole world of theological exegesis, ethics, dogmatics and preaching which I had so far held to be fundamentally trustworthy began to be shaken to its foundations."5

But perhaps the fundamental and comprehensive factor in Barth's theological transformation was his removal from the sheltered environment of academic study and the position of pasteur suffragent at Geneva to the industrial town of Safenwil and to the total

---

3) ibid., pp.290f.; cf. Eberhard Busch, Karl Barth: His life from letters and autobiographical texts, trans. by John Bowden (London, 1976), pp.40ff.

4) Eberhard Busch, Karl Barth, p.68; cf. Karl Barth, 'Nachwort', pp.294f.

5) Karl Barth, 'Nachwort', p.293, my translation.

demands of a pastoral and preaching ministry:

> "He discovered the complete irrelevance of this religious Christianity for the actual content of most men's lives, the uselessness of talk of "the higher things" or "authentic existence" for the problems of working conditions and elementary justice which plagued his congregation. He sat in his study on Sunday morning, watched the people out walking on their day off, and wondered why they should come in to hear him. He discovered, that is, the same thing that religiously enthusiastic young pastors still regularly discover, and turn to clinical work or non-directive counseling or teaching about religion or a nervous breakdown: that he had nothing much to say."6

This growing sense of unease with theological liberalism prompted Barth, in association with his life-long friend Eduard Thurneysen, to pursue a "wholly other" theological foundation.[7] It was already clear that the future could not rest with the theological inheritance of Schleiermacher[8] and the caricature of the theology of Luther and Calvin which Barth and Thurneysen had derived from their previous studies effectively prevented them from

---

6) R. W. Jenson, God after God: the God of the Past and the God of the Future, seen in the work of Karl Barth (Indianapolis and New York, 1969), pp.5f.; cf. Barth's own sense of dissatisfaction concerning his ministry at Safenwil (Eberhard Busch, Karl Barth, p.64).

7) Karl Barth, 'Nachwort', p.294

8) Karl Barth, 'Evangelical Theology in the 19th Century' in God, Grace and Gospel, trans. by J. S. McNab, Scottish Journal of Theology Occasional Papers, No. 8, ed. T. F. Torrance and J. K. S. Reid (Edinburgh and London, 1959), pp.55-74 (p.58).

immediately seeking a new beginning by a fresh appraisal of the "old orthodoxy". It also became increasingly apparent that the religious socialism of Leonhard Ragaz and Hermann Kutter was, of itself, inadequate for such a reformulation. Though Barth had first been made aware of the claims of religious socialism through the influence of his father it was through his friendship with Thurneysen that he had become better acquainted with the teachings of Hermann Kutter and Christoph Blumhardt "of which hitherto I had only taken incidental notice".[9] Through Kutter Barth "simply learnt to take the great word 'God' onto his lips with renewed earnestness, responsibility and gravity",[10] and from the younger Blumhardt he began to discover the meaning of Christian hope by considering the eschatological nature of Jesus' message. However, while Barth was later to express reservations concerning the dangers of a secularization of the Christian message by religious socialism, the tendency not just to combine but to identify the Socialist expectation with the Christian expectation of the Kingdom of God,[11] he was already

---

9) Karl Barth, 'Nachwort', p.293

10) ibid., my translation.

11) C.D.II.1.p.634

suspicious of certain elements in Kutter's writings.[12]

In fact a new theological basis was discovered simply through the attempt to read and expound the Old and New Testament Scriptures: "they began to speak to us - in a very different way than that which, in the school of what was then 'modern theology', we supposed we should have heard them."[13] In this elementary manner Barth came to recognize the true subject of Scripture's witness: not man and his religion but God and His coming Kingdom.[14] As never before Barth devoted himself to read the text of the letter to the Romans and to write (primarily for his own edification) that which he heard. Certainly this exercise was not without reference to a host of other authors, J. T. Beck, Dostoevsky, Spitteler, Kierkegaard and particularly Franz Overbeck,[15] but Barth's first commitment was to speak unequivocally

---

12) Karl Barth, 'Nachwort', p.294. Certainly the socialist movement continued to be an influence in Barth's thinking but the concensus opinion is clearly correct in regarding as an over-statement the thesis of F. W. Marquardt that Barth's conception of the relationship between Christ and all men derived from his socialist presuppositions (F. W. Marquardt, Theologie und Sozialismus: Das Beispiel Karl Barths (München u. Mainz, 1972); cf. John Thompson, Christ in Perspective: Christological Perspectives in the Theology of Karl Barth (Edinburgh, 1978), pp.148f.) and H. Diem 'Die Christologie Karl Barths in der Sicht von Friedrich Wilhelm Marquardt', Kerygma und Dogma, 20 (1974) 138-157.).

13) Karl Barth, 'Nachwort', p.294; cf. Eberhard Busch, Karl Barth, p.97.

14) R. W. Jenson, God after God, p.6.

15) Karl Barth, 'Nachwort', p.295.

of God and His Godness, His infinite qualitative distance from man's religion, man's ethics, man's culture and from man himself. In contradistinction to his theological inheritance Barth reaffirmed the No of God's Kingdom, concurring with the view of Overbeck that this eschatological No had been betrayed by the religion of historical Christianity;[16] if true Christianity was to be reaffirmed it could only be at the expense of this Christian religion.

One symptom of the inherent subjectivity of 19th century Liberalism was its total evading of the theme of eschatology. To speak of the "last things" is to speak of God Himself, the irreducible subject of the event of His revelation. The possibility of an eschatology implies the possibility of an authentic objective knowledge of God and the abandonment of eschatology by theological Liberalism was indicative of its denial of such a possibility. The attempt to reinterpret theology in terms of the individual's self-consciousness necessitated a symbolic understanding of Biblical statements which expressed the being and activity of God in ontological or historical terms.[17] A similar reduction to subjectivity

---

16) cf. Eberhard Busch, Karl Barth, pp.115f.

17) cf. T.F.Torrance, Karl Barth: An Introduction to his Early Theology, 1910-1931 (London, 1962), pp.73ff.

was characteristic of German Pietism in the 19th century since its emphasis upon the personal nature of religious experience reduced eschatology to a purely individual and inward hope. Through this centrality of individual experience and individual consciousness "personality" (Persönlichkeit) had become the idol of the 19th century.[18] Moreover, while Johannes Weiss and Albert Schweitzer had recognized the eschatological character of the message and ministry of Jesus Christ they had neutralized their discovery by imprisoning it as an aspect of the time conditioning of the Gospel.[19] Barth's reassertion of the eschatological nature of the Christian message in both the first and the second editions of his commentary on Romans was not only a thunderous repudiation of of this religious anthropocentricity, it was also the affirmation of the possibility and actuality of an authentic, objective knowledge of God.[20]

Negatively the intention of "dialectical theology" was to effect a total break from the subjectivsm of 19th century theology

---

18) Karl Barth, Der Römerbrief (first edition) (Berne,1919),p.202 Note Barth's recognition of the coincidence of Liberalism and Pietism (Eberhard Busch, Karl Barth und die Pietisten Die Pietismuskritik des jungen Karl Barth und ihre Erwiderung (München,1978), pp.58ff.).

19) T.F.Torrance, op.cit.,pp.78f.; cf. C.D.II.1.pp.636f.

20) Karl Barth, The Epistle to the Romans translated from the sixth edition by Edwyn C.Hoskyns (Oxford 1933) here-after referred to as Romans. This second edition of Barth's Der Römerbrief, published in 1922 by Christian Kaiser Verlag of Munich, was actually a complete rewriting of his interpretation of the text.

and the tendency to speak of God by speaking of man "in an exalted tone",[21] to exclude every erroneous conception of the continuity between God and man (including the secular optimism of religious socialism) by recognizing the essentially eschatological form of revelation. Questions of human existence and human ethics can only truly be considered from the "ultimate perspective of eternity".[22] In this sense Barth tended towards a conception of eternity in terms of timelessness, an eschatological "Moment" that is transcendentally above man's time:[23]

> "Being the transcendent meaning of all moments, the eternal 'Moment' can be compared with no moment in time."24

Later Barth was to acknowledge the imbalance of this post-temporal conception of eternity though he continued to consider it to be a necessary emphasis in relation to the distorted supra-temporal view of eternity posited by 19th century Liberalism:[25]

> "...we had not seen the biblical conception of eternity in its fulness. The result was that we could not speak about the post-temporality of God in such a way as to make it clear that we actually meant to speak of God and not of a general idea of limit and crisis."26

---

21) Karl Barth, The Humanity of God, trans. by John Newton Thomas and Thomas Wieser (London and Glasgow, 1961), p.36.

22) T. F. Torrance, Karl Barth: An Introduction..., p.63; cf. Karl Barth, Romans, p.449.

23) Karl Barth, Romans, pp.497ff., cf. Karl Barth, The Resurrection of the Dead, trans. by H. J. Stenning (London, 1933), pp.109ff.

24) Karl Barth, Romans, p.498.

25) C.D.II.1.pp.634ff.; cf. Karl Barth, The Humanity of God, pp.37ff.

26) C.D.II.1.p.635. While admitting an earlier imbalance Barth nowhere denies the validity of post-temporality as an authentic aspect of God's eternity.

However, it would be quite wrong to infer that Barth's concern, even at this early stage, was merely to deny and not to affirm. Even here it was Barth's purpose to assert positively that which Overbeck had asserted negatively, to contend for the reality of this objective, eschatological knowledge of God, to attain to the Yes of Blumhardt's proclamation of Christian hope by submitting to Overbeck's No.[27] If the initial emphasis of Barth's single theological transformation was a negative concentration upon the No of God this must be understood as a prerequisite of the positive affirmation of God's Yes that was to follow, a necessary purgation of the anthropocentric debris of Liberal Neo-protestantism. Initially it was inevitable that, in order to eliminate every false conception of the continuity between God and man, the utter distinction between God and man should be dialectically stressed.[28] But the inherent continuity of Barth's theological development is established by a recognition that this divine No is not withdrawn in Barth's later writings, instead it comes to be considered exclusively in the context of the divine Yes.[29] It was Barth's determination to deny

---

27) T.F.Torrance, Karl Barth: An Introduction...,p.43

28) T.F.Torrance, Karl Barth: An Introduction...,pp.84f.; cf. R.H.Roberts, 'Eternity and Time in the Theology of Karl Barth: An essay in Dogmatic and Philosophical Theology' (dissertation, Edinburgh,1975),pp.33ff.

29) T.F.Torrance, Karl Barth: An Introduction..., p.53; cf. G.C. Berkouwer, The Triumph of Grace in the Theology of Karl Barth, trans. by Harry R.Boer (Grand Rapids,1956),p.37

only in order to affirm that distinguished him from other dialectical theologians of the period who were "united mostly in their negations".[30]

When this inherent continuity of Barth's theological development is not recognized the degree of change in emphasis between the writing of Romans and the later volumes of the Church Dogmatics can be greatly over-estimated. Thus Van Harvey suggests that there is a fundamental shift in the meaning of faith between these stages of Barth's development:

> "Ironically enough, it is Barth, the one who launched the ship of dialectical theology onto these chartless seas, who now seems frightened by its course and who has tried to bring the helm about 180 degrees. Consequently the understanding of faith, which he propounded so powerfully in his commentary on Romans, has been repudiated in his later writings. The earlier view, he now believes, leads inevitably to what one might call a theological agnosticism, which is to say, it does not take seriously the unique revelation of the knowledge of God in Jesus Christ. Hence, Barth's later works represent the attempt to unfold the objective knowledge of God that he believes is given to man in a real historical event." 31

Van Harvey illustrates this transformation with the example of Barth's understanding of the Resurrection. According to Van Harvey, Barth maintained in Romans a fundamental distinction between

---

30) R.W.Jenson, God after God, p.68

31) Van A.Harvey, The Historian and the Believer: The Morality of Historical Knowledge and Christian Belief (London, 1967), pp.153f.

faith and history whereby the Resurrection was not to be considered as a historical event at all (Van Harvey interprets this as essentially the same emphasis as that of Rudolph Bultmann). However, in the Church Dogmatics the Resurrection comes to be viewed not only as a real event but as the real event of time and space. What seems to elude Van Harvey is that the distinction between these emphases lies not so much in a change in Barth's understanding of faith as in the particular motive in the two instances. In Romans Barth's purpose is to deny the simple continuity of the Resurrection with all other events (an emphasis which continues in the Church Dogmatics). In the Church Dogmatics Barth's purpose is to affirm that the Resurrection, even though it does not fall into the same historical-scientific categories of other events, is nonetheless a real event in time and space.[32] While not denying a definite movement in Barth's thought the direction of that movement is consistent and not inconsistent. The seeds of Barth's later and developed concern for actuality are already present in Romans. Barth's thinking (like that of any other theologian) develops and matures but it is misleading to postulate distinct changes in his theological development

---

32) cf.pp. 88ff. of this thesis.

or subsequent changes of direction:[33]

> "If that which we then thought we had discovered and brought forth was no last word but one requiring a revision, it was none the less a true word. As such it must remain, and still cannot be bypassed; rather it constitutes the presupposition of that which must be further considered to-day. He who may not have joined in that earlier change of direction, who still may not be impressed with the fact that God is God, would certainly not see what is now to be said in addition as the true word concerning His humanity."[34]

This "revision" within Barth's theological development occurred through his original concern to affirm both the possibility and the actuality of an objective knowledge of God, a concern to speak of God in terms of God rather than in termsof man and thus a concern to begin with the reality of His self-revelation. Whatever its merits or demerits as an interpretation of Anselm his essay on Anselm's Proslogion is perhaps the most significant expression of Barth's theological method and crucial for an understanding of this

---

33) R.W.Jenson maintains that Hans Urs von Balthasar is mistaken in the contention that the transition from Romans to the Church Dogmatics is the transition from dialectic to analogy. Jenson suggests that analogy plays the same part in Romans as in Barth's later writings and that, rather than being opposing phenomena, analogy and dialectic are two aspects of the one phenomenom (R.W.Jenson, God after God,p.202; cf. Hans Urs von Balthasar, Karl Barth: Darstellung und Deutung seiner Theologie (Köln,1951). For this view of Barth's development as continuous rather than discontinuous see also E.H.Friedmann, Christologie und Anthropologie: Methode und Bedeutung der Lehre vom Menschen in der Theologie Karl Barths (Münsterschwarzach 1972),p.40

34) Karl Barth, The Humanity of God, p.38

revision in his theological development:[35]

> "...in this book on Anselm I am working with a vital key, if not the key, to an understanding of that whole process of thought that has impressed me more and more in my Church Dogmatics as the only one proper to theology."36

In this brief but brilliant work Barth discusses the scientific character of the theological task, the relation between faith and reason and the authentic object of theology. The only valid basis for rational speaking about God is the actuality of His objective self-revelation; the rationality of theological language is determined by the rationality of its object.[37] Thus the task of theology is to seek understanding of the reality of revelation with which it is confronted and its essential attitude must be that of faith.

It is this concern for the reality of revelation and an objective knowledge of God in His Word, a concern for that which is actual, which is the essence of Barth's mature theological method. For this reason Barth is seriously misrepresented by those who

---

35) Karl Barth, Anselm: Fides Quaerens Intellectum: Anselm's Proof of the Existence of God in the Context of his Theological Scheme, trans. by Ian W. Robertson (London, 1960); cf. Colin E. Gunton, Becoming and Being: The Doctrine of God in Charles Hartshorne and Karl Barth (Oxford, 1978), p.123 & T. F. Torrance, Karl Barth: An Introduction..., pp.182f.

36) Karl Barth, Anselm, p.11 (preface to the second edition). The first German edition of this essay was published by Christian Kaiser Verlag of Munich in 1931. cf. T. F. Torrance Theological Science (Oxford, 1969), pp.6f.

37) cf. Karl Barth, Evangelical Theology: An Introduction, trans. by Grover Foley (London and Glasgow, 1963), p.88.

suggest that a "Christomonism" or "Christ-principle" is the centre-point of his theology.[38] Barth continually warns against the tendency to view Jesus Christ as the embodiment of a principle; a principle deals with abstract and general truths whereas in Jesus Christ one is confronted by the concrete story of particular events associated with a particular person.[39] The name "Jesus Christ" itself expresses the unity of His person and His work and militates against this reduction of Christology to a mere concept or idea.[40] The climax of Barth's theological transformation was the recognition and identification of Jesus Christ as the actual event of God's self-revelation, the sole and authentic location of objective knowledge of God. The definitive object of theological reflection is not man and his religion but neither is it the absract concept of an _eschaton_, it is Jesus Christ Himself, the _Eschatos_:[41]

> "Not one word of what is said in the _Commentary on Romans_ is withdrawn. But where abstract eternity was, Jesus of Nazareth now stands. ...
> If one went through the _Commentary on Romans_ and replaced the tangential intersection of time and eternity with

---

38) G. W. Bromiley, 'Karl Barth' in _Creative Minds in Contemporary Theology_, ed. P. E. Hughes (Grand Rapids, 1966), pp.27-62; also Colin Brown, _Karl Barth and the Christian Message_, (London, 1967), p.12, cf. p.138.

39) _C.D_.II.2.p.4, _C.D_.IV.3.pp.173ff.: In this latter passage Barth criticizes G. C. Berkouwer (op.cit.) for considering the essence of his theology to be the "Triumph of Grace" rather than the particular person of Jesus Christ.

40) cf. John Thompson, op.cit., pp.4ff. & W. Schlichting, _Biblische Denkform in der Dogmatik: Die Vorbildlichkeit des biblischen Denkens für die Methode der 'Kirchlichen Dogmatik' Karl Barths_ (Zürich, 1972), pp.277ff.

41) cf. T. F. Torrance, _Karl Barth: An Introduction..._, p.79; cf. R. H. Roberts, 'Barth's Doctrine of Time: its nature and implications' in _Karl Barth: Studies of his Theological Method_, ed. S. W. Sykes (Oxford, 1979), pp.88-146 (p.109).

the story narrated by the second article of the Apostles' Creed, he would obtain the theology of the Church Dogmatics."42

This identification of Jesus Christ as the Eschatos implied a corrective to Barth's earlier concentration upon the post-temporality of God's eternity and the dialectical opposition of eternity and time, transcendence and immanence, itself a denial of both the possibility and the actuality of Incarnation.[43] An eschatological faith which focuses upon Jesus Christ as the Eschatos is determined by the Already as well as the Not Yet. God's self-revelation in Jesus Christ is noetically provisional since the eschatological future involves the ultimate unveiling of things hitherto hidden. But God's self-revelation in Jesus Christ cannot be ontically provisional since it cannot be transcended, the eschatological future does not consist of new saving events or truths. The consequence of Barth's initial concern to affirm the Godness of God was the identification of authentic "Godness" with the ontic actuality of the person and work of Jesus Christ, the recognition of His transcendence within His immanence, the No of His eschatological judgment within the Yes of His gracious election:[44]

---

42) R.W.Jenson, God after God, p.71.

43) T.F.Torrance, Karl Barth: An Introduction..., p.79.

44) The fallacy of so-called Barthianism consists of an accentuation of God's Godness without the recognition that it is the Godness of this God in concreto and not in abstracto.

> "In Barth, spatial transcendence has been replaced by a dynamic transcendence; a transcendence that happens, and is therefore narrated (perceived by ear, not eye); a transcendence of act, event, of identity in difference. It is a transcendence that comes to expression when the story of Jesus of Nazareth, crucified and risen, is narrated."45

This dynamic transcendence of God which is actual in Jesus Christ is not dialectically antithetical to His immanence, it is rather the ontological possibility of His immanence; the transcendence of God consists in His specific freedom to be immanent in Jesus Christ.[46] This freedom of God, as Lord, to be immanent in the event of His self-revelation is the basis of Barth's claim concerning the exclusivity of revelation: if God's transcendence is His freedom in the event of revelation then any supposed knowledge of God that is independent of His self-revelation, independent of this specific freedom in Jesus Christ, cannot, by definition, be authentic knowledge of God. God is truly known exclusively in that event in which He is and remains the Lord, in the event of His Word where He has caused Himself to be known: "...we cannot discern the being of God in any other way than by looking where God Himself gives us Himself to see".[47] Knowledge of the true God can never be at man's disposal. Rational speaking about God must be determined

---

45) Colin E. Gunton, 'Transcendence, Metaphor, and the Knowability of God', J.T.S., 31 (1980), 501-516 (p.512).

46) ibid., p.513.

47) C.D.II.1.p.261.

by the rationality of its specific object, not an object at man's disposal (Objekt) but the object which stands over against man and confronts him (Gegenstand):

> "God is never an object in the sense of being at the disposal of human knowledge in its ordinary operations, or amenable to criteria of truth which takes no account of the specific and unique nature of this object, namely, that it is always Subject. Thus, Barth maintains that we are the object of the Divine Subject's saving grace—we are the object to whom the Subject addresses his Word. In this way, Barth has thrown the cognitive relation into reverse."[48]

Thus the Lordship of God in this specific event represents the starting point of Barth's theology; the phrase "God reveals Himself as the Lord" indicates who Barth means when he uses the word "God":[49]

> "An exposition of Barth's arguments in his development of the doctrine of the Trinity will reveal that his phrase 'God reveals himself as the Lord' performs for him the same function that 'that than which no greater can be conceived' performed for Anselm: it provides him with reasons for using the word God in rational discourse."[50]

The exclusivity of this claim of revelation caused Barth to abandon a projected second volume of Christian Dogmatics[51] and begin afresh with the first volume of Church Dogmatics, excl-

---

48) P.C.Almond, 'Karl Barth and Anthropocentric Theology', S.J.T., 31 (1978) 435-447 (p.440).

49) C.D.I.1.pp.295ff.

50) Colin E. Gunton, Becoming and Being, p.125.

51) Karl Barth, Prolegomena zur Christlichen Dogmatik: Die Lehre vom Worte Gottes (München, 1928).

uding any supposed extraneous philosophical support for the doctrine of God and His Word.[52] In the light of His self-revelation authentic knowledge of God is necessarily knowledge of the One who reveals Himself as the Lord, the One who loves in freedom, the One who freely relates Himself to us in Jesus Christ.[53] For Barth, as for Anselm, authentic knowledge of God as the One who reveals Himself as the Lord implies not only the impossibility of His non-existence but also the form of His existence:

> "There is no possibility of knowing the perfect God without knowing His perfections. The converse is also true: knowledge of the divine perfections is possible only in knowledge of the perfect God, of His loving in freedom."54

Whereas the term "perfection" denotes a distinctive "attribute" of God alone, the term "attribute" could imply a general characteristic "attributed" to God in common with others. For this reason Barth discards the classical concept of attribution.[55] The knowledge of who God is in Himself, of the perfections of His existence, is not derived by attributing to Him independent conceptions of love and

---

52) C.D.I.1.pp.xi ff.

53) C.D.II.1.pp.257 ff.

54) ibid.,p.322

55) ibid.,pp322ff.

freedom, immanence and transcendence, but by considering (nachdenkend) the actuality of his "happening" in the event of His Word. Theological speaking about God's spatiality and temporality must be determined by His actual spatial and temporal relatedness to man in Jesus Christ. Specifically, Barth's conception of God's eternity is a direct and necessary outworking of his distinctive theological method.

b) The authentic temporality of God's eternity:

While Barth's theological contribution could only be distorted by the vain attempt simplistically to reduce it to a single all-pervading theme yet it remains a valid claim that the issue of God's relatedness to man in space and time forms the centre of his entire dogmatic enterprise. Barth's intention to present a thoroughly Trinitarian theology is determined by his resolve to consider the actuality of God's self-revelation in Jesus Christ as an event of space and time. Therefore an informed consideration of Barth's theology or any single aspect of it must begin with the attempt to comprehend the manner of God's spatial and temporal relatedness to man as it is understood by Barth.

While it is the aim of the first part of this thesis to concentrate upon the temporality of the divine event the parallel question of spatiality must continually inform this inquiry. It is interesting to note that Barth questions the traditional juxtaposition of omnipresence and eternity as the relatedness of God to space and time.[56] Though he later considers omnipresence and eternity as the prototypes of space and time respectively,[57] and, though he admits an "undeniable relationship" between God's omnipresence and eternity, Barth denies that they should be considered as "parallels".[58] His reasons for this reticence are twofold. Firstly he distinguishes between them by considering eternity as a perfection of God's freedom as such, albeit as qualified by and identical with His love, whereas he understands omnipresence (along with omnipotence and glory) as a perfection of God's freedom operative in His love. Secondly he objects to the juxtaposition in the older theology since both omnipresence and eternity were grouped under a general negative conception of divine infinity and thereby considered in terms of God's non-spatiality and timelessness. In fact both objections derive from the anthropocentricity of the older theological method which tended to consider omnipresence and eternity as a response to the problems of created existence, a theological method in which God is confronted by man and his questions rather than vice-versa, a theological method which issued in man speaking about God as

---

56) C.D.II.1.pp.464ff.

57) ibid., p.612.

58) ibid., p.465.

the negative image of Himself. Yet Barth's objections to this juxtaposition are surely less than persuasive. His determination to speak positively of God in terms of the actuality of His self-revelation and his consequent rejection of this negative conception of infinity need not, of itself, dissolve the juxtaposition of God's omnipresence and eternity. Moreover, the somewhat elusive distinction which Barth draws between omnipresence and eternity seems quite arbitrary and perhaps more motivated by systematic tidiness than by theological necessity. Surely both omnipresence and eternity must be considered as perfections of God's love in freedom and the freedom of God's love.[59] Indeed, to conceive of God's eternity as "an attribute of God's freedom as such",[60] in distinction to His omnipresence, tends towards a conception of eternity other than in the context of His actual relatedness to man in Jesus Christ, a tendency in Barth to which attention must be given later in this chapter.

Barth begins his account of eternity as a Perfection of the Divine Freedom by rejecting any definition of eternity in terms of "an infinite extension of time both backwards and forwards".[61]

---

59) To the extent that the systematic arrangement of Barth's discussion of the specific divine perfections appears to be less than convincing one may be left with the impression that throughout these two sections (C.D.II.1.pp.351ff.) he may have been too motivated by "systematic tidiness".

60) ibid., p.465.

61) ibid., p.608.

This concept of everlastingness would still be characterized by the very features which, according to Barth, distinguish God's eternity from time as man experiences it. It is in this sense (and in this sense alone) that Barth understands eternity as "non-temporality", as lacking the separation, distinction and contradiction intrinsic to man's time. Conversely Barth also rejects the common identification of eternity with timelessness:

> "The theological concept of eternity must be set free from the Babylonian captivity of an abstract opposite to the concept of time."62

This misrepresentation of eternity as an abstract projection of the negation of time is a direct consequence of the theological method rejected by Barth, the theological method according to which God is defined by defining man negatively, the theological method which identifies transcendence as an abstract absolute otherness. As Colin Gunton observes, this method tends towards a quantitative conception of transcendence:[63] the greater the degree of abstraction from man's finitude, the greater the degree of God's transcendent infinitude. But the greater the degree of abstraction from man's finitude, the less the degree of the knowability of the trancendent

---

62) ibid.,p.611

63) Colin E.Gunton,'Transcendence, Methaphor, and the Knowability of God.'pp.501ff.

God.[64] The "God" of this theological method remains imprisoned within his own transcendence. The God who in Jesus Christ has happened in space and time cannot possibly be identified with this un-free abstraction:

> "On the contrary, He is infinite in a manner in which the antithesis and mutual exclusiveness of the infinite and the finite, non-spatiality and timelessness on the one hand and spatiality and temporality on the other, do not enclose and imprison Him, so that He is confined by His being omnis mensurae aut termini expers.[65]

The affirmation of God's eternity ought to inform us positively of that which God is , not that which He is not,[66] yet the theologically bankrupt method of negation inevitably issues in the effective denial of God's knowability:

> "A negatively conceived transcendence, suggested in Aqunias' teaching that we can know of God only what he is not, which in its turn is part of the legacy of Augustine's pervasive employment in theology of the contrast between the sensible and intelligible worlds, finally came home to roost in Kant's placing of God among the noumena, the unknowable objects of thought. If God is in principle unknowable, then theology must either change its character, as Schleiermacher taught, or disappear, as it seems about to do in some areas of the discipline."[67]

---

64) cf. R.W.Jenson, God after God,p.134; cf. C.D.II.1.pp.465ff.

65) C.D.II.1.p.467

66) ibid.,p.613

67) Colin E.Gunton, 'Transcendence, Methaphor, and the Knowability of God.'p.516

It is Barth's concern to speak of God in terms of the event of His self-revelation, a concern for that which is actual, that preserves him from the dissolution of time into the abstract timelessness that is inherent in this theological method of negation.[68] The scientific task of authentic theology is to make an appropriate response to its object (Sache), namely the actualization of God's self-revelation in His Word. T.F.Torrance observes that Barth uses the German word Wirklichkeit in the sense of Aktualität rather than Realität "because of the relation between Aktualität and Akt, actuality and act, which it involves."[69] The question of God's knowability must not be considered in abstracto but in concreto, on the basis of the actual knowledge of God in His Word,[70] and in concreto the Word of God is the actualization of His self-revelation; it is itself the act of God:[71]

---

68) cf. R.H.Roberts,'Eternity and Time in the Theology of Karl Barth',pp.64f.

69) T.F.Torrance, Karl Barth: An Introduction..., p151. Note that Eberhard Jüngel also prefers to use Wirklichkeit in this active sense: E.Jüngel,'Die Welt als Möglichkeit und Wirklichkeit: Zum ontologischen Ansatz der Rechtfertigungslehre' in Unterwegs zur Sache: Theologische Bemerkungen, ed. E.Wolf, Beiträge zur evangelischen Theologie, 61 (München,1972),pp.206-233

70) C.D.II.1.pp.3ff.; cf. C.D.I.1.pp.187ff.

71) C.D.I.1.pp.143ff.; cf. C.D.I.2.p.45

> "The distinction between word and act is that mere word is the mere self-expression of a person, while act is the resultant relative alteration in the world around. Mere word is passive, act is an active participation in history. But this kind of distinction does not apply to the Word of God. As mere Word it is act. As mere Word it is the divine person, the person of the Lord of history, whose self-expression is as such an alteration, and indeed an absolute alteration of the world, whose _passio_ in history is as such _actio_."72

Barth's distinctive conception of God's eternity can only be considered within the context of this primary concern for actuality, indeed, any attempt to understand this conception other than from the standpoint of this concern is doomed to distortion.[73] Only by taking time can revelation be revelation[74] and if theology is to attain a true conception of God's eternity it must begin with the event in which His eternity becomes time; it must begin with the actuality of the Incarnation:[75]

> "In Jesus Christ it comes about that God takes time to Himself, that He Himself, the eternal One, becomes temporal, that He is present for us in the form of our own existence and our own world, not simply embracing our time and ruling it, but submitting Himself to it, and permitting created time to become and be the form of His eternity."76

---

72) _C.D._I.1.p.144; cf. _C.D._III.1.pp.344ff., where Barth states that God's affirmation of creation itself means His actualization of creation.

73) cf. R.H.Roberts,'Eternity and Time in the Theology of Karl Barth',p.283

74) _C.D._I.2.p.50

75) _C.D._II.1.p.616ff.

76) ibid.,p.616

That God's eternity has actually occurred in time implies the prior possibility that God is able to be eternal in this way, that His eternity does not necessarily exclude the inclusion of the time of His Word. God is not bound by this possibility as if it were an *a priori* necessity for Him to take time to Himself, yet His eternity must include His genuine readiness for time, His gracious unnecessitated readiness to become temporal in His Word.[77] This readiness of God's eternity is positively understood as His time for us in Jesus Christ, the time of the One who loves in freedom, the time of His patience and, therefore, the possibility of our time for Him.[78] The affirmation that God reveals Himself itself signifies that God has time for us.[79] God's eternity is not the negation of time but His divine readiness to create time,[80] His readiness to have time for man and, therefore, His readiness to give man time for Him. Thus the temporality of creation corresponds to God's grace as the Creator and finds its counterparts in the time of the history of the covenant and salvation.[81] The authentic temporality of God's eternity is therefore the ontological basis of the temporality of creation. The possibility of Christian existence as our time for God depends upon the prior possibility that His eternity includes His time for us:

---

77) ibid.,p.618

78) ibid.,pp.611f.

79) *C.D.*I.2.pp.45ff.

80) *C.D.*III.1.p.68

81) ibid.,p.71

> "In our creaturely time, although it is our time, and therefore the time of our sin, He has given us His divine time. He allows us our time in order that we may always have time for Him—no, in order that in it He may always have His time for us, revelation time."82

God's eternity is "non-temporal" since God cannot be possessed or dominated by beginning, succession and end in their separation, distinction and contradiction. But God's eternity is authentically temporal since it possesses and controls all beginning, succession and end:[83] "God's eternity is itself beginning, succession and end."[84] It is not that God is authentically in time but that time is authentically in Him.[85] To deny the reality of this authentic temporality of God's eternity would be to deny the actuality of the Incarnation.[86]

Barth's positive conception of God's eternity as His authentic temporality is both paralleled and confirmed by his conception of God's omnipresence. God's omnipresence is not an absolute non-spatiality, an aspect of an abstract infinity, it is rather His authentic spatiality, the perfection of His being in which He is preeminently present.[87] God's omnipresence consists in His freedom

---

82) C.D.II.1.p.62

83) C.D.II.1.pp.610f.

84) ibid.,p.611

85) C.D.III.1.p.68

86) ibid.,p.618

87) C.D.II.1.pp.468ff.

to be present to everything that is not Himself but is distinct from Himself, the freedom to be present to the universe created and preserved by Him without being identical to it:[88]

> "God possesses His space. He is in Himself as in a space. He creates space. He is and does this so that, in virtue of His own spatiality, He can be Himself even in this created space without this limiting Him or causing Him to have something outside Himself, a place apart from Himself, a space which is not His space too in virtue of His spatiality, the space of His divine presence. Or, to express it more positively, God possesses space in Himself and in all other spaces. He does this as the being who is completely present in the spatiality that belongs to Him. There is no place where He is not present in His essence, which includes, of course, His knowledge and power. There is no place where He is less present than in all others. On the contrary, He is everywhere completely and undividedly the One He always is, even if in virtue of the freedom of His love He is this in continually differing and special ways."89

Here again the possibility of God's being present to that which is distinct from Himself must be understood as His divine freedom and not as any supposed a priori necessity. God's omnipresence is His freedom to possess space, both in Himself and distinct from Himself, as the One He is, as the free Lord He is. Moreover this divine freedom is no mere abstraction, it is rather God's specific transcendent freedom to be present in His Word to man in space and time, to be present as the One who loves in freedom. The affirmation of God's omnipresence and eternity does not imply that He is limited or possessed by space and time but that He Himself

---

88) ibid., pp.461f.

89) ibid., p.470.

possesses space and time in order that He might be related to man and that man might be related to Him in Jesus Christ:

> "...while the Incarnation does not mean that God is limited by space and time, it asserts the reality of space and time for God in the actuality of His relations with us, and at the same time binds us to space and time in all our relations with Him."90

Barth maintains that it is this positive temporality of God's eternity, rather than its secondary character as "non-temporality", which is the predominant interest of Scripture since the concern of the Bible is not to refer to any abstract conception of eternity but to speak of the Living God Himself in His actual relatedness to men. Thus the Bible displays no hesitation in refering to God in temporal terms, in speaking of His "years and days".[91] Moreover, Barth argues that Boethius's classic definition of eternity as *interminabilis vitae tota simul et perfecta possessio* (the "total, simultaneous and complete possession of unlimited life") is only valid if it is taken as relating specifically to the eternity of God instead of as relating to an abstract conception of the eternity of being.[92] Interpreted in this manner the definition identifies God as the *possessor interminabilis vitae*, as the One who possesses life in freedom, as the possessor of "perfect" life, as the Living God. Thus the

---

90) T.F.Torrance, *Space, Time and Incarnation* (Oxford, 1969), p.67.

91) *C.D.*II.1.p.610.

92) ibid., p.611. For Barth neither God's eternity nor man's time can be considered as mere abstractions.

definition becomes an affirmation of God's authentic temporality, albeit a temporality the authenticity of which distinguishes it positively from time as man experiences it.

c) The pure simultaneity of God's time:

Having established that God's eternity is authentically temporal it is now necessary to focus attention on that which, according to Barth, distinguishes eternity as God's time from man's time, its character as "non-temporality". It is crucial to recognize with Barth that time is neither a constant nor an absolute existing in its own right to which God is subject.[93] Colin E. Gunton is surely correct when he observes that Process Theology's identification of God as the event that contains all other events involves a virtual deification of time itself and is thus a modern form of idolatry.[94] Space and time are a "continuum of relations given in and with created existence" and without which that existence would be "indeterminable and unintelligible".[95] For God to reveal Himself to men in Jesus Christ would therefore be meaningless if this self-revelation was not an event within space and time.[96] Yet God

---

93) T.F.Torrance, Space, Time and Incarnation, pp.60f.; cf. C.D.II.1.pp.609f.

94) Colin E. Gunton, 'Transcendence, Metaphor, and the Knowability of God', pp.508ff.; Colin E. Gunton, Becoming and Being, p.178.

95) T.F.Torrance, Space, Time and Incarnation, p.61; cf. C.D. III.2.p.438.

96) The denial of this spatial and temporal structure of revelation and of Christian belief is the underlying fallacy of so-called "demythologization" (ibid.).

Himself can never be dominated by the categories of space and time; as Creator His relationship to creation and its spatial and temporal structures remains that of the transcendentally free Lord. Specifically, God is not dominated by beginning, succession and end in their separation, distance and contradiction. This constitutes the "non-temporality" of His eternity.[97]

> "...if we are to achieve a positive Christology that does not fall prey to the absolutism of time or eternity, we must hold firmly to the bipolarity of the New Testament's approach: that this life is both fully temporal and yet is the place where the eternal is present."98

In contradistinction to the authentic temporality which is God's eternity Barth understands time in the succession and division of past, present and future as man's fallen time:[99]

> "...the time we think we know and possess, "our" time, is by no means the time God created. Between our time and God-created time as between our existence and the existence created by God there lies the Fall."100

The conception of eternity as timelessness (which was generally characteristic of classical metaphysics and which is inherently antithetical to a doctrine of Incarnation) derived from the mythological projection of a rejection of this "fallen time".[101] As a perfection

---

97) C.D.II.1.p.608.

98) Colin E. Gunton, Yesterday and Today: A study of continuities in Christology (London,1983), p.127.

99) C.D.I.2.p.47; cf. C.D.III.2.pp.511ff.

100) C.D.I.2.p.47.

101) Colin E. Gunton, Becoming and Being, p.178.

of the freedom of God's love and in distinction to the fallen time experienced by man, God's eternity is the possession of time in the duration which is lacking to man's time, the possession of beginning, middle and end in pure simultaneity instead of succession and division.[102] The event of the Incarnation implies that "we are compelled neither to escape time because it is fleeting nor to impose upon its fleetingness an absoluteness that it does not have (for example, by divinizing evolution). For in what happened to Jesus, we are presented with time that is established through and beyond its decay."[103] God's eternity is therefore the one simultaneous occasion in which beginning, middle and end, past, present and future, coinhere:[104]

> "Even the eternal God does not live without time. He is supremely temporal. For His eternity is authentic temporality, and therefore the source of all time. But in His eternity, in the uncreated self-subsistent time which is one of the perfections of His divine nature, present, past and future, yesterday, to-day and to-morrow are not successive, but simultaneous."105

This pure simultaneity of God's time is that which distinguishes His eternity as authentic temporality. Barth only refers to the "non-temporality" of God's eternity in relation to the freedom

---

102) C.D.II.1.p.608; cf.C.D.III.1.pp.67f.

103) Colin E.Gunton, Yesterday and Today,p.128

104) C.D.II.1.p.608; cf. C.D.III.2.p.526

105) C.D.III.2.p.437

of His authentic time from the contradiction and separation of man's fallen time. God's eternity is not timeless but the continuity of God's eternity overcomes the limits of time.[106] God's eternity includes past, present and future but the omnipotence of God's knowing and willing excludes their opposition as Not Yet, Now and No More; it includes a before and an after but not a No-Longer and a Not-Yet.[107] It is in this simultaneity that God's time is "real time" rather than a negation of time, just as God's omnipresence is "real space" rather than a negation of space.[108]

It is not, however, Barth's intention to collapse the temporal distinctions of beginning, succession and end, past, present and future into a simutaneous unity, rather he intends to retain these temporal distinctions within the contemporaneous simultaneity of God's time.[109] The tendency to forfeit the distinctions of time within an eternal unity appears to be a feature of Wolfhart Pannenberg's conception of eternity. Although he refuses to contrast eternity and time he speaks of eternity as the truth and unity of all time beyond the flow of time as past, present and future; the

---

106) C.D.II.1.p.618

107) ibid.,p.612; cf. John Macquarrie, Christian Hope (London and Oxford,1978),pp.23f.

108) C.D.II.1.p.613

109) R.H.Roberts,'Eternity and Time in the Theology of Karl Barth,p.64

concurrence of all events in an eternal present.[110] Only because Barth retains the distinctions of time, albeit in their "pure simultaneity", within his conception of God's eternity can he maintain this eternity as the ontological basis of time:

> "God in himself is the possibility of there being time, of occurrences with a before and an after, with a departure and a goal. He is this possibility because he has for himself departure and goal,and so can be departure and goal for other beings."[111]

Since God's eternity is "real time" it is the prototype, foreordination and source of time:[112] "God has time because and as He has eternity."[113] Eternity, as God's "real time", is the basis of His creation of Man's time.

Similarly, that God can have "time for us" in Jesus Christ finds its absolute basis in His eternity as His readiness for this time.[114] In Jesus Christ God's being for us takes the form of space and time but this form of His being for us has its prototypes in His omnipresence and eternity.[115] In Jesus Christ God re-creates

---

110) W.Pannenberg,'Time, Eternity and Judgment' in What is Man? Contemporary Anthropology in Theological Perspective, trans. by D.A.Priebe(Philadelphia,1970),pp.68-81(p.74;cf.p.81).

111) R.W.Jenson,God after God,p.129

112) C.D.II.1.pp.611f.; cf. C.D.III.1.p.67

113) C.D.II.1.p.611; cf. p.474: "...God is present to other things, and is able to create and give them space, because He Himself possesses space apart from everything else."

114) ibid.,p.618

115) ibid.,p.612

His true time amidst man's fallen time which is not so alien to Him that He cannot graciously heal it and raise it to His eternal time.[116] Therefore the time of God's Word is real time, the fulfilment of time, and only in relation to this Word, only in contemporaneousness with Jesus Christ, can man know real time.[117] As a living act of God's real time the event of His Word cannot be imprisoned as a particular act of the historical past in a manner which denies its contemporaneity:[118]

> "The incarnate Word of God is. But this means that it was and will be. But again it was never "not yet," and it will never be "no more." On the contrary, it is "now" even as it is "once" (and to that extent "no more"); and it is also "now" even as it is "then" (and to that extent "not yet"). It is a perfect temporal present, and for that very reason a perfect temporal past and future. It enters fully into the succession and separation of the times which together constitute time, and transforms this succession and separation into full contemporaneity."[119]

---

116) ibid.,pp.617 f.; cf.C.D.III.1.pp.73 ff.

117) C.D.I.2.pp.66 ff.; cf. R.H.Roberts,'Eternity and Time in the Theology of Karl Barth',pp.282 f.

118) C.D.I.1.p.145 f.; cf. R.H.Roberts,'Eternity and Time in the Theology of Karl Barth',p.66

119) C.D.III.1.pp.73f.; cf.C.D.I.1.p.120. It is this conception of God's Word as an act of His eternity which preserves Barth from the apparent impasse which exists between the theological accounts of contemporaneity in the writings of Rudolf Bultmann and Oscar Cullmann.

Just as past, present and future, in their distinction but not their separation, are 'compresent' to God in the simultaneity of His eternity, so past, present and future, in their distinction but not their separation, are included and not excluded in the contemporaneity of the living event which is God's Word. The word 'compresence' is included in the Oxford English Dictionary albeit as a rare word no longer commonly used.[120] Its usage in the 17th century was within the context of the Eucharistic debate with reference to Luther's teaching that the body and blood of Christ were 'present together' in, with and under the elements of bread and wine without the latter substance being transubstantiated. It is because of this former context and usuage that the employment of the word is appropriate here to affirm the presence together of distinct substances, events or phenomena without the forfeiture of the distinctions between them:[121]

---

120) "Compresence.Obs.rare...Presence together; co-presence... Compresentiality...The quality of being present together. So Compresentation...(The Oxford English Dictionary, Vol. II,C (Oxford,1933), p.743.).

121) Colin Gunton uses the word 'co-presence' to affirm the same dynamic tension but the word 'compresence' is preferred here for the historical reasons stated in the text and also because a single word is to be preferred to a hyphenated word (cf. Colin E. Gunton, Yesterday and Today pp.111ff.).

> "God's act (which is his revelation) is a past fact of history but it is <u>also</u> 'an event happening in the present, here and now'. God's act happens, has happened and indeed will happen; but it is each of the three, without abrogation of any, its being an 'accomplished fact'. The adherence to both 'historical completeness' <u>and</u> 'full contemporaneity' is extremely important in Barth's exposition. Without it his account would slide on the one hand into secularity... or, on the other, it would move into an eternalisation."122

Towards the end of Barth's exposition of eternity as a perfection of God's freedom he defines the distinctions of God's authentic temporality in terms of the pre-temporality, supra-temporality and post-temporality of His eternity.[123] In these authentically temporal distinctions God in His freedom possesses, conditions and comprehends all time in the simultaneity of His eternity: "He preceeds its beginning, He accompanies its duration, and He exists after its end. This is the concrete form of eternity as readiness for time."[124] Only if God's eternity includes these authentically temporal distinctions can the Christian message be distinguished from a myth or a dream.[125]

The eternal God is pre-temporal since "His existence pre-

---

122) R.H.Roberts,'Eternity and Time in the Theology of Karl Barth',p.107; cf. R.W.Jenson,<u>God after God</u>,p.125

123) <u>C.D.</u>II.1.p.619ff.

124) ibid.,p.619

125) ibid.,p.620

cedes ours and that of all things."[126] In the beginning which precedes our existence and the existence of everything distinct from Himself God in Himself was no less Himself. To deny this pre-temporality of God's eternity is to forfeit the freedom of His love, the graciousness of His relatedness to men. Only God as the One whose existence precedes all other beginnings can freely create, freely reconcile and freely redeem. The pre-temporality of God's eternity preserves creation, reconciliation and redemption as the action of His freely electing will in Jesus Christ. As such the pre-temporality of God is not merely a speculative inference from the Gospel but an element of the Gospel itself, a direct analysis of God's Word. However, This pre-temporality of God's eternity must not be stressed to the detriment of His supra-temporality and post-temporality. Barth detects such an over-emphasis in the Reformers' pre-occupation with a particular conception of election and providence according to which man's whole salvation has already been decided in the eternal past.[127] Within this system human life with its decisions,responsibilities and possibilities is reduced to a mere appendix in relation to the divine decision of the eternal past and the future expectation of fulfilment is clouded by gloom and even hopelessness. But God's eternity is not exclusively pre-temporality;

---

126) ibid.,p.621

127) ibid.,pp.631f.

His eternity is not left behind by the present and future but simultaneously includes and comprehends the present and the future.[128]

The eternal God is supra-temporal since His eternity "embraces time on all sides."[129] As supra-temporality God's eternity is not "timeless" but "causes itself to be accompanied by time",[130] it is the pure duration (in contrast to man's fleeting duration) in which the eternal God determines that He will be present in all time as the One who loves in freedom and that all time will be compresent to Him: "God's eternity is in time. Time itself is in eternity":[131]

> "Eternity did not cease when time began, to begin again when time ceases. Eternity is in the midst, just as God Himself is in the midst with us."132

In His supra-temporality God freely actualizes His love within space and time; as the One who is above us He is with us to be sought and found in space and time.[133] God's supra-temporality is the revelation of His eternity in time and therefore it is the foundation for a consciousness of the meaning of time, a consciousness of the beginning, succession and goal of the past, the present and the future. The event of revelation in Jesus Christ is the supra-

---

128) cf. C.D.II.2.pp.181ff.

129) C.D.II.1.p.623

130) ibid.

131) ibid.

132) ibid.,p.624

133) ibid.

temporal presence of the eternal God in space and time on which a true time-consciousness depends.[134] Yet the over-emphasis upon this supra-temporality of God's eternity which characterized theology in the 18th and 19th centuries was far more dangerous than the Reformers' stress upon the divine pre-temporality.It involved the attempt to compress the eternal God within man's time to the extent that religious man himself, his needs, possibilities and experiences, became the object of theology. The pre-temporality of God's eternity was considered at worst as an irrelevant speculation and at best as a mere introduction to the statement of God's eternal presence. The post-temporality of God's eternity remained an unacknowledged theological appendix:[135]

> "...the conception of eternity had lost in depth and perspective, so that finally the point was reached where the assertion of it was hardly if at all to be distinguished from the denial of its contents."136

God's eternity cannot consist exclusively in this supra-temporality and remain His supra-temporality. The eternal God is present within time as the free Lord of time, as the One who precedes its

---

134) ibid.,pp.626ff.

135) ibid.,pp.632f.

136) ibid.,p.632. A similar charge could be brought against any notion in which the eternal God is virtually identified with the process of time and human history (Colin E.Gunton, 'Transcendence, Metaphor, and the Knowability of God', pp.508ff.

beginning and exists after its end. As the One who loves in freedom He cannot be possessed by time nor identified with the process of time. He is present in time as the One who is above time, this is His supra-temporality:

> "God in His supra-temporality is to be distinguished from a mere sum or principle of time by the fact that He is also pre-temporal and post-temporal. He is not, therefore, bound to our time as such a principle would be, but time is in His hands and at His disposal."137

The eternal God is post-temporal since He is after time as the One who is when time ceases. In His post-temporality God is the goal towards whom we move: "the goal and the end beyond which and over which another goal and end cannot exist."[138] The post-temporality of God's eternity is God Himself in the perfection of this goal, in the "Sabbath rest" after the completion of all His works ad extra, in His final judgment when "all that has been will be before Him what it must be" and He will be "all in all".[139] The po st-temporality of God's eternity stands before us as the final revelation of God and His Kingdom, not as a novel event but as the ultimate unveiling of the One already knowable as the Lord in His revelation:[140]

---

137) C.D.II.1.p.638

138) C.D.II.1.p.629

139) ibid.,p.630

140) ibid.,pp.630f.

> "God is also post-temporal eternity, the eternity to which we move. To this extent He is the God of all hope, the imminent peace which is prepared and promised to His people, into which it has not yet entered but will enter. God has and is also that which so far we do not have and are not. He therefore embraces time and us too from a position in front of us. Thus in having Him we have really everything—including what so far we do not have. His is the kingdom. He is the Last. He is the One who is all in all. It is only then, at the goal and end of time, that He will be revealed as this and no longer veiled at all. But He is this already in Himself. He was it from the beginning."141

The recognition of this post-temporality of God's eternity was the essence of the distinctive eschatological message of the Blumhardts by which they opposed the purely individual hope that was characteristic of Pietism, the eschatological message that the younger Blumhardt, together with Kutter and Ragaz, later combined (or identified) with the expectations of Socialism.[142] Barth acknowledges that his rejection both of the secularization of eschatology by Religious Socialism and the evasion of eschatology by Pietism and Liberalism derived initially from his over-emphasis upon the post-temporality of eternity.[143]

> "It was necessary and right in face of the Immanentism of the preceding period to think with new seriousness about God's futurity. But it was neither right nor necessary to do this in such a way that this one matter was put at the head of all Christian teaching, just as the previous epoch had wanted to make what they claimed to be the knowledge of God's presence the chief point in Christian doctrine."144

God's eternity does not consist exclusively in His post-temporality;

---

141) ibid.,p.631

142) ibid.,pp.633f.

143) ibid.,pp.634ff.

144) ibid.,p.636

the One who will be is the One who was and the One who is. Barth's theological thought could only develop in a positive and Trinitarian direction on the basis of a new consciousness of the pre-temporality of eternity which had characterized the theology of the Reformers and even a cautious perception of God's supra-temporality as the truth which lay behind the errors of theology in the 18th and 19th centuries.[145]

The pitfalls of an over-emphasis upon the post-temporality of God may best be illustrated by a brief analysis of Wolfhart Pannenberg's conception of the ontological priority of the future (a thing is in essence that which it will become). This futurist ontology is an outworking of an eschatological epistemology which pervades his whole theology: truth is not identified as a timeless essence of unchanging reality but as a process which can only finally be comprehended at the universal end of history.[146] Pannenberg not only attempts to apply this eschatological epistemology to the whole of reality,he also effectively identifies this futuristic totality of truth and the universal end of history with the being of God.[147] According to Pannenberg the Hebrew manner of considering God's being was not in terms of His timelessness

---

145) ibid.,pp.637f.

146) W.Pannenberg,'What is Truth?' in Basic Questions in Theology,vol.II, trans. by G.H.Kehm (London,1971),pp.1-27

147) ibid.,p.27

but His rule, a rule which has not yet fully come.[148] Thus God's being which is His rule, is in the process of becoming.[149] Pannenberg attempts to avoid the apparent logical implications of development and change in God which arise from this conception of His being in process by reference to the supposed retroactive force of God's future being: God's being in the future is the ontic as well as the noetic ground of His being in the present and past.[150] But does this elusive conception of the ontological priority of the future have any real meaning or valid reference to reality; is it any more than a verbal contortion? the distinction between Pannenberg's problematic notion that a thing is in essence that which it will become and the Biblical attestation of God as the One "who was and is and is to come"[151] is indicative of the distinction between an unbalanced assertion of an eschatological post-temporality and Barth's conception of the mutuality of pre-temporality,

---

148) W.Pannenberg, Theology and the Kingdom of God, Eng. trans. ed R.J.Neuhaus (Philadelphia,1975), pp.52ff. This somewhat tendentious interpretation of the Old Testament affirmation of God's reign is characteristic of the way in which all theology and all knowledge are made to conform to a presupposed eschatological framework.

149) ibid.,p.56

150) ibid.,pp.62ff.

151) Revelation 4: 8

supra-temporality and post-temporality as forms of God's eternity.[152]

Barth's assertion of the mutuality of the divine pre-temporality,supra-temporality and post-temporality derives from his understanding of eternity, not as a speculative, philosophical abstraction, but as the "real time" of the living God Himself.[153] Eternity is a perfection of the living God: "God lives eternally".[154] Pre-temporality, supra-temporality and post-temporality are the manner in which the living God is Himself related to time:

> "Eternity is really beginning, really middle, and really end because it is really the living God. There really is in it, then, direction, and a direction which is irreversable. There really is in it an origin and goal and a way from the one to the other. Therefore there is no uniformity in it. Its forms are not to be exchanged or confused."155

For this reason Barth can refer to the "mutual indwelling and interworking" of these three forms of eternity in terms of a "perichoresis" as in the doctrine of the Trinity itself. Eternity is the living

---

152) While Jürgen Moltmann's earlier theology, as a Theology of Hope, may have been guilty of a similar imbalance in his conception of the God with "future as his essential nature" (Jürgen Moltmann, Theology of Hope: On the Ground and the Implications of a Christian Eschatology, trans. by J.W.Leitch (London,1967),p.141 & passim) account must be taken of the correctives, if not retractions, implicit in his more recent emphasis upon the eternal Triunity of God (Jürgen Moltmann, The Trinity and the Kingdom of God: The Doctrine of God, trans. by Margaret Kohl (London, 1981).

153) C.D.II.1.pp.638ff

154) ibid.,p.640

155) ibid.,p.639

God Himself as the One who is pre-temporal, supra-temporal and post-temporal in authentic distinction and pure simultaneity, without "separations or distances or privations."[156] For this reason also Barth links the eternity of God, as a perfection of the Divine Freedom, with the glory of God.[157] God's glory is God Himself as the One He is, as the One who loves in freedom, as the One who makes Himself known as this God.[158] God's glory is "the self-revealing sum of all divine perfections. It is the fulness of God's deity, the emerging, self-expressing and self-manifesting reality of all that God is."[159] Therefore, God is eternal as the One He truly is, as this glorious God, as the One who loves in this specific freedom:

> "God endures in glory. It is not His being as such, mere abstract being, which is eternal. God has no such being. His being is eternal in glory. For the specific nature of God's eternity, the distinction and unity in which He is eternal, is also and as such the specific nature of God as the God of glory."160

This leads to a final observation regarding Barth's

---

156) ibid.; cf. p.660

157) ibid.,pp.640ff.

158) ibid.,p.641

159) ibid.,p.643

160) ibid.,pp.640f.

exposition of God's eternity, namely the relationship between the eternity of God and the constancy of God. God is who He is in His pre-temporality, supra-temporality and post-temporality, without rivalry or separation but in pure duration, because in His eternity He is constant as the One He is. The unity of the triune God as Father, Son and Spirit is a unity that includes order and succession, beginning and end "all at once in His own essence",[161] a unity in movement but without fleetingness or separation, without diminishment or change. The freedom of God's eternity is His freedom to be true to Himself, to be constant as this Triune God. God's eternity is His constancy in time on the basis of which "we can and may put our trust in Him".[162] This conception of God's constancy is neither in conflict with the affirmation of His livingness nor in conflict with Barth's understanding of His eternity as authentic temporality, it rather affirms that as the living God and in His authentic temporality "He is not Himself subject to or capable of any alteration, and does not cease to be Himself":[163]

> "...there neither is nor can be, nor is to be expected or even thought possible in Him ... any deviation, diminution or addition, nor any degeneration or rejuvenation, any

---

161) ibid.,p.615

162) ibid.,p.609

163) <u>C.D</u>.II.1.p.491

> alteration or non-identity or discontinuity. The one, omnipresent God remains the One He is. This is His constancy."164

Barth rejects the classical identification of God as the "immutable" (by which, according to Polanus, God must be conceived as the pure immobile) since such a conception would necessarily prohibit His freedom for relatedness to that which is distinct from Himself.[165] The authentic "immutability" of God cannot be equated with any philosophical abstraction but must be determined by a recognition of the actual "immutability" of God in the event of His self-revelation. For this reason Barth prefers to speak of God's constancy than His "immutability" since the latter is both "suspiciously negative" and retains its historical connotations of motionlessness.[166] God's livingness, which includes His authentic temporality, is affirmed by the declaration of His constancy but forfeited by the arbitrary attribution of motionlessness:[167]

> "His immutability is not a holy immobility and rigidity, a divine death, but the constancy of His faithfulness to Himself continually reaffirming itself in freedom."168

Despite the futuristic orientation of his conception of eternity

---

164) ibid.

165) ibid.,pp.493f.

166) ibid.,p.495

167) ibid.,pp.455ff.; cf. C.D.IV.1.pp.561f

168) C.D.IV.1.p.561

Pannenberg also considers the livingness of God to be that which distinguishes His constancy from the classical notion of "immutability":

> "...the eternal God of the Bible is a living, active God. ... In his eternal faithfulness to himself he is the source of history, through which he embraces all things in his omnipresence. Only for that reason can he be the God who works in history, in distinction to the god of Greek philosophy."169

For this reason it may be preferable to abandon the word "immutable" altogether:

> "...the God who has revealed Himself in Jesus Christ as sharing our lot is the God who is really free to make Himself poor, that we through His poverty might be made rich, the God invariant in love but not impassible, constant in faithfulness but not immutable."170

In distinction from any abstract "immutability" the constancy of the living God is confirmed and expressed in His actual relatedness to creation in space and time as a reality distinct from Himself.[171] God's constancy consists in the fact that, in the real history which He has in and with the world created by Him, He "does not become nor is He other than He is in Himself from eternity and in eternity",[172] God's total relatedness to creation in salvation and judgment occurs in conformity with Himself.[173] This conception of the constancy of God does not conflict with His omnipotence but rather identifies the authentic omnipotence of the living God. The power to do everything would not be the extension

---

169) W. Pannenberg, '<u>Time, Eternity, and Judgment</u>', pp. 75f.

170) T. F. Torrance, <u>Space, Time and Incarnation</u>, p.75

171) <u>C.D</u>. II.1.pp.499 ff.

172) ibid., p.502

173) ibid., pp.503 ff

of power but its limitation and removal since it would imply the jeopardizing of God's true omnipotence by a possibility for that which, according to His constancy, would be impossible. God's omnipotence, like His constancy, must not be considered as an absolute abstraction arbitrarily attributed to the divine being but as a perfection of God the character of which is determined by His own being. God's omnipotence consists in His power to be Himself and therefore to be constantly true to Himself:

> "It can be said that God can do "everything" only if the "can" is understood to mean that He Himself in His capacity to be Himself is the standard of what is possible, and if the "everything" is understood as the sum of what is possible for Him and therefore genuinely possible, and not simply the sum of what is "possible" in general. God cannot do everything without distinction. He can do only what is possible for Him and therefore genuinely possible. This does not imply any limitation of His omnipotence. Rather, it defines His omnipotence as His and therefore true omnipotence."174

The constant will and being of God which is the meaning and secret of the history of salvation as His relatedness to creation is Jesus Christ Himself: "He is immutably this God, and not another".[175] Since God is the same both in His revelation and in eternity Jesus Christ is Himself the authentic and constant will and being of God both in His relatedness to Himself and His relatedness to that which is distinct from Himself.[176] The constancy of the living God therefore consists in His free limitation of Himself to be unalterably this gracious God in Jesus Christ:[177]

---

174) ibid., pp.532 f

175) ibid., p.513

176) ibid., pp.512 ff.; cf. p.324

177) ibid., pp.518f.

> "The God in whose essential nature it lies to do this, not of necessity but in free love, is the constant God. But this "constancy" also involves the fact that He has actually done this in free love. Therefore God is constant, He does not alter, when He becomes and is one with the creature in Jesus Christ. For this happening is simply God Himself, His free life, in which He is inexhaustible, untiring, incapable of being diverted from His purpose. God does not contradict Himself in this act, but confirms and reveals Himself as the One He is, and as the Creator and Reconciler of His creation."178

Barth's exposition of God's eternity is an attempt to take account of both its authentic temporality and its pure simultaneity, to retain the distinctions of past, present and future but as com-present to God in pure duration, to affirm the actual livingness of God but in the constancy of His eternal conformity to Himself. The common criticism of Barth's account is therefore nothing if not predictable, namely that Barth is trying "to have it both ways", that he is "halting between two opinions".[179] Is it not inherently meaningless to affirm both the authentic temporality and the pure simultaneity of God's eternity? How can "eminent temporality" include a quality of "non-temporality"? Is not this to stretch language beyond the bounds of rationality? Is it not that duration and simultaneity have at least the appearance of being contraries?[180]

---

178) ibid., p.515

179) Perhaps Barth's conception of God's omnipresence in terms of both remoteness and proximity could be cited as an instance of a similar equivocation (C.D.II.1.pp.461 f.)?

180) Colin E. Gunton, Becoming and Being, p.179

Colin Gunton instances Barth's ambiguity by reference to his utilization of Boethius's definition of eternity with reference to God's eminent temporality, while H. P. Owen follows Aquinas in regarding the statement as "the definitive formulation of classical theology's equation of eternity with timelessness".[181] (But does Barth's employment of this definition necessarily implicate him in a previous interpretation of it, particularly when he has delineated his own alternative application of the statement in terms of God's livingness?). Colin Gunton suggests that this apparent ambiguity regarding eternity is the source of difficulties throughout Barth's theology, particularly that he has "failed to maintain the full temporal reality of the revelation event":[182]

> "The root of the ambiguity would then seem to be a persistent tendency of Barth's to contaminate the temporality of revelation with a conception of revelation as a timeless theophany, which then reappears in the attempted combination of eminent temporality and timeless eternity."183

While similar criticisms are expressed by a wide range of theological writers[184] particular attention must be given to Richard Roberts's profound analysis of Barth's conception of eternity since

---

181) ibid., p.180; cf. H. P. Owen, Concepts of Deity (London, 1971). p.19. Note that Owen himself suggests that Barth's attempts to speak of God as both timeless and temporal are "instances of sheer self-contradiction" (p.107).

182) Colin E. Gunton, Becoming and Being, p.181.

183) ibid.

184) Colin Gunton refers especially to R. W. Jenson, J. Moltman (in Theology of Hope) and H. Bouillard (H. Bouillard, Karl Barth. vol.I: Genèse et évolution de la théologie dialectique & vols.II & III: Parole de Dieu et existence humaine (Paris, 1957).

he not only summarizes these widespread criticisms but also offers his own incisive strictures.[185] The criticisms proposed by Roberts are set in the context of his own deep appreciation and respect for Barth's theological work as "the greatest and doubtless the last movement in the western tradition of attempts to surmount the antitheses of man and God, eternity and time, ... in living synthesis."[186] Yet while Roberts acknowledges Barth's achievement to be "breath-taking"[187] and while he recognizes that any ambiguity in this "synthesis" arises from Barth's concern "to give theological understanding to the insights of Scripture into the relationship of eternity and time"[188] he also considers the ambiguity of Barth's synthesis to be systematic and therefore fundamentally debilitating. According to Roberts, the very fact that R. W. Jenson considers Barth's conception of time in terms of a "historicizing" of revelation while Heinz Zahrnt contrastingly views it as a radical de-temporalization of theology is itself indicative of a fundamental ambiguity.[189] It should be noted however, that in his dismissal

---

185) R. H. Roberts, 'Eternity and Time in the Theology of Karl Barth'; cf. 'Barth's Doctrine of Time; its nature and implications' .

186) R. H. Roberts, 'Eternity and Time in the Theology of Karl Barth' p.476

187) ibid., p.389

188) ibid., p.109

189) ibid., p.92; cf. Heinz Zahrnt, The Question of God: Protestant Theology in the Twentieth Century, trans by R. A. Wilson (London, 1969).

of Barth's Trinitarian theology as an eternalization of the whole historical process Zahrnt makes virtually no reference to Barth's conception of the authentic temporality of God's eternity, the compresence of all time, history and decisions in God's pure simultaneity, but appears to continue with that definition of eternity as infinite time past, specifically rejected by Barth:[190]

> "...how can anything still happen when everything has already 'happened' in eternity?...
> The basing of the events of salvation upon a timeless event in the perfect tense results for Barth in an irreparable loss of concrete historical reality."[191]

Irrespective of any ambiguity in Barth, Zahrnt's comments are more indicative of a refusal to take serious account of the dipolarity which characterizes Barth's conception of God's eternity, a determination to consider one strand of his teaching in isolation, one-sidedly inferring a monistic timelessness without reference to Barth's concern for actuality and his consequent rejection of such abstractions.[192]

At the centre of the criticisms of Barth by Roberts is the view that Barth's conception of God's eternity as "real time" involves the effective denial of contingent reality. God and creation cannot be related contingently if that relationship is determined by any necessary fact or statement. Therefore, if the 'possibility'

---

190) H. Zahrnt, <u>The Question of God</u>, pp.112 ff.

191) ibid., p.113

192) cf. ibid., p.114

of revelation is determined by the 'reality' of an eternal covenant of creation and election the contingency of creation in relation to God is forfeit.[193] If all reality is determined by the actus purus et singularis (interpreted as 'real time') as a consequence of an underlying identity between ontology and temporality "then could not the whole massive architectonic be thought of as teetering on the brink of the abyss of timelessness, once the dialectic of 'real time' had been exposed?"[194] According to Roberts this 'real time' of God's being in act can only be regarded as 'temporal' in a "very Pickwickian sense",[195] as "nominally 'timeful', but in reality 'timeless'".[196] Barth's concept of 'real time' is so lacking in the characteristic features of time as experienced by man as to render the ascription 'time' meaningless:[197]

> "Despite Barth's Herculean labours does not there remain a certain logical problem and conceptual difficulty in asserting that eternity is the prototype of time when it lacks exactly those aspects of transience and succession which are inevitably associated with time?"198

---

193) R. H. Roberts, 'Eternity and Time in the Theology of Karl Barth', pp.326 f.

194) ibid., p.470

195) ibid., p.476

196) ibid., p.463

197) ibid., pp.462 ff.; cf. R. H. Roberts, 'Barth's Doctrine of Time: its nature and implications', p.88

198) R. H. Roberts, 'Eternity and Time in the Theology of Karl Barth', p.313

While Roberts acknowledges the reductive nature of this interpretation of the Church Dogmatics and while he also recognizes the complexity of Barth's argument which resists "simplistic reduction"[199] such mitigating considerations do not detract from the gravity of his criticisms. If Barth's interpretation of God's eternity is only nominally temporal it lapses at once into abstract timelessness. Moreover, if this merely nominal temporality is posited as the ontological basis of time then the possibility of authentically contingent reality is excluded. Yet Roberts levels an even deeper censure against Barth which penetrates the very heart of his theological method and underlies all other criticisms, namely the censure of what Roberts refers to as the "totalitarian" structure of Barth's theological method:

> "One major factor influencing in different ways both the devoted disciples and the disaffected has been the great intellectual offence offered by the assertion of a reality about which so much could be said at such length. As we have seen, this reality is a single one which brooks no rival or opposition. It either exists and demands submission in the 'acknowledgement' of faith or it cannot exist for those who refuse to grant its totalitarian demands."200

Ultimately Roberts' criticisms of Barth derive from his predetermined response to the question of whether or not "in theological investigation a creative encounter is made which demands intellectual and conceptual adjustment as ontology determines

---

199) ibid., pp.470 f.

200) R. H. Roberts, 'Barth's Doctrine of Time: its nature and implications', p.145.

epistemology."[201] Thus Roberts attempts to assess the achievements of the Church Dogmatics according to "the common tests of rationality",[202] refusing to "capitulate his own rationality in the face of the apparent rationality of revelation".[203] That Roberts resists Barth's conception of God's eternity as 'real time' since it lacks the characteristic features of time as experienced by man is surely an outcome of his rejection of this totalitarian theological method. But this rejection of the totalitarian demands of the rationality of revelation implies their replacement by the totalitarian demands of an autonomous rationality determining the acceptability or non-acceptability of any rationality of revelation.

It is the essence of Barth's theological method that actuality determines rationality, that the event of revelation determines epistemology, that the act in which God is known determines the form and manner of His knowability. It is not that Barth is anti-rational but that, in his concern for reality, he recognizes that authentic rationality must take account of the actuality of the event in which God reveals Himself and thus be determined by it.[204]

---

201) R. H. Roberts, 'Eternity and Time in the Theology of Karl Barth', p.312

202) ibid., p.473

203) ibid., p.464

204) cf. T. F. Torrance, Theological Science, p.9

T. F. Torrance clearly expresses the epistemological task implicit in this theological method towards the beginning of his study of Theological Science:

> "Our primary task, epistemologically, is to focus our attention on the area where God is actually known, and seek to understand that knowledge in its concrete happening, out of its own proper ground, and in its own proper reference to objective reality."205

It is therefore both irrational and unscientific to admit independent presuppositions prescribing the form and manner of God's knowability.[206] This impartiality "to anything and everything outside of or beyond the object" constitutes that which Torrance considers to be a "proper circularity" and that which Roberts dismisses as "unsatisfying".[207] Thus Brian Johanson is correct in recognizing that Roberts in fact "repudiates everything that is essential to Barth's theology".[208] It is precisely because the event of God's revelation is temporally actual that Barth affirms the time of this divine event as 'real time' despite its lack of the features of

---

205) ibid., p.25 f.

206) ibid., p.26; cf. pp.34 & 54

207) ibid., pp.35 f.; cf. R. H. Roberts, 'Eternity and Time in the Theology of Karl Barth' pp.313 ff.

208) Brian Johanson, 'Review Article of Karl Barth: Studies of his Theological Method', King's Theological Review, 4 (1981), 37-43 (pp.40f & 42); cf. R. H. Roberts, 'Barth's Doctrine of Time: its nature and implications', p.146. Johanson is probably also correct when, in response to Roberts's portrayal of Barth's work as "the stricken, glorious hulk of some great Dreadnought", he suspects that "on the day when all theological ships are tested on the great sea of eternity ... it will be Roberts's theology that will sink unnoticed like some unknown rowing boat in which he valiantly but hopelessly tried to rescue Barth from himself." (ibid.).

fleetingness characteristic of time as experienced by man. The rationality of temporality and spatiality is determined by the actuality of the event of God's self-revelation in time and space. It is surely not 'totalitarian' to insist that the inherent rationality of this actual event must determine the subsequent rationality of our attempts to comprehend it. Conversely, it is both 'totalitarian' and 'irrational' to insist, as Roberts appears to do, that the inherent rationality of this actual event must be discarded or at least adjusted in the light of a presupposed and autonomous rationality.

Moreover, Roberts interprets Barth's conception of eternity as a denial of contingency since he, like so many of Barth's critics,[209] "appears to force him to say what he does not say"[210] insisting upon resolving the dynamic tension of Barth's account of eternity into either a monistic timelessness on the one hand or an anthropocentric secularity on the other. Although Roberts, following Jenson, recognizes the tendentious dangers of reading Barth one-sidely both critics seem strangely compelled to do so.[211] The dipolarity of Barth's Doctrine of God, the genuine freedom in which God genuinely relates Himself to reality that is genuinely distinct

---

209) cf. H. Bouillard, Karl Barth, vol.II.pp.73ff.; vol.III. pp.291f.; H. Zahrnt, The Question of God, p.114; R. W. Jenson, Alpha and Omega: A study in the Theology of Karl Barth (New York, 1963), pp.161 ff.

210) Brian Johanson, op.cit., p.41.

211) R. H. Roberts, 'Eternity and Time in the Theology of Karl Barth', pp.470f.; cf.R. W. Jenson, God after God, pp.151 ff.

from Himself, is the means by which the contingency of that distinct reality is preserved. God's eternity, as His authentic temporality, comprehends the past, present and future of all reality _without_ the forfeiture of the distinctness and contingency of that reality. God's constancy _does not exclude_ the reality of His history as the living God in free relatedness to His creation.[212] However, the nature and manner of this contingency of created reality must be clearly delineated not as an autonomous contingency but as a created contingency in relation to God's freedom, straining language with T. F. Torrance to speak of a "contingent necessity":

> "Since it was created out of nothing, it might have been quite different from what it is, but now that it has come into being it has a contingent necessity in that it cannot not be what it now is. Considered in itself, then, there is only _the_ world, this world that has come into being, but considered from the side of God's creation it is only one of all possible worlds. Thus we must think of God's relation to the world in terms of an infinite differential, but we must think of the world's relation to God in terms of a created necessity in which its contingence is not negated."[213]

In the course of his discussion of the development of New Testament Christology Colin Gunton utilizes a helpful (though limited) illustration of this 'contingent' or '_a posteriori_' form of necessity:

---

212) _C.D._II.1.p.502. Note how briefly Roberts reviews Barth's exposition of God's constancy (R. H. Roberts, 'Eternity and Time in the Theology of Karl Barth', pp.134 ff.)

213) T. F. Torrance, _Space, Time and Incarnation_, p.66. This distinction, best identified as that between an _a priori_ and an _a posteriori_ necessity, is of crucial importance to Barth's Doctrine of God; cf. chapter 4 of this thesis.

> "It is sometimes remarked that a great piece of music, viewed as a completed work, has about it an impression of necessity. A single note altered anywhere would destroy it. Yet few would want to suggest that while he was composing it the composer was compelled to develop it as he did. It is only as we view it 'backwards' that its inherent necessity is conceived and understood."214

This authentic form of the world's contingency in relation to God is only jeopardized when the essential dipolarity of God's relatedness to the world is disregarded or 'resolved'. According to Barth the irreducible tension of this dipolar structure is demanded by the manner of God's actual relatedness in space and time as the One who loves in Freedom. David Ford is correct when, in response to Roberts's quest for a "clear conceptual resolution of the relation of time to eternity", he interprets Barth as "suggesting that there can be no such resolution".[215] Furthermore, the implications of

---

214) Colin E. Gunton, Yesterday and Today, p.71. For a further illustration of this form of necessity with reference to a musical performance see Daniel W. Hardy, 'Christian Affirmation and the Structure of Personal Life' in Belief in Science and in Christian Life: The relevance of Michael Polanyi's thought for Christian Faith and Life, ed. T. F. Torrance (Edinburgh, 1980), pp.71-90 (p.74). It is this 'contingent necessity' of creation in Barth's thought that is expressed by Wilfried Härle in terms of the being of creation as ontologically grounded in the grace of God (Wilfried Härle, Sein und Gnade: Die Ontologie in Karl Barths Kirchlicher Dogmatik (Berlin and New York, 1975), pp.70ff. & 270ff.).

215) David Ford, 'Barth's interpretation of the Bible' in Karl Barth: Studies of his Theological Method, ed. S. W. Sykes (Oxford, 1979), pp.55-87 (p.75).

Roberts's criticisms are more deeply exposed by Brian Johanson:

> "To reject these complementarities as 'ambiguous', 'contradictory', and 'equivocation' is possible only if one rejects the wholeness of Jesus Christ."216

In his own penetrating (though much underrated) analysis of Barth's concept of eternity, R. W. Jenson, previously to R. H. Roberts, draws attention to this irreducible tension that characterizes Barth's dipolar understanding of the Doctrine of God. Barth's conception of eternity could be interpreted, and is probably correctly interpreted, in terms of God's radical temporality, yet an examination of that which constitutes the radicalness of God's temporality tends towards a notion of God's temporal transcendence reminiscent of traditional theology's concept of timelessness:[217]

> "Just as the Commentary on Romans can be read as the perfected theology of a religion of timeless eternity, so the Church Dogmatics can be read as the most perfect eternalizing yet achieved of the gospel's themes and story. It is clear that this is the opposite of what Barth intends, and that when we read his theology so we are reading it wrongly——but there is something that compels us to read it wrongly in this way."218

Jenson, unlike many other critics of Barth already mentioned, is therefore confident that Barth is misunderstood when his exposition is resolved into a restatement of monistic timelessness, that his analogy of time and eternity "is not intended to be the

---

216) Brian Johanson, op.cit., p.41

217) R. W. Jenson, God after God, pp.151 ff.

218) ibid., p.152

platonic analogy of moving time to unmoving eternity",[219] but he is concerned to ascertain why, when Barth so resolutely banishes "the Cheshire cat of timeless eternity", the grin of that cat "decidedly lingers on".[220] Jenson locates the source of this "ambiguity" in the manner by which Barth expresses God's transcendence, the particular form of His dipolarity. According to Barth God's transcendence consists in the freedom of His relatedness which implies a distinction between "God-in-himself" and "God-for-us" even though the latter is identified as the image of the former.[221] For Jenson such a distinction understood in terms of God's temporality "can only be" the distinction "between timelessness and time".[222] Thus Barth's use of analogy as a means of referring to God's transcendence is itself the source of his ambiguity.[223]

By way of alternative Jenson proposes the possibility of considering God's transcendent freedom in terms of His futurity.[224] In antithesis to any conception of God's transcendence as His supposed immunity to the danger of an open future Jenson suggests that the resurrection appearances of Jesus are the revelation of

---

219) ibid., p.154
220) ibid., p.153
221) ibid.
222) ibid.
223) ibid., p.154
224) ibid., p.155 & pp.157 ff.

God's "futurity to what already is":[225]

> "If the futurity of God is thus the structure of his trinitarian life with and for us, we do not need to safeguard God's freedom by the clumsy device of calling the "dispensational Trinity" the "image" of an "immanent Trinity." For futurity _is_ the condition of freedom. God is free over against the realized actualities of his trinitarian life with us, because he is always ahead of them; he always can be otherwise triune than he has so far been. This freedom _is_ his trinitarian life. It is a permanent, transcendent freedom, because it is love's complete but never-ended openness to the future. Just so, as love's openness, this unpredictability of God is gospel and not threat: we do not know what God will be, but we know that every new event of his eternal creativity will be seen, when it has occurred, as an inevitable step in the life of the good God we have known."226

Jenson is at his most brilliant when elucidating Barth's theology and at his most rhetorical and problematical when expounding his own alternative. Having perceptively exposed, throughout his analysis, an imbalance of Barth's Trinitarian concept of time towards the past the only alternative offered by Jenson is a far more elusive Trinitarian concept of time which is unbalanced towards the future. If God's transcendence consists in His futurity and if His futurity implies that He "can be otherwise triune than he has so far been" how can a meaningful belief in His actual revelation in the past and the present be retained? God cannot authentically actualize Himself in the event of His self-revelation if the transcendence of His essential nature consists, not in His free constancy, but in an indeterminate futurity. Jenson accepts that the extent to which his proposals are either a

---

225) ibid., p.159

226) ibid., p.174

perversion or a fulfilment of Barth's theology is a matter for another to judge.[227] Such a judgment must tend towards the former alternative since Jenson's proposals, far from being an adjustment, amendment or fulfilment of Barth's theology, actually distort the very foundation of Barth's Doctrine of God, forfeiting the actuality of His free self-revelation in favour of a futurity and consequent provisionality reminiscent of Pannenberg's futurist ontology and Moltmann's Theology of Hope.[228]

Moreover, Jenson's dissatisfaction with Barth's account of God's transcendence is less than persuasive since he appears to misconstrue the precise manner of God's dipolarity in Barth's theology, reading into Barth's use of "image" and "analogy" a distinction and consequent ambiguity that simply are not there. While Barth's conception of the dipolarity of God's being preserves the transcendent freedom of His relatedness *ad extra* it does so without constituting any ambiguous distinction since this transcendent freedom is as much the form of His relatedness *ad intra* as it is the form of His relatedness *ad extra*. Both in Himself and for us God is the One who loves in freedom.[229] It is this radical identity within both the immanent and the economic Trinity that distinguishes Barth's doctrine of God from traditional theology's notion of absoluteness and the consequent notion of a timeless eternity. God's eternity

---

227) ibid., p.193

228) cf. above pp.55ff.

229) cf. chapter 4 of this thesis.

is the compresence, in pure simultaneity, of His actual time for us.

However, the substance of Jenson's criticisms consists in the observation, for which there is a general consensus amongst Barth's critics,[230] that, despite the Trinitarian structure of his conception of eternity, there is a persistent orientation towards pastness and completion and a consequent weakness with reference to futurity. Even within Barth's discussion of the three forms of God's eternity one can detect an observable reticence in his account of God's supra-temporality, a hesitation understandably motivated by Barth's concern to totally disassociate himself from the erroneous immanentism which vitiated the theology of the 19th century. This reticence, which is wholly unnecessary within the Trinitarian structure of Barth's conception of eternity and which continually undermines the clarity with which he affirms the actuality of eternity as God's time, finally "comes home to roost" in Barth's similarly debilitating and structurally unnecessary reticence with reference to the doctrine of the Spirit.[231]

---

230) cf. Colin E. Gunton, Becoming and Being, pp.181 ff.; Jürgen Moltmann, Theology of Hope, pp.37 ff.; David Ford, op.cit., pp.84 f.; B. C. Hanson, 'Hope and Participation in Christ: A study in the Theology of Barth and Pannenberg' (dissertation, Princeton, 1970), p.53

231) Colin E. Gunton, Becoming and Being, pp.164 f. & 218; cf. chapter 6 of this thesis.

II The Concept of Eternity and the Time of Jesus Christ

a) The Easter time of Jesus Christ:

Since Barth's distinctive conception of eternity as God's time is an outcome of his theological method whereby all theological assertions are determined by the actuality of God's self-revelation it is now necessary to focus attention upon that actuality, the specific occurrence of God's authentic temporality in the time of Jesus Christ. The actuality of God's temporal relatedness to man and the freedom of that relatedness can only realistically be affirmed Christologically, as an exposition of the actual event of the Word becoming flesh, of the Word becoming time.[1] The actual temporality of God is the occurrence of His temporality among us as 'the Lord in our midst':[2]

> "In Jesus Christ it comes about that God takes time to Himself, that He Himself, the eternal One, becomes temporal, that He is present for us in the form of our own existence and our own world, not simply embracing our time and ruling it, but submitting Himself to it, and permitting created time to become and be the form of His eternity."3

R. W. Jenson observes that it is Barth's essentially Trinitarian conception of God's temporality, a conception determined by the actuality of the resurrection of Jesus Christ, that distinguishes Barth from the markedly non-Trinitarian conception of eternity expressed by Schubert Ogden who effectively forfeits any positive

---

1) C.D.I.2.p.50; cf. C.D.II.1.pp.616 ff.

2) C.D.I.1.pp.399 f.; cf. C.D.III.2.pp.437 ff.

3) C.D.II.1.p.616

content of temporality through his rejection as "mythological" of the possibility of God acting in history:[4]

> "Unless we are willing to let the event of Christ be constitutive for the event of God, the attempt to speak of God's temporality will necessarily involve smuggling in determinants from the christological tradition without methodical warrants for so doing."5

The lifetime of Jesus, the history which was the span between His birth and His death, was temporal in the same manner that the lifetime of all men is temporal. The time of the Incarnation is necessarily genuinely temporal, historical time.[6] But, unlike other men, Jesus has "a further history", the time between His resurrection (Auferweckung) and ascension, His "Easter history".[7] For Barth it is this Easter time of Jesus Christ, the time of His presence as the risen One (Auferstehung), that is determinative for a valid conception of time and eternity. He even maintains, in contrast to Oscar Cullmann, that it was the constraint of this

---

4) R. W. Jenson, God after God: the God of the Past and the God of the Future, seen in the Work of Karl Barth (Indianapolis and New York, 1969, p.150; commenting on S. M. Ogden, The Reality of God and other essays (London 1967); cf. Colin E. Gunton, Becoming and Being: The Doctrine of God in Charles Hartshorne and Karl Barth (Oxford, 1978), pp.48 ff.

5) R. W. Jenson, God after God, p.150

6) C.D.III.2.pp.440 f.; cf. C.D.I.2.p.50

7) C.D.III.2.p.441

particular history which determined and formed the New Testament authors' understanding of time.[8] This Easter time of Jesus Christ is His Easter history, not just a timeless idea but an actual event with an objective content within time and space, a happening "once upon a time".[9] For all the distinction between this Easter time of Jesus Christ and the lifetime which preceded it nonetheless it must be recognized as His concrete existence in time and space:[10]

> "If Jesus Christ is not risen——bodily, visibly, audibly, perceptibly, in the same concrete sense in which He died, as the texts themselves have it——if He is not also risen, then our preaching and our faith are vain and futile; we are still in our sins. And the apostles are found "false witnesses," because they have "testified of God that he raised up Christ, whom he raised not up" (I Cor. 15 14 f.). If they were true witnesses of His resurrection, they were witnesses of an event which was like that of the cross in its concrete objectivity."[11]

Since it an actual event of time and space the resurrection of Jesus Christ is objectively true, its truth does not depend upon the acceptance or rejection of the report about it. Barth

---

8) ibid., pp.443 f. Barth's basic criticism of Cullmann's work refers to the lack of any real significance which the latter accords to the resurrection in his "reconstruction of the New Testament conception of time and history". This central aspect of Barth's criticism is strangely ignored by Cullmann in his response to his critics; Oscar Cullmann, Christ and Time: The Primitive Christian Conception of Time and History, trans. by Floyd V. Filson, 3rd edition (London, 1962), pp.xvii ff.

9) C.D.III.2.p.442; cf. C.D.IV.1.pp.333 ff.

10) C.D.IV.3.p.312

11) C.D.IV.1.pp.351 f.

totally rejects the "demythologizing" proposal of Rudolf Bultmann whereby he locates the truth of the Easter event in "the rise of faith in the risen Lord".[12] The New Testament texts refer primarily not to the formation of an Easter faith by Jesus' disciples but to the foundation of that faith by Jesus Christ Himself; to the incontrovertible fact which "compelled and drove the disciples to this faith":[13]

> "Faith in the risen Lord springs from His historical manifestation, and from this as such, not from the rise of faith in Him."14

It is hardly surprising that Barth, in the light of his methodological concern for actuality, should regard Bultmann's existentialist interpretation of Scripture and his demythologization of such acts of God as looking "suspiciously like docetism".[15]

However, while Barth so clearly affirms the actuality of this Easter time of Jesus Christ as an event of time and space, while he even refers to it as an occurrence in human history which

---

12) C.D.III.2.pp.443 ff., commenting on Rudolf Bultmann, 'New Testament and Mythology' in Kerygma and Myth: A Theological Debate, vol.I,ed. H. W. Bartsch, trans. by R. H. Fuller (London, 1953), pp.1-44 (p.42).

13) C.D.IV.1.pp.339 ff.; cf. Karl Barth, 'Rudolf Bultmann - An Attempt to Understand Him' in Kerygma and Myth: A Theological Debate, vol.II,ed. H. W. Bartsch, trans. by R. H. Fuller (London, 1962), pp.83-132 (p.100 f.).

14) C.D.III.2.p.443

15) Karl Barth, 'Rudolf Bultmann - An Attempt to Understand Him', p.111; cf. C.D.III.2.p.448 & pp.451 ff.

"must be like all other history in regard to its historicity",[16] he is careful not to define or restrict the 'historicity' of this event in any 'positivistic' sense. The event of the crucifixion of Jesus Christ can be referred to as 'historical' in the sense that it can be understood to have occurred as a result of human decisions and actions, although to restrict this reference and not also to understand it as a result of God's decision and action, as an event of His judgment and salvation, would be to misunderstand it.[17] But the event of the resurrection (Auferweckung) occurs in a "historical sphere of a different kind",[18] it does not occur in any sense as the result of human decisions and actions but purely as a result of God's decision and action, as a pure act of God.[19] Barth observes that while the New Testament gives a full account of the crucifixion of Jesus Christ there is "no real account of His resurrection"; the resurrection (Auferweckung) is presupposed by the accounts of "appearances of the Resurrected", the presence of the risen One (Auferstehung). Perhaps this should be understood as itself indicative of the non-describable character of the resurrection (Auferweckung) as a pure act of God.[20] Moreover, the event of the resurrection remains beyond the scope of the

---

16) C.D.IV.1.p.298

17) C.D.IV.1.p.300

18) ibid.,p.334

19) ibid.,p.300

20) ibid.,pp.334 f.

historical investigation, verification and proof that are the concerns of much modern scholarship. Within the limits prescribed by this 'positivistic' understanding of historicity the event of the resurrection cannot be described in terms of history but in terms of "saga" or "legend". However, even if the event of the resurrection cannot be referred to as history "in this sense", even if the terms "saga" and "legend" are admitted, this is certainly not to imply that the event never actually occurred or that it occurred only as the development of Easter faith among the disciples:[21]

> "The event is not perhaps "historical" in the modern sense, but it is fixed and characterised as something which actually happened among men like other events, and was experienced and later attested by them."22

For this reason, because it is a pure act of God beyond any "historicist" concept of history, Barth refers to the event of the resurrection as a "pre-historical" happening, an utterly unique event.[23] The German word Urgeschichte is probably better rendered as 'primordial history' or 'primal history' than as 'pre-history' since Barth's reference is to a history that is first in order, the primary ground of history, and not simply to that which chronologically precedes history.[24] Eberhard Jüngel notes that

---

21) ibid.,pp.335 f.

22) C.D.IV.2.p.143; cf. John Thompson, Christ in Perspective: Christological Perspectives in the Theology of Karl Barth (Edinburgh, 1978), p.95

23) C.D.IV.1.p.336

24) Colin E. Gunton, 'Karl Barth's Doctrine of Election as part of his 'Doctrine of God', J.T.S., 25 (1974) 381-392 (p.388)

while Barth (rejecting his unhistorical use of the term in his commentary on Romans[25]) employs the word Urgeschichte in his Christian Dogmatics to express the relationship between revelation and history,[26] he rejects the term in the first volume of the Church Dogmatics[27] only to re-employ it when expounding the Doctrine of God and the Doctrine of Election.[28] Jüngel is surely correct in the observation that, far from being an inconsistency of Barth's development, the term is re-employed in a thoroughly Trinitarian context.[29] Barth's final use of the term Urgeschichte is with reference to the eternal event of electing love between the Father and the Son which occurs in time, not just in the Incarnation and the event of the resurrection of Jesus Christ, but in the totality of the pure acts of God in Creation, Reconciliation and Redemption that are the actualization of His eternal covenant with man in Jesus Christ.[30] The event of the resurrection is

---

25) Karl Barth, The Epistle to the Romans, translated from the sixth edition by Edwin C. Hoskyns (Oxford, 1933) pp. 248 ff.

26) Karl Barth, Prolegomena zur christlichen Dogmatik (Munich, 1927) pp. 230 ff.

27) C.D. I.2. pp. 57 f.

28) C.D. II.2. pp. 7 ff.

29) Eberhard Jüngel, The Doctrine of the Trinity: God's Being is in Becoming, trans. by Horton Harris, Monograph Supplements to the Scottish Journal of Theology, eds. T. F. Torrance and J. K. S. Reid (Edinburgh and London, 1976), pp. 75 f.

30) Surprisingly Jüngel only seems to refer to Barth's use of the term in relation to the event of the Incarnation and the divine decision which precedes it (ibid., p. 76).

Urgeschichte not just because it is a pure act of God beyond positivistic historical verification but because, as a pure act of God, it is the actualizing of the event of His electing love which is the primary basis of all history. Similarly the event of creation is Urgeschichte, not just because it is history which cannot be seen or comprehended, not just because it "is not history in the historicist sense",[31] not just because from a 'positivistic' perspective it is wholly "non-historical",[32] but because, as the beginning of all time, it is "ultimately a reflection and counterpart of the time of grace".[33]

When Barth refers to the event of creation and the event of resurrection negatively as 'non-historical' in the 'positivistic' sense, or positively as urgeschichtlich, he is certainly not implying that these events never actually occurred since he refuses to be confined by historicist terminology. Not all history is 'historical' in this historicist sense, indeed, in its immediacy to God every event of history could be defined as 'non-historical' since this immediacy to God, its ultimate significance and "decisive elements or dimensions", its character as Urgeschichte, is neither perceivable nor comprehensible from a 'positivistic' standpoint.[34] The event of creation is exclusively Urgeschichte, exclusively 'non-historical' in the historicist sense, since, as a pure act of God in which

---

31) C.D.III.1.p.78

32) ibid.,p.79

33) ibid.,p.76

34) ibid.,p.80

"Creator and creature confront each other only in immediacy", it is a genuine happening that is wholly beyond the scope of historicist methodology.[35] Because the event of creation has this character Barth recognizes elements of 'saga' in the Scriptural account of the event, though he explicitly uses the word 'saga' "in the sense of an intuitive and poetic picture of a pre-historical reality of history which is enacted once and for all within the confines of time and space."[36] Similarly, the event of the resurrection of Jesus Christ is exclusively Urgeschichte since, as a pure and unique act of God, it "has actually happened although it cannot be grasped historically".[37] This unique event of the resurrection cannot be grasped in any other way than by faith. The disciples were encountered by the risen Jesus Christ in such a way that "they were placed in the decision of faith or lack of faith".[38] Even if it were possible to suppose that the Easter event had the character of 'history' in the historicist sense it would still be impossible, by purely historicist method, to account for its significance to the disciples and to the Christian community for revelation, reconciliation and redemption;[39] the total significance and reality of this event consist in its being exclusively an act of God, exclusively Urgeschichte.

---

35) ibid.

36) ibid.,p.81; cf. C.D.I.1.pp.326 ff. Note that in using the word 'saga' of the creation accounts Barth intends to distinguish these narratives from 'history' in the historicist sense on the one hand and from 'myth' on the other (C.D. III.1.pp.81 ff.).

37) C.D.IV.1.p.336

38) C.D.IV.1.p.728

39) ibid.,p.729

It is not surprising that Barth should again be accused of ambiguously attempting to 'have it both ways' by holding together two logically incompatible assertions:

> "How can Barth both claim the resurrection as a historical fact (albeit only describably indirectly, through saga-like realistic stories) and also refuse to base his conclusions on ordinary historical investigation?"40

Van Harvey, in the course of his examination of the relationship between faith and historical knowledge, argues that to affirm the resurrection of Jesus Christ as a real event of time and space while denying the appropriateness of testing that claim in the manner by which such claims are normally verified is lacking in moral integrity.[41] This form of criticism rests on the premise that all events must be verifiable by modern historicist method if they are to be accepted as 'historical'. Barth dismisses this 'positivistic' assumption of uniformity as "sheer superstition":

> "It is sheer superstition to suppose that only things which are open to "historical" verification can have happened in time. There may have been events which happened far more really in time than the kind of things Bultmann's scientific historian can prove."42

---

40) David Ford, 'Barth's interpretation of the Bible' in Karl Barth: Studies of his Theological Method, ed. S. W. Sykes (Oxford, 1979),pp.55-87 (p.80); cf. A. Brandenburg, 'Der Zeit- und Geschichtsbegriff bei Karl Barth', Theologie und Glaube 45 (1955) 357-378 (pp.377f.).

41) Van A. Harvey, The Historian and the Believer: The Morality of Historical Knowledge and Christian Belief (London, 1967), pp.153 ff. Note that Van Harvey assumes a greater degree of development in Barth's thought between Romans and the Church Dogmatics than the texts appear to allow (ibid., cf. K. Barth, Romans, p.30).

42) C.D.III.2.p.446; cf. C.D.IV.1.pp.336 f.

The presupposition that all events can be established as 'historical' by a uniform method of verification arbitrarily excludes the possibility of a unique occurrence. Just as Barth's understanding of the resurrection of Jesus Christ as Urgeschichte precludes the possibility of it being verified by such historicist methods, so his critics, by their demand that all events must be verifiable by this form of scrutiny, preclude the possibility of such a unique event occurring.[43] This 'positivistic' epistemology must itself be indicted as 'lacking moral integrity' if an open-mindedness to the possibility of the unique, the possibility of revelation, the possibility of God being God in this way and in this actuality, is also a mark of epistemological 'morality'. This historicist critique of Barth again rests upon the issue of whether actuality determines rationality or whether an independently presupposed rationality, which excludes the possibility of a specific actuality, can itself be rational.[44]

Wolfhart Pannenberg also opposes the dualistic distinction between event and significance that underlies the historical positivism of E. Troeltsch and Rudolf Bultmann's existentialist differentiation between Historie and Geschichte. However, he also rejects Barth's concept of Urgeschichte as a further form of epistemological dualism, making Barth an unintentional ally of positivism.[45]

---

43) cf. David Ford, op.cit.,p.80

44) cf. C.D.III.2.p.447. Van Harvey is certainly aware that such counter arguments exist but he seems inexplicably oblivious to their force (cf. Van Harvey, op.cit.,pp.205 ff.)

45) W. Pannenberg, 'Redemptive Event and History' in Basic Questions in Theology, vol.1, trans. by George H. Kehm (London,1970),pp.15-80; cf. A. D. Galloway, 'The New Hegelians', Rel. St., 8 (1972), 367-371 (p.368).

Pannenberg proposes a thoroughly monistic understanding of revelation and history. Both the factuality and the significance of the resurrection of Jesus Christ must be knowable to unprejudiced human reason.[46] Specifically Pannenberg rejects the possibility of a single event being both a 'veiling' and an 'unveiling' of God, the possibility of a real event in time and space being knowable only in faith and through a distinct work of the Holy Spirit.[47] According to Pannenberg the Holy Spirit must be understood, not as a supplementary factor limiting the accessability of revelation, but as an inherent factor within the actual reporting of the Christ event.[48]

In one sense Pannenberg's contention is a classic 'I win if I change the rules' argument: he affirms the historicity of the resurrection by rescuing the term 'historicity' from the methodology of positivism, but it is in this positivistic sense that Barth considers the resurrection as 'non-historical'. However, Pannenberg's criticisms in essence challenge the very basis of Barth's doctrine of God and His revelation. By insisting upon a monistic conception of revelation within history, Pannenberg must necessarily forfeit a dipolar conception of God Himself. Only as the One who remains the free

---

46) W. Pannenberg, 'What is Truth?' in Basic Questions in Theology, vol.2, trans. by George H. Kehm (London, 1971), pp.1-27(p.26).

47) W. Pannenberg, 'Insight and Faith' in Basic Questions in Theology, vol.2, pp.28-45 (especially pp.43ff.); cf. W. Pannenberg, The Apostles Creed: In the Light of Today's Questions, trans. by Margaret Kohl (London, 1972) pp.128ff.

48) W. Pannenberg, Jesus——God and Man, trans. by Lewis L. Wilkins and Duane A. Priebe (London, 1968) p.174.

Lord in the very event of His self-revelation, only as the One who loves in freedom, is God the free Lord in Himself.[49] For Barth the event of the resurrection of Jesus Christ, as necessarily a pure act of God, must have the character of Urgeschichte since it is the act of the One who remains free as the One He is even in that act. The reality of the event of resurrection can only be penetrated in faith and through the work of the Holy Spirit because it is an event of the One who is Lord, an urgeschichtlich event.[50] Pannenberg's rejection of this category of Urgeschichte derives directly from his relegation of any direct self-revelation of God to the universal end of history and his consequential conception of the resurrection as an apocalyptic prolepsis of that end of history rather than as itself the event of God's self-revelation in freedom.[51]

While the Easter-time of Jesus Christ is, in one sense, a time like all other times, an actual occurrence in time and space, it is also wholly distinct from all other times inasmuch as the risen Jesus Christ is free from the limitations of time; He is not subject to any passing away or change. In comparison to our time the

---

49) cf. T. F. Torrance, Theological Science (Oxford,1969),pp.37ff.

50) cf. C.D.IV.1.pp.728 ff.

51) W. Pannenberg, 'Redemptive Event and History' passim; cf. W. Pannenberg Jesus - God and Man,pp.66 ff. & 225 ff.

Easter time of Jesus Christ is "mastered time"; He lives as the Lord of time; His Easter time is also the time of the eternal God.[52]

> "The resurrection of Jesus Christ tells us ... that as the Crucified "He lives and reigns to all eternity" (Luther), that as the One who was, having been buried, He is not of the past, He did not continue to be enclosed in the limits of the time between His birth and death, but as the One who was in this time He became and is the Lord of all time, eternal as God Himself is eternal, and therefore present in all time."53

As the actual occurrence of God's eternity in time and space the Easter time of Jesus Christ is not only the revelation of that eternity as God's authentic temporality in pure simultaneity, not only the revelation of His true presence in time as the One who is truly free in time, it is also the revelation of the reality, significance and goal of all time. Time itself is real because, in the light of this Easter time of Jesus Christ, God becomes time. Time is not an absolute since, in this Easter time of Jesus Christ, God is not dominated by time but remains the free Lord of time. All time, as created time, has a goal and significance because this Easter time of Jesus Christ is the revelation of the eternal decision of God, the revelation of His eternal covenant with man in Jesus Christ actualized in time:[54]

---

52) C.D.I.2.p.52; cf. C.D.III.2.pp.463 ff. & C.D.IV.4.p.24

53) C.D.IV.1.p.313

54) C.D.III.2.pp.455 f. In order to dispute some of the assumptions underlying many recent approaches to 'Christology' Colin Gunton draws analogies from music and from developments within modern science to illustrate and support this relative nature of time and the possibility of a transcendent yet contingent rationality being located within it (Colin E. Gunton, Yesterday and Today: A study of continuities in Christology (London, 1983), pp.119ff.).

> "Since God in His Word had time for us, and at the heart of all other times there was this particular time, the eternal time of God, all other times are now controlled by this time, i.e., dominated, limited and determined by their proximity to it."55

Because God's eternal decision is revealed in the Easter time of Jesus Christ as actualized in human history it is identified as the goal and significance of all human history, as the "substance of all the preceding history of Israel and the hope of all the succeeding history of the Church."[56] In the Easter time of Jesus Christ it is revealed that the history which is the actualization of God's eternal covenant with man in Jesus Christ is not "dead history" but "eternal history", "the history of God with the men of all times, and therefore taking place here and now as it did then."[57] The Easter time of Jesus Christ was, therefore, not only the revelation of God's eternity in its distinction from man's 'fallen' time but also the revelation of His eternal decision in Jesus Christ "to give man a share in this time of His, in His eternity":[58]

> "The answer given by the life of Jesus to the questions of God and man makes His time the time which always was when men lived, which always is when they live, and which always will be when they will live. It makes this life at once the centre and the beginning and end of all the times of all the lifetimes of all men."59

---

55) ibid.,p.455

56) <u>C.D</u>.II.2.p.53

57) <u>C.D</u>.IV.1.pp.313 f.

58) <u>C.D</u>.III.2.p.451

59) <u>C.D</u>.III.2.p.440

However, the Easter time of Jesus Christ is not just the revelation of God's eternity, it is this simply because it is primarily the revelation of the eternal God Himself. As exclusively an act of God, independent of any human decisions or actions, the resurrection of Jesus Christ was the self-attestation of God.[60] The significance of the Easter time of Jesus Christ for the apostolic community was, therefore, that "in this time the _man_ Jesus was manifested among them in the mode of _God_."[61] As such the Easter time of Jesus Christ was itself the revelation of the preceding time of His life and death, the revelation that this whole time was the time of "the appearance and presence of God",[62] the revelation that this lifetime is His eternal time, the revelation that fulfilled time is "the time of the years 1-30."[63] This perception had been hitherto inaccessible in its totality to the apostles, only in the light of this Easter time was the presence of the reconciling God in Jesus Christ no longer a paradox, no longer a 'veiled' deity,[64] only in the freedom of God's grace could that reconciling presence be recognized.[65] The pre-Easter lifetime of Jesus Christ

---

60) _C.D_.IV.1.pp.301 f.

61) _C.D_.III.2.p.448

62) ibid.,p.454 f.

63) _C.D_.I.2.p.58

64) _C.D_.III.2.pp448 f.; cf. _C.D_.IV.1.p.301

65) _C.D_.IV.1.pp.304 f.

is only the unveiling of the reconciling God, only the revelation of the time He has for us in Jesus Christ, only the revelation of His grace, on the basis of the Easter time of Jesus Christ. It is not that this Easter time in any way transcends the lifetime and death of Jesus Christ but that in it the reality and significance of that lifetime and death are made known:

> "What the disciples came to see in the appearances of the Resurrected was no more and no less, but initially just the same, as what will one day be manifest to all eyes. They saw the full extent of His work and influence as achieved in His life and death."66

b) <u>The pre-Easter time of Jesus Christ:</u>

As the revelation of the eternal God and thereby the revelation of God's eternity, the revelation of His authentic pre-temporality, supra-temporality and post-temporality, the temporality of Jesus Christ "does not consist merely in the fact that He is", it consists also in the fact that He will be and has been.[67] That the Easter time of Jesus Christ signifies His being in the present and His futurity is a theme to which this chapter must return but it is necessary in the first place to consider further the relationship between the Easter time of Jesus Christ and His pre-Easter time.

---

66) *C.D.*IV.3.p.301; cf. John Thompson, op.cit .,pp.93 f.

67) *C.D.*III.2.p.474

For the apostolic community the Easter time of Jesus Christ primarily identified the reality of His immediate pre-Easter time, His lifetime and death. Who Jesus is in the to-day of His Easter time He was already in the yesterday of His pre-Easter time; who He is recognized to be by the apostles in His unveiled to-day He was already in His veiled yesterday.[68] In the light of His Easter time the pre-Easter time of His lifetime and death, no less than His Easter time itself, is the time of the Incarnation, the time of the One who, as Lord of time, freely becomes time for us.[69] Barth therefore thoroughly repudiates the spurious distinction between the Jesus of history and the Christ of faith that has vitiated so much recent New Testament study:[70]

> "It was neither a "historical Jesus" nor a "Christ of faith" which they knew and proclaimed, neither the abstract image of one in whom they did not yet believe nor the equally abstract image of one in whom they afterward believed. Instead, they proclaimed concretely the one Jesus Christ who had encountered them as the one who he was, even when they did not yet believe in him. Having their eyes opened by his resurrection, they were able to tell who he was who had made himself known to them <u>before</u> the resurrection. A twofold Jesus Christ, one who existed <u>before</u> and another who existed <u>after</u> Easter, can be deduced from New Testament texts only after he has been arbitrarily read into them. From the viewpoint even of "historical criticism," such an operation ought to be considered profoundly suspect."71

---

68) ibid., cf.p.448

69) ibid.,p.455

70) cf. John Thompson, op.cit.,pp.26 f.

71) Karl Barth, <u>Evangelical Theology: An Introduction</u>, trans. by Grover Foley (London and Glasgow, 1963), p.32; cf. <u>C.D</u>.IV.2.p.165.

Colin Gunton has argued similarly that, while there may be an observable diversity of ways in which the New Testament writers speak of Christ, they each "see him as in some way or other the presence of the eternal God in time".[72] Therefore any attempt to consider Jesus 'historically' apart from this essentially theological context is doomed to failure. If the person of Jesus Christ is not interpreted within this theological context assumed by the New Testament writers He is not seen at all:[73]

> "In so far as a Christology wishes to make use of the New Testament, it can only be as the intellectual quest of those who seek understanding of the faith in the present Christ which has been received in worship, biblical exploration, experience or some other means. This is because the New Testament knows of no other Jesus than the one who was past but has become present and will be in the future. It also knows of no other Jesus than the one whom it understands from the beginning as God's presence in time."74

Perhaps because he places such emphasis upon the Easter time of Jesus Christ as the time of revelation, the unveiling of that which previously was veiled, Barth has been criticized for his seemingly limited concern for the pre-Easter time of Jesus' lifetime and death. Colin Gunton comments upon Barth's "apparent lack of interest in the historical figure of Jesus",[75] and even John Thompson in his highly appreciative study of Barth's Christology suggests that the "ordinary human life and history of Jesus", though always affirmed, play a "minor, dependent role" leaving the impression that "these real aspects of Christ's humanity are... under-

---

72) Colin E. Gunton, Yesterday and Today, p.125.

73) ibid.

74) ibid., p.83

75) Colin E. Gunton, Becoming and Being, p.185; cf. R. W. Jenson, Alpha and Omega; A study in the Theology of Karl Barth (New York, 1963), p.140

estimated and underplayed".[76] Yet even if Barth should be guilty of such an underestimation it should be considered against the background of the misconceived concern for a supposed 'historical Jesus' that had dominated 19th century theology. Only in the light of His Easter time, but genuinely in the light of His Easter time, is Jesus truly recognized as the One He actually was in His pre-Easter lifetime. While Barth considers that the New Testament offers nothing in the nature of a "biographical portrait" in the sense of a modern character-sketch but only a "fragmentary picture" of the character of Jesus he attributes this to the singular character of the "real human person" attested by the New Testament writers, a person "so unique and to that extent so alien, that there are no categories in which to grasp it".[77] The New Testament certainly portrays this man as a man, but it has done so and could have done so only in the manner that "God and His revelation and Word and works can be attested by men".[78] Despite Barth's dismissal of the 'Jesus of history' movement as the deluded quest for a Jesus who never actually existed in history, the quest for a Jesus distinct from the One He was actually revealed to be in His Easter time, this ought not to be misinterpreted as a lack of interest in the actual pre-Easter time of Jesus. If Barth is guilty of such an under-

---

76) John Thompson, op.cit.,p.75

77) C.D.IV.2.p.165

78) ibid.

estimation the indictment could only be framed in terms of 'word space' specifically allocated to an account of Jesus' pre-Easter time. Against this 'lack of word space' must be held the emphatic passages in which Barth specifically affirms the reality, the nature and the import of this pre-Easter time:

> "Does not the apostolic to-day derive its mystery, power and dignity wholly and utterly from this yesterday. Here in this yesterday it takes place first and properly that the kingdom of God comes and is proclaimed in parable, but also by signs and wonders. Here it is that the reconciliation of the world with God is accomplished on the cross. Here it is that the foundations of the community are laid. Here it is that the great dividing line is secretly but very really drawn which marks off the new age from the old. Here there lives and moves and acts and suffers the Lord who reveals Himself as such at the resurrection, and then in the power of this revelation builds, maintains and rules His community until the new age is consummated. Here this Lord, the true Son of God, is also true Man, born of the Virgin Mary and made like one of us. _Et incarnatus est!_ Above all He is and therefore has been in this perfect. He would not be if He had not previously been."[79]

However, the pre-Easter time of Jesus Christ which was identified in its authenticity to the apostolic community was not limited to the immediate pre-Easter time of His lifetime and death but included the prophetic time of the Old Testament, the time of the history of the people of Israel in which the history of Jesus Christ "has not actually occurred, but is objectively prefigured".[80] Earlier Barth had considered the time of the Old Testament as the time of the witness to the expectation of the fulfilment of

---

79) _C.D_.III.2.pp.474 f.

80) _C.D_.III.2.p.475

revelation, but in so describing the Old Testament witness he refused to define the form of its expectation in terms of a simple "not yet":[81]

> "Where expectation is genuine, "previously" does not mean "not yet"; just as, where recollection is genuine, "subsequently" does not mean "no longer." Genuine expectation and genuine recollection are testimonies to revelation, mutually as different as expectation and recollection are different, but one in their content, in their object, in the thing attested, and also one in that for them this thing attested is neither merely future nor merely past; as "future" and as "past" it is present."82

The Old Testament, like the New Testament, witnesses to revelation as the free and concrete action of God.[83] Jesus Christ is the true content and theme of this witness to the extent that the kings, priests and prophets of the Old Testament really announce and signify Jesus Christ as the king, the priest and the prophet, the self-manifestation of God as the upholder and proclaimer of the covenant.[84] The Old Testament, like the New Testament, witnesses to revelation as that in which God remains the hidden God, declaring His hiddenness in the very act of His self-revelation. Since its witness is to this hiddenness the crucifixion of Jesus Christ comprises the actual fulfilment of the Old Testament's expectation.[85] Finally the Old Testament, like the

---

81) *C.D.*I.2.pp.70 ff.

82) ibid.,p.70

83) ibid.,p.80 ff.

84) ibid.,pp.83 f.

85) ibid.,pp.84 ff.

New Testament, witnesses to revelation as the presence to man of God as the coming One and as such its witness is prophecy to be believed in or to be rejected rather than prediction which can be controlled experimentally by logic.[86] In these ways Jesus Christ was "already manifest as the expected One in the time of the Old Testament."[87] In the course of his exposition of Jesus as the Lord of Time Barth maintains that, since in Old Testament time the actual history of Jesus is "objectively prefigured and subjected by reason of the action of the same God who later brought it to pass", we cannot say of Jesus "that He was "not yet" in this time before His time, just as we cannot say of the time after His earthly life, the time of the apostles and the community, that He is "no longer.""[88] In the light of the prophetic time of the Old Testament the lifetime, death and Easter time of Jesus cannot be considered as an "arbitrary intervention of God."[89] The Easter time of Jesus Christ is therefore the revelation of that which was prefigured but already a reality in Old Testament time, the reality "of the covenant between God and this people; the declaration of the election of this lost people."[90] This single reality that was revealed in the Easter time of Jesus Christ and that was previously

---

86) ibid.,pp.94 ff.

87) ibid.,p.78

88) C.D.III.2.p.475

89) ibid.

90) ibid.

concealed in His lifetime and death was also previously concealed in the Old Testament time of its prophetic prefiguration:

> "He was the Lord of this history too, because He was the goal and meaning of this time before. Hence it is no blasphemy but the sober truth, no allegorical fancy but the assertion of the most proper sense of the Old Testament, if we give Him the name of Him who already in the Old Testament called Himself the One who is and who will be."91

During his discussion of the prophetic office of Jesus Christ under the heading The Light of Life Barth outlines the manner in which the prophecy which is the actual life of Jesus Christ transcends the Old Testament.[92] In distinction to the prophets of the Old Testament Jesus Christ is Himself the divine Logos which He speaks. Rejected by Israel He speaks to the nations and to the world as such and He speaks on the basis of the covenant which is actually fulfilled in Him. Finally, He is Himself the mediator between God and men, the One in whom the act of reconciliation proclaimed by the prophets actually occurs. In this sense none of the Old Testament prophets is "a true type or adequate prefiguration of the prophecy of Jesus Christ".[93] However, this is not to deny a genuine anticipation of the prophecy of Jesus Christ, a genuine type and prefiguration, not in the Old

---

91) ibid.,p.476

92) C.D.IV.3.pp.49 ff.

93) ibid.,p.52

Testament prophets but in the history of Israel itself.[94] The history of Israel, like the history of Jesus Christ, is itself an actual event that occurs in history, it is an event that is not an end in itself but has universal significance as the summons of God to men of all nations. In its totality and interconnexion it certainly speaks of the conflict and contradiction between God and His people but it does so on the basis of the actuality of the grace of the covenant, not just in its futurity but in its proximity. Finally, as the attestation of a living unity between God's action and that of His people, it has a mediatorial character as exemplary and representative history.[95] While Barth admits that the prophecy which is the history of Israel is certainly not identical with the prophecy which is the history of Jesus Christ, nonetheless, it is Messianic prophecy, itself saying earlier what the history of Jesus Christ says later. As such, it constitutes the "pre-history" of Jesus Christ, the word of its prophecy being His "fore-word".[96] Moreover, while the prophecy of the history of Israel was true and genuine because it was authentically the presence and action of Jesus Christ Himself, it was this in an utterly concealed and hidden form as His mediate and indirect presence and action.[97] The "not yet" that qualifies and delimits the "already" of this "pre-history" of Jesus Christ is

---

94) ibid.,p.53

95) ibid.,pp.53 ff.

96) ibid.,pp.65 f.

97) ibid.,pp.68f.

the same "not yet" of His hiddenness that qualifies and delimits His pre-Easter time in its entirety. This "not yet" must not obscure the reality of the "already"; the reality of the one covenant, the one Prophet, the one Mediator, who is the same "yesterday and to-day."[98] In this way Barth affirms the contemporaneity of the history of Jesus and the history of Israel, albeit as a hidden contemporaneity perceptible only in faith and in the light of His Easter time; thus a contemporaneity that is hidden in a parallel manner to the hiddenness of His pre-Easter lifetime and death. In this way also Barth specifically repudiates Oscar Cullmann's rejection of any such contemporaneity of the history of Jesus and the history of Israel as an inevitable outcome of Cullmann's presupposed "linear" conception of time.[99]

Yet even in the prophetic history of Israel beginning with the covenant made by God with Abraham the limit of the pre-Easter time of Jesus Christ is not reached:

> "The covenant which God made with Abraham and his seed, and which was fulfilled in Jesus, was not an arbitrary intervention of God and therefore something wholly new in history. It was simply the initial stage in the execution of the purpose God intended when He caused history to commence in and with creation and therefore in and with the beginning of time generally."100

---

98) ibid.,pp.70 f.

99) C.D.III.2.pp.481f.; cf. Oscar Cullmann, Christ and Time, pp. 131 ff.

100) C.D.III.2.p.476

In the light of His Easter time the apostolic community came to recognize the man Jesus, the event of His history, as the real object of God's determination in the event of creation, as the fulfilment of the covenant and therefore as the internal basis of creation. The pre-Easter time of Jesus Christ must therefore include this "primal history" (Urgeschichte) of the event of creation (itself a "history" beyond "historical" investigation).[101] Moreover, even beyond the event of creation an "eternity of God" that does not include the time of Jesus Christ as the primal decision and eternal will of God before the event of creation and before all time is inconceivable in the light of His Easter time and its inherent significance.[102] The eternal Word of God which was with God in the beginning and which was God is fully identified in the Easter time of Jesus Christ as *this* Word:[103]

> "The *οὗτος* here refers to the incarnate Logos. It is He who was "in the beginning." and not only that, but even before this beginning He was with God and was Himself God, participating in the divine being and nature, before created time began, in the eternity of God."104

Barth categorically rejects the concept of a supposed *λόγος ἄσαρκος*; the eternal Son must not be considered *in abstracto*

---

101) ibid.,pp.476 f.

102) ibid.,p.477

103) ibid.,p.484; cf. *C.D*.IV.1.pp.51 ff. & *C.D*.IV.2.p.33

104) *C.D*.III.2.p.484; cf. *C.D*.IV.2.pp.33 f.

but in concreto, in the actuality of the event of His revelation.[105] Such an abstraction would be indicative of the attempt to overlook the gracious decision of God to be Deus pro nobis in Jesus Christ and idolatrously to reintroduce a supposed Deus absconditus. The authentic and eternal Word of God is not identified as this indeterminate λόγος ἄσαρκος but as the Word made flesh, the life, death and resurrection of the man Jesus Christ in space and time. This Word made flesh which is the decision of God in time to be Deus pro nobis is none other than the actualization of the One authentic Word which is His decision in eternity.[106] The event of the Incarnation, the actual occurrence of the Word becoming flesh, is not indicative of a change in the being of God but is the actualization of His true, eternal being; the being of God is identical to His gracious decision in Jesus Christ to be this Deus pro nobis:

> "... the incarnation makes no change in the Trinity. In the eternal decree of God, Christ is God and man. Do not ever think of the second Person of the Trinity as only Logos. That is the mistake of Emil Brunner. There is no Logos asarkos, but only ensarkos. Brunner thinks of a Logos asarkos, and I think this is the reason for his natural theology. The Logos becomes an abstract principle. Since there is only and always a Logos ensarkos, there is no change in the Trinity, as if a fourth member comes in after the incarnation."107

It is bewildering that in his earlier work Robert Jenson, in contradistinction to Barth, should seek to reaffirm a concept of a λόγος ἄσαρκος "in strict correspondence to the Creator's mysterious

---

105) C.D.IV.1.p.52

106) ibid.

107) Karl Barth, Karl Barth's Table Talk, recorded and edited by John D Godsey, S.J.T. Occasional Papers No. 10 (Edinburgh and London,1963),p.49; cf. C.D.II.1.pp.515 ff.

work of judgment"; a "hidden Lord of history" whose rule "cannot be understood directly from His grace in Christ"; who is "the same God but God in a different way".[108] Who is this "hidden God" who expresses Himself in an indeterminate Word? Is it not that a truly Trinitarian theology of revelation is forfeited if God is other in Himself than He is in the event of His revelation, in the event of His Word becoming flesh? Jenson maintains a dipolar conception of God as a means of preserving the freedom of His grace in revelation and reconciliation but here dipolarity tends to lapse into duality as the logical outcome of the positing of a <u>λόγος ἄσαρκος</u>.

That the man Jesus Christ is the self-identification of God who has completely defined Himself in this event of His revelation, in this event of His Word made flesh, represents the fulcrum of Barth's Trinitarian theology. This full self-identification of God is effectively nullified by the assertion of a postulated <u>λόγος ἄσαρκος</u>.[109] At the very centre of Barth's theology his concept of eternity and his doctrine of election coincide.[110] Creation and time itself are preceded by God's eternal election of this man Jesus Christ; it is the history of this man which is the content of

---

108) R. W. Jenson, <u>Alpha and Omega</u> pp.166 f.

109) cf. E. Jüngel, '...keine Menschenlosigkeit Gottes...: Zur Theologie Karl Barths zwischen Theismus und Atheismus', <u>Evangelische Theologie</u>, 31(1971), 376-390 (p.382)

110) cf. John Thompson, op.cit.,pp.99 & 180 f.

the eternal decree and will of God.[111] One cannot therefore speak of any time when the man Jesus Christ was not with God as the content of His gracious election and the beginning of all things,[112] as the "reality which underlies and precedes all other reality as the first and eternal Word of God".[113] The human history of Jesus Christ cannot therefore be considered as "a mere economy of only provisional and practical significance",[114] this Word become flesh is rather the actualization of the eternal being and covenant will of God as Deus pro nobis. God is "immutably this God, and not another".[115] The incarnation is certainly not an act in which God contradicts Himself, nor even an event that is indicative of some change in God's being, rather God's specific eternity is His constancy in all time as this God in Jesus Christ:[116]

> "God has limited Himself to be this God and no other, to be the love which is active and dwells with men at this point and in this way, in Jesus Christ. God has bound Himself in His own Son to be eternally true to His creation. But He has done this Himself, and the fact that He has acted in this and not in any other way has its basis in and from Himself.117

---

111) C.D.IV.2.pp.33 ff.

112) ibid., cf. C.D.IV.1.p.53

113) C.D.IV.1.p.53

114) C.D.IV.2.p.35

115) C.D.II.1.p.513

116) ibid.,p.515

117) ibid.,p.518

This affirmation of Jesus Christ as the actualization of God's eternal covenant and the consequent categorical denial of any possibility of change in God's being and determination contrasts starkly with Jürgen Moltmann's account of "change" in God. Perhaps predictably Moltmann's conception of "change" in God derives from his all-pervading preoccupation with the problems of theodicy. Moltmann, like Barth (though perhaps for different reasons[118]), affirms the reality of God's suffering in the event of the cross, but, unlike Barth, Moltmann is only able to comprehend this event of God's suffering as indicative of "change" within God's Trinitarian being:

> "The cross of Jesus, understood as the cross of the Son of God, therefore reveals a change in God, a <u>stasis</u> within the Godhead: 'God is other.' And this event in God is the event on the cross."119

God cannot be thought of as unchangeable if He is free to love, to become vulnerable, to suffer. Both the history of the Son and the history of the Spirit must necessarily involve a "new" experience within the life of the Trinity, albeit a "new" experience for which God has made Himself open from eternity:[120]

---

118) Moltmann continues to appear more concerned to justify a loving God before suffering man than to justify sinful man before a holy God.

119) Jürgen Moltmann, <u>The Crucified God: The Cross of Christ as the Foundation and Criticism of Christian Theology</u>, trans. by R. A. Wilson and John Bowden (London,1974),p.193

120) Jürgen Moltmann, <u>The Church in the Power of the Spirit: A Contribution to Messianic Ecclesiology</u>, trans. by Margaret Kohl (London,1977),pp.62 f.

> "The relationships in the Trinity between Father and Son are not fixed in static terms once and for all, but are a living history. This history of God or this history in God begins with the sending and delivering up of the Son, continues with his resurrection and the transference of the rule of God to him, and only ends when the Son hands over this rule to the Father."121

The implications of this account of "change" in God both in terms of theological provisionality and a consequent conception of revelation and also in terms of the freedom of God in this act of suffering as an event of His grace will be reviewed both in the final section of this chapter and in chapter four of this thesis. However, in the context of this present chapter it is necessary to expose the presupposed conception of eternity that underlies such passages. To refer to the event of the cross as involving change within the life of the Trinity surely presupposes a conception of eternity in terms of extension in time rather than in terms of the compresence of all time in pure simultaneity to God. The eternal relatedness of the Father, the Son and the Holy Spirit, while certainly not "fixed in static terms" but a living history, an authentic temporality, is not "changed" by this living history which includes the event of the cross simply because this history and this event are actually and authentically included in the eternal determination and being of God. The event of the Word becoming flesh, the Incarnation, crucifixion and resurrection of Jesus Christ, does not imply a change in God's eternal being simply because it is itself the actualization of God's eternal being. Moltmann himself,

---

121) J. Moltmann, <u>The Crucified God</u>, p.265

in his more recent theological work, appears to be moving towards this understanding of the inclusive character of God's eternity by his conception of the redemptive suffering of the cross at the centre of the eternal life of the Trinity, especially as depicted in the iconography of the Eastern Church.[122]

The Easter time of Jesus Christ, the time of His resurrection, is therefore both the revelation and the actualization of His pre-Easter time in its totality, the pre-Easter time of His lifetime and death, His pre-Easter time which was the prophetic time of the Old Testament, His pre-Easter time as the real object of God's determination in the event of creation and, ultimately, His pre-Easter time as the eternal Word of God. Who He was in this pre-Easter time He actually is in His Easter time. Who He is revealed to be in His Easter time He already was authentically in His pre-Easter time. In the light of the Easter time of Jesus Christ past time in its entirety is revealed as His time, the time of which He is Lord:

> "... it is all summed up in Rev.1. 8: "I am—which was." The past to which we look back from the present of the man Jesus is, like this present and the future which lies before it, His time, the time of this man Jesus."123

This pastness of the pre-Easter time of Jesus Christ is in no way in conflict with the present and the futurity of His Easter time.

---

122) Jürgen Moltmann, The Trinity and the Kingdom of God: The Doctrine of God, trans. by Margaret Kohl (London,1981). pp.30 ff. & 158 ff.

123) C.D.III.2.p.478

As the One who already was in this past time He is the One who is always present, the One who comes. The being of Jesus Christ as Lord of Time cannot possibly be limited or qualified by a "not yet" or a "no longer"; He is "the same yesterday and today and for ever".[124] The being of Jesus Christ in the past, the present and the future is precisely the actualization of the authentic temporality and pure simultaneity of the eternity which is the being of God:

> "This eternity includes not only the present and future, but also the past. God's eternity does not invalidate past, present and future, and therefore time; it legitimates them. In it they have their origin and true character. In it yesterday, to-day and to-morrow are one, and in their unity genuine and real. The man Jesus is in this genuine and real yesterday of God's eternity, which is anterior to all other yesterdays, including the yesterday of creation."125

c) The futurity of Jesus Christ:

This chapter began with a consideration of the Easter time of Jesus Christ, specifically with a consideration of the 40 days of His appearances as the Resurrected One (Auferstehung). But to limit the immediate presence of the risen Jesus Christ to this period of 40 days, to qualify His being in the present and the future by a hopeless "no longer", would be to miss the inherent significance of this Easter time. While the event of God's self-revelation has actually occurred in this Easter time of Jesus Christ

---

124) ibid.,pp.477 f.; cf. Hebrews 13.8.

125) C.D.III.2.p.484

the work of Jesus Christ as the Revealer "is not ended or concluded", He "has not yet reached His goal".[126] The salvation which is the issue of His total work is already actualized in Him and anticipated in His Easter time but it is "not yet reached in the situation of the world and man". The Easter time of Jesus Christ is already the anticipatory presence and revelation of the future of salvation but He is still moving towards this final consummation.[127]

To the apostolic community after the event of Pentecost the Easter time of Jesus Christ declared that His presence as the Risen One was not confined to the 40 days of that Easter time but that He was and is "really but transcendentally present";[128] His authentic temporality does not exclude but includes His continuing and actual presence to-day as the One He was in the yesterday of His Easter history:

> "His past history, His yesterday, cannot be understood or portrayed as a thing of the past, a thing of yesterday. The yesterday of Jesus is also to-day. The fact that He lives at the right hand of God means that even now He is absolutely present temporally."129

The true significance of the Easter time of Jesus Christ is that in the power of the Holy Spirit He becomes and is the

---

126) C.D.IV.3.p.327

127) ibid.

128) C.D.III.2.p.467

129) ibid.

Contemporary of the community of His people. The One who was present to the disciples in the 40 days of His Easter history is the same as the One who "encountered them in the outpouring of His Holy Spirit and who is present with His community to this day in the power of the same Spirit".[130] Neither is this real presence arbitrarily restricted to the "sacraments" of baptism and the Lord's Supper since these are a "symbolical expression" of the directness in which the community is gathered in worship around Jesus Himself, the reality of His presence and rule in their lives even apart from worship.[131] While this continuing presence of Jesus in the Spirit to the community is itself an anticipatory pledge of His final return in glory, of the consummation of His Easter history, the Jesus of this ultimate future is nonetheless identical with the One He was in the yesterday of His Easter history and identical with the One He is in the to-day of His real presence to the community.[132]

In the Prolegomena to Church Dogmatics Barth considered the time post Christum natum as the time of recollection, the recollection of the revelation that has actually occurred in the Easter event,[133] but even here this concept of recollection is not a means of confining the temporality of Jesus Christ to the past-ness of His Easter history:

---

130) C.D.IV.3.p.910; cf. Colin E. Gunton, Yesterday and Today,p.131

131) C.D.III.2.pp.467 f.

132) ibid.,p.468

133) C.D.I.2.pp.101 ff.

> "The New Testament is really the witness to recollection of revelation. But because it is the witness to recollection of revelation, the recollection attested by it is thereby extended. Recollection of eternal time, which is what recollection of the risen One is, is necessarily recollection of a time which overarches our time, and which therefore cannot be confined to the datable time with which it is in the first instance related. Recollection of this time must also be expectation of this same time. If it is true that God once had time for us, our whole time must be bounded by the reality of this time of God; i.e., if God really had time for us, then He will also have it. In other words, we have His revelation not only behind us; because we have it behind us, we also have it in front of us."134

The question of whether or not Barth proposes an adequate account of the Holy Spirit will recur throughout this thesis and will be specifically considered in its final chapter. Let it suffice now to observe that, for Barth, the presence of Jesus Christ in the present is not merely a matter of recollection but of contemporaneity; the revelation which was His Easter history is recollected "in order that it should no longer be past but present".[135] Where the Holy Spirit is present the Christian community can understand its existence not as a "mere tradition or recollection of Jesus" nor as resting upon a mere "retrospective vision" but as a "life of direct discipleship" as their "being in Christ":[136]

> "There is no vacuum between Easter and the final appearing as if Jesus Christ were absent and we had to manage on our own, or as if we could only look backwards and forwards to him. He is present as the Eschatos in the full power, promise and presence of the Holy Spirit."137

---

134) ibid.,p.116

135) C.D.III.2.p.467

136) ibid.,; cf. C.D.IV.3.pp.362 ff.

137) John Thompson, op.cit.,p.130; cf. C.D.III.2.p.468

The Easter time of Jesus Christ is moreover, the declaration that the being of Jesus in time "is not merely a being in the present or the past" but is also "a being in the future, a coming being".[138] The Easter time of Jesus Christ does not signify the gradual progression to a better future, it rather proclaims the specific future of Jesus Christ as the One who comes:

> "Redemption does not mean that the world and we ourselves within it evolve in this or that direction. It means that Jesus Christ is coming again. Redemption means the resurrection of the flesh. It means eternal life as deliverance from eternal death."139

Just as the Easter history of Jesus Christ is determinative for His being in the past and the present so also it is determinative for His being in the future. Other than in the light of this Easter time, other than as the specific expectation of Jesus Christ as the One who comes, Christian expectation would degenerate into a fanciful utopian delusion:

> "Clearly, it would not be inconceivable rebus aliter stantibus, i.e., if there had been no resurrection, for our knowledge of Jesus Christ to have been restricted to His past and present, the past somehow prolonged into and determining the present. In this case the apostles and their communities would have contemplated the future in terms of the propagation, intensification and practical realisation of the Christianity which they championed. ... Indeed, there have been whole periods in the history of the Church when this version of the Christian hope has been regarded as necessary both in theory and in practice. The New Testament does not contain a single shred of evidence to support this view. Compared with what the New Testament calls hope, this Utopian version can only be described as a fabrication, however well-meaning and attractive. The salient feature about it is that in the last resort it can do without Jesus. It may know Him as the Jesus of yesterday and to-day, but it know nothing of Him as the One who is εἰς τοὺς αἰῶνας, as the One who comes."140

---

138) C.D.III.2.p.485

139) C.D.II.1.p.78

140) C.D.III.2.pp.487 f.

The eschatological hope of the Christian community cannot possibly be hope "for the attainment merely of abstract blessings" but can only be hope in Jesus Christ Himself, expectation of the future coming of the One who was present already in His Easter history and is present even now in the power of the Holy Spirit.[141] Since Christian hope is grounded upon this recollection of His resurrection and this direct presence created by the fellowship of the Holy Spirit it can only be hope for His imminent coming.[142] The reference to the shortness of this last time does not relate to its temporal duration, "to the few or the many years and centuries of this interval",[143] but rather relates to the internal character of this interval, its limitation and definition by its Lord at its beginning, at its goal and in its progression, and also to the urgency which characterizes this interval and is the consequence of its unknown duration:[144]

> "That which necessarily gives rise to this hope and makes it an imminent hope also makes it a constant hope, renewing it every day, and protecting it against disappointment, frustration and scepticism."145

The forty days of the revelation which was the Easter history of Jesus Christ was already "the great consummatum est",[146]

---

141) ibid.,p.490

142) ibid.,pp.490 f.

143) C.D.III.4.p.582

144) ibid.,pp.580 ff.; cf. John Thompson, op.cit.,pp.134 f.

145) C.D.III.2.p.491

146) ibid.,p.488

already the actualization of this future fulfilment, already the presence of Jesus Christ not only as the One He was and is but as the One who comes. This Easter time of Jesus Christ was therefore the declaration of this precise future, the future of His coming, and, as such, the community's expectation of His coming rests upon the unequivocal pledge which is this Easter history.[147] Whereas for the community the 40 days of the Easter time of Jesus Christ and His ultimate parousia, His final return in glory, appear to be two temporally separate events, in the authentic temporality of the being of Jesus Christ these two are really one single event:[148]

> "The resurrection is the anticipation of His parousia as His parousia is the completion and fulfilment of the resurrection."[149]

The Easter time of Jesus Christ is therefore the revelation not only of His being in the past and present but also of His being in the future, the revelation of His authentic temporality which includes this futurity. There can be no rivalry, progression or difference of degree between the being of Jesus Christ in these three dimensions of time. His presence to-day does not abrogate His presence yesterday. His presence to-day can only be a pledge and anticipation of His presence to come. He is "the same yesterday and today and for ever". The Christian community therefore exists

---

147) ibid.,pp.488 ff. ; cf. C.D.IV.1.pp.115 ff.

148) C.D.III.2.p.490

149) ibid.

in the light of this authentic temporality of Jesus Christ revealed in His Easter time:[150]

> "It may look backwards to His past even as far as the eternal counsel of God. It may look to His present at the right hand of God, from which He rules to-day by His Spirit. Or it may look to the future and His general and conclusive revelation. But in every case it looks only to Him. And in Him it sees the fulness of everything for which those enlightened by Him are thankful, whether present or expected."151

For this reason it may be better to consider the futurity of Jesus Christ proleptically rather than merely eschatologically. Eschatology is usually understood as referring to the doctrine of the "last things" yet, according to Barth, there are no abstract autonomous "last things" apart from or alongside Jesus Christ Himself, the Last One. Since Jesus Christ as the One who comes is already revealed in His Easter history, since His ultimate coming in glory is neither an amplification nor a transcending of His being and action declared in His resurrection but rather the fulfilment and final unveiling of that declaration,[152] it would be more precise to refer to the proleptic, anticipatory character of the being and temporality of Jesus Christ than risk any misunderstanding of an eschatological reference in terms of a supposed futurity of Jesus Christ in any way distinct or independent in relation to His Easter time. The authentically Christian eschatological expectation is for the final revelation of Jesus Christ as the One He truly was and

---

150) cf. ibid.,p.485

151) ibid.,p.492

152) _C.D._IV.3.p.903

is; the Not Yet of His future manifestation is identical to the Already of the revelation which is His Easter history and the Even Now of His real presence in the power of the Holy Spirit:[153]

> "In this eschaton of creation and reconciliation there will not be another Word of God. Jesus Christ will be the one Word and we shall then see the final and unequivocal form of His own glory which even now shines forth from His resurrection into time and history, all times and all histories. The theme of Christian hope, to the extent that it is not yet fulfilled nor cannot be so long as time endures, is the revelation of the fact that neither formally nor materially, theoretically nor practically, can the one Word of God be transcended, as this is now confirmed in and through His self-transcendence, in virtue of which all ears hear and all eyes see all the things which already it is actually given to us to see and hear in Him. The inclusion of the eschatological element, then, does not imply any restriction, but the final expansion and deepening, of our statement that Jesus Christ is the one Word of God."154

This proleptic character of the being and temporality of Jesus Christ in relation to His futurity is both confirmed and clarified by Barth's use of the word parousia. As already noted Barth, using the word parousia simply with reference to the final coming of Jesus Christ in glory, considers the resurrection and the parousia, two temporally separate events from man's perspective, as a single event to Jesus Christ Himself.[155] However later, in the course of his exposition of the Doctrine of Reconciliation, Barth expresses his point with even greater clarity by referring to the resurrection

---

153) ibid.,p.910

154) C.D.IV.3.p.103

155) C.D.III.2.p.490

of Jesus Christ, His real presence in the power of the Holy Spirit and His final return in glory as three forms of the one event of His parousia.[156] Barth notes that originally (in Hellenistic sources) the word parousia simply meant "effective presence" and that in some parts of the New Testament (Barth specifically mentions the Pastorals and II Thessalonians 2.8) it is closely associated with the word ἐπιφάνεια which, again in its Hellenistic origin, denotes "the making visible of concealed divinity".[157] While Barth would not expect either word to be used directly of the pre-Easter lifetime and death of Jesus Christ since it is only in the event of Easter that the incarnate Word is revealed and seen in His glory,[158] and while Barth admits that in the New Testament the words usually refer to the third and final eschatological form of His presence at His coming in glory,[159] yet in this sense of effective presence and visible manifestation the terms can validly be applied both to His Easter history and to His real presence in the power of the Holy Spirit. In the light of the merging together in John's Gospel of Jesus' coming as the Risen One, His coming in the Spirit and His final return in glory, and in the light of the Synoptic record of Jesus' prophecies concerning the manifestation of the Kingdom of God ἐν δυνάμει, it is invalid to restrict the scope of eschatology

---

156) C.D.IV.3.pp.292 ff.; cf. C.D.IV.1.pp.318 f.

157) C.D.IV.3.p.292

158) ibid.,pp.292 f.

159) ibid.,p.294

to the final coming of Jesus Christ.[160] Both the Easter event and the impartation of the Holy Spirit are eschatological events, events of the last time.[161]

The first form of the single happening which is the parousia of Jesus Christ is the event of His Easter history.[162] This Easter event is the "primal and basic pattern" of the "one and total coming" of Jesus Christ in its other forms.[163] In the resurrection of Jesus Christ His self-declaration has taken place "once for all and irrevocably".[164] In this event the reconciliation which is God's determination for the world and man was fully revealed to the apostolic community.[165] In this event the eternal life which is the overcoming of death and which is God's gift actually occurred.[166] In this event the end of the old and the beginning of the new already took place:[167]

---

160) ibid.,pp.294 f. Barth dismisses as "in its way the greatest triviality of any age" the depressingly common assumption (which first arose within the narrow circle of a particular school of Neo-Liberal theology) that in such references Jesus was "deluded" (ibid.,p.295; cf.C.D.III.2.pp.497 ff.

161) C.D.IV.3.p.295

162) ibid.,p.293

163) ibid.

164) ibid.,pp.296 ff.

165) ibid.,pp.301 ff.

166) ibid.,pp.308 ff.

167) ibid.,p.316

"For it took place in this event that in the appearance of the one man Jesus in the glory of God there was made immediately present as a new but concretely real element in the existence of the world the goal given to the world in and with its reconciliation to God, its future of salvation as redemption from the shadow of death and the antithesis which pursues it, its future of salvation as its completion by the creation of its new form of peace, its being in the glory of God."168

The single event which is the parousia of Jesus Christ also takes place "in the form of the impartation of the Holy Spirit".[169] The presence of Jesus Christ in the promise of the Spirit is the middle form of His parousia and, as such, is His "direct and immediate presence and action among and with and in us."[170] Barth utilizes the ambiguity of the phrase "the Promise of the Spirit" since the presence of Jesus Christ as the Risen One in this middle form is both the promise of His future and final appearing and also itself the promise of His presence now pledged by His resurrection; that He will be really present now by His Spirit is promised and this real presence now is the promise and anticipation of His ultimate presence, His return in glory.[171] This middle form of the one parousia of Jesus Christ is authentically His actual

---

168) ibid.,p.315. Note that Bertold Klappert refers to the appearance of Jesus as the Risen One (Auferstehung) not only as the "anticipation of the parousia" (as quoted by John Thompson) but also as "the prolepsis of the future". (Bertold Klappert, Die Auferweckung des Gekreuzigten: Der Ansatz der Christologie Karl Barths im Zusammenhang der Christologie der Gegenwart (Neukirchen,1971),p.323)

169) C.D.IV.3.p.293; cf. C.D.IV.1.pp.318 f.

170) C.D.IV.3.p.350; cf. C.D.IV.2.pp.322 f.

171) C.D.IV.3.pp.351 ff.

presence here and now:

> "... it is no less genuinely His own direct and personal coming, His parousia, presence and revelation, than was His coming there and then to His disciples in the Easter event, or than will be one day His coming in its final and conclusive form as the Judge of the quick and the dead."[172]

That Jesus Christ is now "at the right hand of God the Father Almighty" does not mean that He is "imprisoned there", it does not detract from or contradict the reality of His presence and action here too.[173] This present day is genuinely a day of His presence, a day of Jesus Christ Himself: "we are contemporaries of Jesus Christ and direct witnesses of His action".[174]

The final and definitive form of the one event of the parousia of Jesus Christ occurs "as the return of Jesus Christ as the goal of the history of the Church, the world and each individual, as His coming as the Author of the general resurrection of the dead and the Fulfiller of universal judgment."[175] In a variety of forms Barth poses the question of why this final form of the parousia is temporally separated from its first form, the Easter event, by its middle form, the presence of Jesus Christ in the promise of the Spirit. Why was not the world at once engulfed by the Easter event as by a tidal wave?[176] Why was it the good

---

172) ibid.,p.356

173) ibid.,p.357

174) ibid.,p.362

175) ibid.,p.293; cf. C.D.IV.1.p.319

176) C.D.IV.3.p.316

will of Jesus Christ to interpose a time qualified by a "not yet" between His own beginning and His own end?[177] Why was not His beginning immediately His goal?[178] Barth clearly maintains that this temporal provisionality is noetic rather than ontic, an apparent absence and not an absence of the efficacy of the Easter event.[179] While for us the tension still exists between this beginning and this goal, a tension in which we can only wait for the conclusive and completed form of the parousia, from God's perspective that which is not yet evident to us is already actual.[180] This temporal provisionality can only be grounded in the good will of Jesus Christ Himself "to be not yet at the goal but still on the way",[181] His good will that His own prophetic work should be continuing towards its goal, His good will that there should be a community both knowing Him and confessing Him:

> "He wills to preserve the world, to cause it to persist, in its present and provisional form, in order that it should be the place where He can be perceived and accepted and known and confessed by the creature as the living Word of God."182

---

177) ibid.,p.331

178) ibid.,p.360

179) ibid.,p.317

180) ibid.,pp.317 ff.

181) ibid.,p.329

182) ibid.,p.332; cf. B. C. Hanson, 'Hope and Participation in Christ: A study in the Theology of Barth and Pannenberg' (dissertation, Princeton,1970), p.69.

In this manner the temporal provisionality between His beginning and His goal, despite the tension and contradiction it involves, is itself a means by which He shows Himself to be gracious.[183] Moreover, the middle form of the parousia of Jesus Christ has "its own specific glory".[184] Even in the transition of our present existence, even in the tension and contradiction that are the characteristics of this present existence, Jesus Christ Himself is really present in the form of the promise of the Spirit for the purpose of our full salvation.[185]

In these three forms of beginning, middle and end the parousia of Jesus Christ is one event.[186] While these three forms must be clearly distinguished as the Easter history of Jesus Christ, His presence in the promise of the Spirit and His final return in glory they must also be understood as "forms of one and the same event".[187] It is not the case that anyone of these three forms is more the parousia of Jesus Christ than any other. Indeed, Barth even considers the relationship of the three forms as a kind of perichoresis in analogy to the doctrine of the Trinity:[188]

---

183) C.D.IV.3.p.333

184) ibid.,p.360

185) ibid.,pp.361 f

186) ibid.,p.293

187) ibid.,p.294

188) ibid.,p.296

"It is not merely that these three forms are interconnected in the totality of the action presented in them all, or in each of them in its unity and totality, but that they are mutually related as the forms of this one action by the fact that each of them also contains the other two by way of anticipation or recapitulation, so that, without losing their individuality or destroying that of the others, they participate and are active and revealed in them."189

This proleptic understanding of the temporality and presence of Jesus Christ which Barth so clearly expresses in his account of the three forms of the parousia is antithetical to the notion of the futurity of revelation posited by Jürgen Moltmann.[190] Moltmann rejects Barth's conception of revelation in its entirety as a further manifestation of "epiphany" religion in which transcendental eternity is presumed to break into history.[191] Barth's identification of the self-revelation of God with the Easter time of Jesus Christ indicates to Moltmann the assumption that the being of God is, in some way, already present and capable of being perceived.[192] According to Moltmann the future revelation of Jesus Christ ought

---

189) ibid.

190) It would be unproductive to compare Barth's position with Wolfhart Pannenberg's understanding of the resurrection of Jesus Christ as a prolepsis of the end of history since the latter's conception derives from his highly problematical theory of the ontological priority of the future with its "retroactive force" combined with a somewhat tendentious interpretation of the apocalyptic significance of Jesus (Wolfhart Pannenberg, Jesus-God and Man, pp.66ff.& 225ff.).

191) Jürgen Moltmann, Theology of Hope: On the Ground and the Implications of a Christian Eschatology, trans.by James W. Leitch (London,1967),pp.40ff.

192) ibid.,pp.52-58

not to be considered as merely the noetic unveiling of something now hidden but rather as the fulfilment of something now promised though not yet actualized, attained or realized.[193] Therefore the resurrection of Jesus Christ ought not be understood as itself the eschatological fulfilment of reconciliation but rather as a promise. pointing beyond itself to that which is not yet present.[194] In explicit contrast to Barth, Moltmann refuses to express either the resurrection or the presence of the Spirit in epiphanic terms since for him the element of provisionality must be understood ontically as well as noetically. This understanding of ontic provisionality is grounded ontologically by Moltmann in his discussion of "change" in God (to which this chapter has already referred).[195] The living history of the Trinity reaches its "centre point" in the crucifixion of the Son but only reaches its conclusion at the end of history when the Son hands over the Kingdom to the Father.[196] It is this concept of the ontic provisionality of the life of the Trinity that gives substance to Barth's reference to Moltmann's principle of hope

---

193) ibid.,pp.58 & 228; cf. M.Douglas Meeks, Origins of the Theology of Hope (Philadelphia,1974), pp.63ff.

194) Jürgen Moltmann, Theology of Hope, pp.86ff.

195) pp. 109ff.of this thesis; cf. Jürgen Moltmann, The Crucified God, pp.187ff.; see also R.Bauckham,'Moltmann's Eschatology of the Cross', S.J.T.,30 (1977) 301-311.

196) Jürgen Moltmann,The Crucified God,p.265.

as a "container without content".[197] While this emphasis may have been modified in Moltmann's more recent work this unbalanced orientation towards the future remains the Achilles' heel of his theology.[198]

In contrast, Barth's definition of God's self-revelation in Jesus Christ excludes the possibility of any ontic understanding of the provisionality of God's being. The future will involve the unveiling of the hidden God, but it will be this hidden God who is unveiled. Certainly the future revelation of Jesus Christ will be a causative as well as a cognitive event, but there is no sense in which this future will reveal One who is ontically distinct from His Word. The event of revelation in Jesus Christ is the actualization of God's own definition of His Godness:

> "...God has defined himself as God in the death and resurrection of Jesus Christ."[199]

Barth's doctrine of God, grounded entirely upon the actuality of His self-revelation, necessitates a noetic, rather than an ontic, concept of provisionality.

Moltmann's denial of this proleptic structure of Jesus

---

197) Karl Barth, 'An Pfarrer Martin Vömel, 10 August 1966' Gesamtausgabe V: Briefe 1961-1968 (Zürich 1975),p.351.

198) cf. pp. 109ff.and also pp. 227ff. of this thesis.

199) E.Jüngel, 'Das Verhältnis von »ökonomischer« und »immanenter« Trinität.' Zeitschrift für Theologie und Kirche, 72(1975) 353-364 (p.356), my translation.

Christ's temporality and presence represents the effective forfeiture of the identity between His being in the past, present and future, rendering the statement of Hebrews 13.8 meaningless. To reject an understanding of revelation in terms of unveiling, to posit an ontic as well as a noetic distinction between the presence of Jesus Christ in His resurrection and in the promise of the Spirit on the one hand and at His final coming on the other, is to imply that Jesus Christ is other at His coming than His presence in His Easter history and in the promise of the Spirit and thereby to forfeit any meaningful conception of the reality of His revelation. The decisive distinction between the conceptions of Jesus Christ's temporality represented by Barth and Moltmann consists in the former's adherence to the proleptic structure of His temporality, to the actuality of His presence yesterday, to-day and for ever as the One who was, the One who is and the One who comes, to the wholly noetic provisionality of His presence then and now:

> "He who comes is the same as He who was and who is. The Resurrected Himself,therefore, is already He who comes, who restricts His coming to the circle of His then followers, and then interrupts it, to resume and complete it at a later point. For what took place in the resurrection of Jesus was already in the concealment and temporal isolation of this event the revelation of the kingdom of God, of the gracious Judge of all men, and of the life of all the dead. Nothing which will be has not already taken place on Easter Day—included and anticipated in the person of the one man Jesus. And so Jesus in His coming is simply the risen Jesus resuming and completing His coming and thus vindicating that beginning and promise.200

---

200) <u>C.D.</u>III.2.p.489

III The Concept of Eternity and the Time of Man

a) God's time and man's time:

Having considered the temporality of God exclusively in the light of His actual temporality in Jesus Christ it is necessary to conclude this first section of the thesis with a consideration of man's time. Just as the authentic temporality which is God's time is identified in the actual time of Jesus Christ so also the nature of man's time can only be authentically recognized in relation to and in distinction from this revelation of God's time. Barth's methodological approach to the question of time and eternity is consistently a reversal of that which is the outcome of a 'Natural Theology' whereby eternity is misconceived in terms of a mythological projection of the time of the creature.[1] For this reason Barth begins his discussion of "Man in His Time" with his exposition of "Jesus, Lord of Time"; he considers man's time exclusively in the context of this revelation of God's time.[2]

The common objections to this exclusive epistemological method, in particular as they are expressed by Richard Roberts,[3]

---

1) C.D.II.1.pp.608f.; cf. Colin E Gunton, Becoming and Being: The Doctrine of God in Charles Hartshorne and Karl Barth (Oxford, 1978), p.178.

2) C.D.III.2.pp.437ff.

3) R. H. Roberts, 'Eternity and Time in the Theology of Karl Barth: An essay in Dogmatic and Philosophical Theology' (dissertation, Edinburgh, 1975), pp.313ff.; cf. R. H. Roberts, 'Barth's Doctrine of Time: its nature and implications' in Karl Barth: Studies of his Theological Method, ed. by S. W. Sykes (Oxford, 1979), pp.88-146 (p.145).

have already been considered in chapter one of this thesis.[4] It is insufficient on the basis of a supposed autonomous rationality to dismiss Barth's conception of God's eternity as 'real time' simply because it lacks the characteristic features of time as experienced by man. Whether 'authentic temporality' is to be located in the actuality of God's self-revelation or in the actuality of man's common experience is ultimately determined by whether this actuality of the event of revelation is admitted or whether it is precluded by the presuppositions of an autonomous rationality.[5] It is the actuality of the event of revelation as 'real time' that determines Barth's methodological approach to the question of time and eternity. This actuality must determine the rationality of the methodological approach simply because it is actual. That God's authentic temporality actually occurs in the event of revelation determines that 'real time' must be located in this event rather than in man's common experience of time:[6]

---

4) cf. chapter one of this thesis; pp. 68ff.

5) cf. T. F. Torrance, Theological Science, (Oxford,1969),pp.25ff.

6) cf. W. Pannenberg, 'Time, Eternity, and Judgment' in What is Man? Contemporary Anthropology in Theological Perspective, trans. by D. A. Priebe (Philadelphia, 1970), pp.68-81 (p.74). Despite Pannenberg's tendency to collapse the distinctions of time into an eternity of simultaneous unity (cf. chapter one of this thesis;pp.45f.) his concern for the historical actuality of the resurrection underlies his recognition that the "truth of time lies beyond the self-centeredness of our experience of time" (ibid.).

> "The fleetingness of time is thus a characteristic not of time as such, but of fallen, alienated, time, and the life of Jesus is the way by which the eternal takes to himself our alienated time and re-creates it as that in which there is construction and not destruction."7

God's temporality is authentic, man's temporality is inauthentic.[8] The fulfilled time of God's self-revelation is genuine, proper time exposing man's time as non-genuine and improper time.[9] Real time, therefore, is not the fallen and lost time experienced by the creature but the fulfilled time of God's revelation, His eternity which is the prototype (Urbild) of the time of the creature.[10] Time, as the form of creaturely existence and in contradistinction to the authentic temporality which is God's eternity, can only be comprehended by the creature in the lostness of past, present and future in their succession, division and even opposition.[11]

---

7) Colin E. Gunton, Yesterday and Today: A Study of continuities in Christology (London, 1983), p.128. Colin Gunton suggests that this possibility of time that is liberated from fleetingness is illustrated by the experience of time generated by music in which the present is not "lost" but "becomes the place where the past is directed to the future". Thus music also suggests the possibility of an order inherent within time itself (ibid., p.122).

8) C.D.III.2.p.438.

9) C.D.I.2.p.66.

10) ibid., cf. C.D.III.1.p.67.

11) C.D.III.2.p.437; cf. C.D.II.1.p.608.

"...eternity is not merely the negation of time. It is not in any way timeless. On the contrary, as the source of time it is supreme and absolute time, i.e., the immediate unity of present, past and future; of now, once and then; of the centre, beginning and end; of movement, origin and goal. In this way it is the essence of God Himself; in this way God is Himself eternity. Thus God Himself is temporal, precisely in so far as He is eternal, and His eternity is the prototype of time, and as the Eternal He is simultaneously before time, above time, and after time. But time as such, i.e., our time, relative time, itself created, is the form of existence of the creature; it is, in contradistinction to eternity, the one-way sequence and therefore the succession and division of past, present and future; of once, now and then; of the beginning, middle and end; of origin, movement and goal."12

Man lives in this time which is a form of his being as a creature created by God; in the inauthentic temporality which is distinct from God's eternity; in the one-way succession of past, present and future, in the connected sequence of "individual life-acts" which constitute his total lifetime.[13] This is the totality of the inauthentic temporality in which he is enclosed. He has no other time as the creature of God than this creaturely time alone. While Jesus has a lifetime like all other men He lives in this time as the Lord of time; the reality and manner of His lifetime is revealed in His Easter time; all time, past, present and future, is identified as His time.[14] Yet man clearly does not live in his time as Lord of time. His past is the time which was once his but which has ceased to belong to him; both memory and oblivion

---

12) C.D.III.1.pp.67f.

13) C.D.III.2.p.438.

14) ibid., pp.440f. & 463ff.

demonstrate the gulf between man's past and man's present. His future is the time which he perhaps will have but which is not his now and which he may never have. His present is no more than the boundary between past and future, a "time between the times" which in actual experience is no time at all, a step between the "no longer" and the "not yet".[15]

The comparison between the time of Jesus and the time of man is not only indicative of the contrast between the Creator and the creature, it is also indicative of God's judgment against man, indicative that man exists in his time as sinful man and thus in alienation from the Creator, is oppressed by the lostness of time.[16] Yet that the man Jesus exists in His time as Lord of time is not only the revelation of the lostness of sinful man in his time but also the revelation that time is positively willed and created by God as a form of human existence.[17] The time of man is therefore "given time". Both man's existence and man's time as a form of that existence are ordained and "given" by God.[18]

---

15) ibid., pp.512ff.

16) ibid., p.517.

17) ibid., pp.517ff.

18) ibid., p.525.

That man's time is "given" time means firstly that man's present can be comprehended in the light of God's present. It is God rather than man who is now primarily and His Now has duration and extension; it includes neither a "no longer" nor a "not yet"; it is the Now in which He is the constant and eternal God who freely loves man in Jesus Christ. For man to exist in the present is for man to be under and with the eternal and constant God who is "for us".[19] Secondly, while man's past is separated from his present, deprived of extension and duration, the will and act of God in giving man time are the meaning and ground of man's being even in this time which is past. Primarily again it is not man who was but God. The Then which is in God's eternity is the Then in which He loved us, the Then in which He willed and gave man time. All that man has been he has been under and with God. Man really is who he was in the whole duration of his past because he was in that past before the God to whom he owed everything and was responsible for everything.[20] Finally, man's future is continually threatened by an undeniable "not yet"; man has no guarantee of his future and may have no future at all. Yet this future is again primarily God's and secondarily man's; it is God who will be in that future and who will still be "for us and faithful to us". Even in this future tense man's time is under and with God, a reality "which is assured and which assures our life". For

---

19) ibid., pp.527ff.

20) ibid., pp.532ff.

this future man is summoned both to trust this eternal God and to be responsible to this eternal God.[21]

That the man Jesus lives in time as the Lord of time means that man's time is "given" time, time willed and created by God, real time despite the sinfulness and lostness of man's experience of it. To recognize the time of man as "given" time is to affirm the reality of this time in distinction from any abstract or speculative conception of time:[22]

> "This Lord of time stands at the beginning of all our attempted thinking about time, ruling and establishing, illuminating and proving. In Him it is the case, and by Him we may know, that time is real and that we have it. In Him God utters His gracious and saving contradiction of man without God and therefore of a concept of time without God, checking self-perverting and ignorant man and arresting the development of all false and cheerless conceptions of time. In Him who, as the eternal Son of God, is the Lord of time, there is shown to us who are not the eternal children of God, and therefore not lords of time, that time is real, that we are in this real time, and how this is the case. As His time, it is the time created and controlled by God and given to men. And we live on the basis of this reality and think on the basis of the promise which it gives. In Him we see ourselves as God willed and created us; in the nature in which God has not ceased to see us, and which has not therefore ceased to be our true nature in spite of all the disruption and error caused by sin."23

Having established positively in the light of the actual time of Jesus Christ that man's time is "given" time, a form of man's existence as the creature ordained and created by God despite the lostness of sinful man's experience of time, Barth turns attention to the limitation of this creaturely time as given by God.[24] The

---

21) ibid., pp.541ff.

22) ibid., pp.551ff.

23) ibid., p.552

24) ibid., pp.553ff.

totality of man's "given" time is not unlimited but limited. The time that is given to man by God is "allotted" time with a definite beginning and a definite end. Man is given this particular span of "allotted" time—no more and no less. Before considering the particular manner of the limitation of man's time as "allotted" time, man's beginning time and ending time, Barth devotes a short sub-section to a response to the protests against this limitation of man's "given" time. The protest against this "only" emanates not merely from the abstract craving for human life but primarily and ultimately from the desire for a "fulfilment of the determination given with its divine creation".[25] That man's "given" time as an allotted span of time lacks duration appears to mean a lack of fulfilment. Man never seems to have enough time to fulfil his determination as the creature of God.[26]

In the first place this limitation of man's time as "allotted" time is a mark of man's existence as a creature distinct from God. It is not that God's eternal time is endless time since His eternity, rightly understood, includes beginning and end. It is rather that this time of God has no fixed span or dimension but God Himself. The life of God in eternity is self-grounded and self-creative but the life of man is not self-grounded nor self-creative; it is the created time over which man has no control; it is the dimension

---

25) ibid.,p.556

26) ibid.,p.557

of creaturely life which has its basis not in man himself as the creature but in God as the Creator; it is therefore the "allotted" time in which beginning and end are distinct.[27]

Secondly, assuming that the desire of human life is to fulfil its positive determination as the life of the creature, that it is content to be creaturely life without usurping the eternity which is the life of the Creator, an unlimited dimension of time by itself would not guarantee the fulfilment of this desire. Unlimited time would imply unlimited opportunity rather than the guarantee of a duration adequate to the fulfilment of man's determination as a creature.[28]

Furthermore, such an unlimited life in which man would not only be able but compelled to continue to aspire to the fulfilment of his determination would really be a worse state. Barth asks whether there could be a better picture of hell than this continual and unsatisfied reaching for perfection by an enduring life in enduring time.[29]

In the fourth place, and positively, this continuing care

---

27) ibid.,pp.558f.

28) ibid.,p.560f.

29) ibid.,p.561f.

and anxiety of man's unsatisfied craving for duration and perfection is rendered irrelevant and superfluous when it is realized that man's life is not limited abstractly but is limited by God. This realization means that within this "allotted" time man's life may be finally satisfied for all its dissatisfaction. The questions of man's beginning and end, man's Whence? and Whither?, do not lead into the void but to this God who Himself limits and allots man's time. Man cannot live as a centrifugal being in unending time without limits or boundaries because his time is set in relationship with the being of God which itself is not a centrifugal being existing in indefinitely enduring time. God's eternity is not unending time but includes beginning and end and He encounters man within the allotted time of these boundaries. For Richard Roberts to question why unending time should necessarily exclude the possibility of this concrete encounter is indicative of a refusal to grasp that it is this eternal God who is the subject of such concrete encounter; that the actuality of the occurrence of God's time in Jesus Christ determines the rationality by which this time is considered and excludes such abstract and hypothetical questions.[30] It is this God who Himself is at the limits of man's "allotted" time; He is before man's beginning and after man's end:[31]

---

30) R.H.Roberts, 'Eternity and Time in the Theology of Karl Barth', pp.415ff.

31) C.D.III.2. pp.562ff.

"He, God, is this beyond. And God is not an "it," a "something," even the negation of a "something." He is absolutely Himself: the One who reveals Himself to us in His Word; who, according to His own Word, is the Creator and Lord of all the reality distinct from Himself; whose sovereignty extends even over chaos, the sphere which He purposely excluded from reality; who, again according to His Word, intervenes and makes Himself responsible for His creature because He loves it; whose aim, again according to His Word, is to manifest the fellowship which He willed to grant it, and continually does so, as His glory embracing even the creature."[32]

Moreover, the fulfilment which man craves for in his "allotted" time arises from that determination of man the creature which is given by God the Creator. The One who gives this determination to man that man should seek this fulfilment is the One who also sets the limits of human life. To recognize this One as the source both of man's determination and of man's "allotted" time is to realize that, while man has a responsibility in the fulfilment of his determination, man is not left to himself to realize this fulfilment. It would be illegitimate for man to seek the fulfilment of this determination other than in the One who gave this determination and also set the limits of man's time:[33]

"It is in Him, who has determined and limited us in this way, that we have the duration and perfection for which we rightly crave." [34]

---

32) ibid.,p.564f.

33) ibid.,p.566f.

34) ibid.,p.566

Finally, God who gives man this determination and who sets limits to man's time is none other than the gracious God, the One who eternally elects Himself for man and man for Himself. It is this gracious God who limits man's lifetime and who sustains man's life even in the span of time allotted to it. During the span of man's lifetime it may appear that it is not with God alone that man has to do. If man's lifetime were unlimited he might even be tempted to continue indefinitely on the basis of this delusion. But at the limits of man's life he is confronted exclusively with the gracious God and with the fact that He is this gracious God. And this is no mere speculation, for the man Jesus, whose lifetime was also restricted but who was also Lord of time, is Himself God for us; He is Himself the free grace of God with which man is confronted:[35]

> "It is impossible to regard human nature in the light of the existence of this man without realizing that it is good and salutary for us to have a limited life in a restricted time because here the grace of God is near and clear to us. But we cannot realise this except as we regard human nature in the light of the existence of this one man."36

Having positively responded to the protests against the nature of man's time as "allotted" time Barth turns attention to the specific limits of man's time, to its beginning and its end. Since man's beginning is constantly receding as that which is behind, it appears to be a less disquieting limitation than man's end. Yet the alarming feature of man's beginning is the connotation it has for man's end. That man has a beginning means that there was a time when man was not, a time of man's non-being, but this suggests

---

35) ibid.,pp.567ff.

36) ibid.,p.571

that the border of man's end may also have this character of non-being. None of the attempted theological solutions to the question of man's beginning in any way alleviates the daunting implication that the non-being from which man comes is the non-being to which man moves. In this manner the nature of man's beginning casts a shadow over his total being in time.[37]

However, while nothing can alter the fact that man comes from non-being this does not imply that he comes from nothing. God is not nothing nor chaos and it is this eternal, gracious God who sets the limits of man's "allotted" time. In the time before man's beginning God already was; He already was the eternal, gracious God who even then was not without man but for man; even then He was the One who eternally elects Himself for man and man for Himself. Man does not come from nothing but from the being, speaking and action of this eternal God. Understood in this way man's beginning is not a shadow over his total being in time but a promise:[38]

> "...the eternal and gracious God, who is the boundary of our beginning, will surely guarantee the whole of our life, the span which we are given and its final end."39

As with the boundary which is man's beginning so the boundary of man's end again poses the question of whether this limit

---

37) ibid.,pp.572ff.

38) ibid., pp.576ff.

39) ibid.,p.577

of man's allotted time is also the edge of the abyss of negation. Life desires life but this boundary implies that man will not be able to live any further. In this manner the death which is man's end overshadows his total being in time with anxiety and care. The Old Testament provides Barth with ample evidence of man's consciousness of this shadow of death which menaces human life;[40] death is "not only a place where man will be, but also a power which holds him in thrall (Ps.49 15)."[41] How can this end of man's "allotted" time be God's good determination for man His creature? Man's beginning was a positive emergence from non-being to being but man's end appears negatively as the opposite prospect.[42] Moreover, if death as man's end means his return to the One who called him from non-being to being the shadow is actually intensified since, "between our emergence from God and our final confrontation with Him, there stands the fact of the abysmal and irreparable guilt which we have incurred from the beginning of our existence, are still incurring and will increasingly continue to do so until the end".[43] In this sense death actually encounters man as the sign of God's judgment which can only mean man's rejection. Death as it actually encounters us, as this sign of God's judgment, certainly

---

40) ibid.,pp.587ff.

41) ibid.,p.590

42) ibid.,pp.593ff.

43) ibid.,p.596

cannot be seen as God's good determination for man; He did not create us to live under this threat.[44] But this form of death as a sign of judgment is again evidenced by the Old Testament and more especially by the New Testament witness to the meaning of the death of Christ.[45]

At the end of man's "allotted" time he is not only confronted with death but also with God; it is not death itself that must be feared at man's end but God Himself.[46] Yet even in this death, even under the sign of His judgment, God is the gracious God who is for man:[47]

> "He is the gracious God, and for us men, even when He places us in death under the sign of His judgment, and in this sign, but only in this sign, is undoubtedly against us. Indeed, it is just as the One who is so palpably against us that He is so much the more mightily for us. If the fire of His wrath scorches us, it is because it is the fire of His wrathful love and not His wrathful hate."48

Once again this comfort in the face of death as the boundary of man's "allotted" time is not based upon mere speculation but upon the actuality of the time of Jesus Christ. It is in Jesus Christ that the eternal God is the gracious God. It is in Jesus Christ that He

---

44) ibid.,pp.596ff.: Barth describes this threat as a minus standing in front of a bracket and "cancelling every other prospect".

45) ibid., pp.598ff.

46) ibid., pp.607ff.

47) ibid., pp.609ff.

48) ibid., p.609.

has taken upon Himself the sin and guilt of all and rescued man from this judgment which man has rightly incurred. It is in Jesus Christ that God has made death the mere sign of His judgment. Without Jesus Christ man would still be under the judgment of God itself and thus irretrievably lost. While the Old Testament affirms God's sovereignty even over death this hope is given substance and content in the New Testament witness to the death and resurrection of Jesus Christ.[49] For man to continue to be anxious in the face of death as the judgment of God is for man to commit the sin of willing that which God does not will but has rejected in the cross of Jesus Christ. The sin of care is exposed by the event of Jesus Christ living at the very point where man's time is limited by man's end. The sin of care is the failure to know that the end of life is hope in the light of the resurrection of Jesus Christ. In care man faces death not as light and hope but as darkness and hopelessness.[50] Man's hope in the face of death rests unreservedly in Jesus Christ and in Him alone:

> "...in the light of the New Testament it is not too much to say that God's existence is our full consolation, assurance and hope in death. For God's existence is visibly and concretely actualised in Jesus Christ as this fulness which excludes any lack."51

After briefly summarizing his arguments thus far Barth

---

49) ibid.,pp.613ff.

50) C.D.IV.2.pp.467ff.

51) C.D.III.2.p.616

points out that the underlying presupposition of the whole exposition has been the equation between the end of man's "allotted" time with death as the sign of God's judgment. Yet the death of Jesus Christ as an atonement for the sin of man was not the inevitable but rather the freely accepted end of His human existence:[52] "His human life might have ended in quite a different way".[53] In order for Jesus Christ to stand in man's place under the judgment of God and take this particular end upon Himself it was necessary for Him to share man's human nature and finitude;" He had to be able to die".[54] In order for this redemption accomplished in Christ to take effect for him man too has to be finite; he has to be able to die. Without such a boundary set for man he would be preserved from the position of having to throw himself conclusively, definitively and exclusively on God. That man is finite and mortal, that his being in time is limited by God as "allotted" time, is therefore determined and ordered by God's good creation. There is no absolute but only a relative necessity involved in the identity between man's end and man's judgment.[55]

Since man actually exists as a sinner before God and

---

52) ibid.,pp.627ff.

53) ibid.,p.629

54) ibid.,p.630

55) ibid.,pp.630ff.

actually faces death as a sign of God's judgment, and since the actual death of Jesus Christ was this death of God's judgment in man's place, Barth is obviously restricted to a "narrower compass of biblical demonstration" to support his argument.[56] Yet he finds such support in the narrative accounts of the translation of Enoch, the death of Moses and the departure of Elijah, also in the New Testament distinction between a "first" death and a "second" death and the preference for the term "to fall asleep" when referring to the former.[57]

While it may be admitted that Barth's argument in this final passage is quite complex his conclusion is both clear and crucial. In the light of the death and resurrection of Jesus Christ there can be no continuing absolute identity between man's end and death as the judgment of God. Moreover, since the event of Jesus Christ is the actualization of God's eternal determination for Himself and for man, this determination of man must include the finitude of his being as a creature in a time "allotted" by God Himself. This conclusion is crucial not only for a valid understanding of the basis of man's participation in God's eternal life (see below) but also for a valid understanding of the Incarnation as primarily _propter nos homines_ and secondarily _propter nostram salutem_.[58]

---

56) ibid.,p.633

57) ibid.,pp.633ff.

58) cf. _C.D._IV.1.pp.47ff. and discussion in chapter five of this thesis; pp. 237ff.

This is the point at which the concept of time and the doctrine of Election meet since the true meaning of man's time is located not in itself but in the particular time in which God actualized His eternal will, the time He took to establish His covenant with man in Jesus Christ.[59]

b) <u>The gift of eternal life:</u>

This chapter began with a reaffirmation of the distinction between God's time and Man's time. The aim of the first section of this chapter was to clarify that, while man as the sinner experiences his time as lost time, this time of man as a creature is nonetheless willed,"given" and "allotted" by God as part of His good determination of the creature. Yet even understood in the light of the time of Jesus Christ as "given" time and "allotted" time this time of man is still distinct from the eternity which is God's time. Only God lives in this His eternal time. Only God lives an "eternal life"; if man is to receive eternal life it can only be on the basis of God's gracious will to "live in fellowship" with man. It is this eternal life as the actualization and preservation of God's fellowship with him that is promised to man as his destiny:[60]

---

59) C.D.III.2.p.456

60) C.D.IV.1.p.111

> "God's command applies to me inasmuch as, being his child, I am an heir of eternal life. In speaking with me, he promises me his presence as my redeemer from the provisional state in which I am here and now his creature, and from the contradiction in which I am here and now a Christian, and he thus bids me wait for this future of his and hasten toward it."61

The resurrection of Jesus Christ is the concrete demonstration of the will and resolve of God to give man a share in the eternity which is His time;[62] in electing man from all eternity for fellowship with Himself God elects man for this eternity.[63] This promise of eternal life is that man's present form will not be "dissolved or done away or destroyed, which would mean death", rather it will be taken up into a new form given by God though not "proper to it in its creatureliness:[64]

> "Since, then, God alone can be its future, the life of a creature after death cannot in any sense or circumstances be anything other than its life from God and for God, i.e., the life which is not its own but is given to it by God. God alone is above death and after it. He alone has immortality (I.Tim.6 16). If a creature is to have immortal life, i.e., the life which defies and overcomes death, which leaves it behind, which is no longer threatened by it, then in no circumstances can this be simply its autonomous continuation in life. It can be only its new life from God and with God."65

The objections expressed by G.C.Berkouwer to Barth's

---

61) Karl Barth, Ethics, ed. Dietrich Braun, trans. by Geoffrey W.Bromiley (Edinburgh,1981),p.461

62) C.D.III.2.p.451

63) C.D.II.2.p.265

64) C.D.IV.3.p.311

65) ibid.,pp.310f.

expression of eternal life as the 'eternalizing' of ending life (which Berkouwer seems to interprete as effectively implying man's non-existence after death rather than man's existence)[66] seem to discount such passages as those previously quoted in which Barth speaks unequivocally of eternal life as eternal life. Fundamentally Berkouwer's objections would appear to derive from a failure to grasp the essential significance of Barth's conception of eternity. God's eternity is not some static abstraction but the authentically temporal location of His being. As the eternal God He is the living God. For man to participate in this eternity can only mean a participation in this livingness, a preservation of fellowship. For Barth the eternalization of man's life means that this "mortal will be swallowed up in life", our life will "fully, definitively and manifestly participate in that καινότης ζωῆς (Rom.6 4)".[67] Moreover the promise to man of eternal life is rooted in the Resurrection life of Jesus Christ as the concrete demonstration of this eternal life of God - hardly in the form of a static abstraction or mere recollection of His pre-Easter life. B. C. Hanson offers an interesting observation regarding the logic of Berkouwer's objections:

> "...the issue of apokatastasis in Barth's theology is an important issue only if Barth holds to continued personal existence after death. If man's existence after death is just to be an object of God's memory, then no one should

---

66) C.D.III.2.p.624; cf. G. C. Berkouwer, The Triumph of Grace in the Theology of Karl Barth, trans. by Harry R. Boer (London, 1956), pp.158ff. & 328ff.

67) C.D.III.2.p.624.

> waste time debating whether all men or only some men may or must attain to that status. The issue is important only if men continue a conscious, personal existence after death. Since Berkouwer discusses the apokatastasis problem at some length, it would appear that he does not take his own criticisms of Barth's conception of an afterlife too seriously. And since Barth often defends himself against some charges of universalism, it is an indication of his own belief in a continuing personal life after death."68

Human life is characterized by a continual discontinuity which must be arrested if man is to live in fellowship with God and participate in His eternal life.[69] This discontinuity is ultimately perceived in death and in the anticipatory shadow which death casts over the total duration of life. The Resurrection of Jesus Christ is the revelation of His Lordship and victory on man's behalf over death and the discontinuity it represents. But even in this eternal life in which the discontinuities of man's life are overcome man "will still be in his time".[70]

> "His divinely given promise and hope and confidence in this confrontation with God is that even as this one who has been he will share the eternal life of God Himself. Its content is not, therefore, his liberation from this-sidedness, from his end and dying, but positively the glorification by the eternal God of his natural and lawful this-sided, finite and mortal being."71

---

68) B C.Hanson, Hope and Participation in Christ: A Study in the Theology of Barth and Pannenberg' (dissertation, Princeton, 1970), pp.91f.

69) C.D.IV.2.pp.317ff.

70) C.D.III.2.p.521

71) C.D.III.2.pp.632f. Barth illustrates his point with reference to the 'fetching home' of Elijah: "...the life which Elijah the prophet lived before and with God was not extinguished when his end came, but...he now lives it before and with God as never before." (ibid., p.636.).

For man to hope for eternal life does not mean that he hopes to be changed into some different form of being, neither does he hoped to be merged into the being of God. Such a pagan form of hope could have no possible meaning or relevance for man's existence in the present (For this reason Barth is cautious regarding the use of the phrase 'resting in God'). Any such conception implies a false understanding not just of the being of man and his hope but also of the being of God Himself:

> "...we must be careful not to form pagan conceptions of God and the eternal life that he lives and the eternal life that He promises to man, as though at bottom God was a supreme being with neither life, nor activity, nor history, in a neutrality which can never be moved or affected by anything, a being with which man can ultimately be united only in rest or in some kind of passive enjoyment or adoring contemplation. The God who is Father, Son and Holy Spirit, active and revealed to us as the eternally living God in Jesus Christ, is not in any sense this supposedly "supreme"being. And unless we say something very much more, restand enjoyment and contemplation are not the right words to describe a being in the depth of fellowship with Him."72

God is the Lord and therefore the content of the promise given to man for his future in fellowship with God must correspond to the being of God as the Lord; it must correspond to the being of God who is " historical even in Himself and much more so in His relationship to the reality which is distinct from Himself".[73] Barth accordingly prefers to speak of the eternal life of man as a being like that of the angels (Luke 20 36), a being

---

72) C.D.IV.1.p.112

73) ibid.

of man with God the Lord as his active ruler; a being in the service of God. The future that the Christian hopes for is a being in a co-operation of service with God, a being in His kingdom and therefore under Him. In that the creatureliness and identity of man will not be destroyed, the distinctness and antithesis of man in relation to God will remain, even in man's participation in the being and life of God as God's covenant partner:

> "It will be a being not only as object, but as an active subject in the fellowship of God with the created world and man, a being in a partnership with God which is actively undertaken and maintained, a being in man's own free responsibility with God for the cause of God." 74

The illness which led to Barth's death in December 1968 halted his work on volume four of the Church Dogmatics (The Doctrine of Reconciliation) and prevented the commencement of volume five (The Doctrine of Redemption). It is unfair and probably incorrect to suggest that Barth's failure to produce this fifth volume was for other than purely chronological reasons, though his reticence concerning the work of the Holy Spirit (which is suggested as a deeper reason for the absence of this volume) will be discussed in the final chapter of this thesis.[75] Barth's detailed outworking of the nature of eternal life presumably would have been one of the subjects to be dealt with in this fifth volume. In its absence little more can be said than that already recounted, though the essential consistency of the development of Barth's thought through the course

---

74) ibid.,p.113

75) See pp. 303 ff. of this thesis.

of the Church Dogmatics should provide a sufficient basis for a responsible projection. Barth's own tentative suggestions concerning the shape of his proposed echatology are quoted by Eberhard Busch in his biography of Barth:

> "How did Barth himself mean to understand eschatology? 'I can only give an indication: the "old" and "new" worlds are indirectly identical, the new already present in the old in that its reconciliation in Jesus Christ has already taken place. What is still to come is its manifestation (i.e., "apocalyptic" eschatology!)' - its general, final, universal revelation! In other words: "Eternal" life is not another, second life beyond our present one, but the reverse side of this life, as God sees it, which is hidden from us here and now. It is this life in relationship to what God has done in Jesus Christ for the whole world and thus also for us. So we wait and hope - in respect of our death - to be made manifest with him (Jesus Christ who is raised from the dead), in the glory of judgment, and also of the grace of God. That will be the new thing: that the veil which now lies over the whole world and thus over our life (tears, death, sorrow, crying, grief) will be taken away, and God's counsel (already accomplished in Jesus Christ) will stand before our eyes, the object of our deepest shame, but also of our joyful thanks and praise."76

Eternal life is therefore not a form of existence that is totally discontinuous with man's present existence within the world but is rather the unveiling of the reality of man's present existence within the world under the Lordship of God; the final unveiling of man's authentic existence as the covenant partner of God. Similarly Markus Barth recalls a conversation with his father in the summer of 1961 (or possibily one or two years earlier) concerning the possible shape of the fifth volume of the Dogmatics. While the

---

76) Eberhard Busch, Karl Barth: His life from letters and autobiographical texts (London,1976),p.488; quoting a letter to W.A.Visser't Hooft 8 March 1953.

discussion centred upon the relevant Biblical texts (I Thessalonians and I Corinthians 15) Markus Barth recalls that his father was strengthened rather than shaken in the hypothesis that he had previously maintained, namely that the eschaton did not involve additional saving events or truths but rather involved the revelation of things hitherto hidden.[77]

c) The provisionality of Christian existence:

That which is already 'actual' in Christian existence is the Christian's present participation in the person and work of Jesus Christ. Through the person and work of the Holy Spirit the Christian, in time and space, already participates in that which is eternal, namely in God's eternal election of man actualized in Jesus Christ.[78] Despite the provisionality and temporality of the Christian's existence the actuality of that existence is already valid because the Holy Spirit is the temporal presence of that which is eternally present:[79]

> "Therefore for us life in the Holy Spirit means "already," even in the midst of the "not yet," to stand in the full truth of what, considered from our "not yet," is pure future but on the strength of this "already" pure present, in which therefore we can already live here and now, expecting the annulment of the duality."80

---

77) Letter from Markus Barth to John E.Colwell, 7 July 1980.

78) The precise nature of this participation and of the noetic and ontic work of the Spirit will be discussed in chapter six of this thesis,pp. 295ff.

79) C.D.II.1.pp.157ff.

80) ibid.,p.158

A similar understanding of the actuality of Christian existence is expressed by Karl Rahner in a discussion of the hermaneutics of eschatological assertions.[81] An eschatological assertion is not merely a statement about man's future, a supplementary assertion to statements concerning his past and present, it is rather a statement in which man's being in the present is referred to this eschatological future and thus is an assertion concerning man's actual eschatological being in the present; knowledge of this eschatological future is "an inner moment of the self-understanding of man".[82]

> "Knowledge of the future will be knowledge of the futurity of the present: eschatological knowledge is knowledge of the eschatological present."[83]

Man's eschatological future is the ultimate revelation of the salvation that has been actualized in Jesus Christ, but this salvation is already the true life of man in Jesus Christ through the power of the Holy Spirit, his future life in Jesus Christ is already his hidden but authentic present life in Jesus Christ. God's gracious Word does not say that he will be this new man but that he already is this new man; it speaks "of the present irruption of this future, of the advent of the new man here and now".[84] It is therefore necessary to speak of Christian existence as both proleptic and eschat-

---

81) Karl Rahner, Theological Investigations, IV, trans. by Kevin Smith (Baltimore and London, 1966), pp. 323ff.

82) ibid., p.331

83) ibid., p.332

84) C.D.IV.3.p.249

ological, a genuine anticipation of a future life since that future life is already man's hidden life in the present.[85] It is in this sense that every statement concerning Christian existence in the present is itself an eschatological statement, a statement that refers to a consummation and fulfilment in the future.[86] By faith man in the present recognizes his true life as that which has been actualized in Jesus Christ; as a life of direct discipleship, as a "being in Christ".[87] In hope man in the present recognizes his future eternal life as that which is now hidden in Jesus Christ:

> "We believe that we are redeemed, set free, children of God, i.e., we accept as such the promise given us in the Word of God in Jesus Christ even as and although we do not understand it in the very least, or see it fulfilled and consummated in the very least, in relation to our present. We accept it because it speaks to us of an act of God on us even as and although we see only our own empty hands which we stretch out to God in the process. We believe our future being. We believe in an eternal life even in the midst of the valley of death. In this way, in this futurity, we have it. The assurance with which we know this having is the assurance of faith, and the assurance of faith means concretely the assurance of hope."88

The time of the Christian community within the world has as its beginning the end of the 40 days of the Resurrection

---

85) Hanson refers to the "teleological framework" of Barth's theology in distinction to the "futurist framework" of Pannenberg's theology (B.C.Hanson,'Hope and Participation in Christ',pp.137ff.

86) C.D.I.1.pp.462ff.

87) C.D.III.2.p.467

88) C.D.I.1.p.463

appearances of Jesus Christ. As the Lord of time this post-Easter time is also His time, the time of Jesus Christ present with His Church by His Spirit. In this sense the time of the Christian community is also the time of the risen Jesus Christ.[89] Yet the New Testament not only relates the time of the Christian community to the time of Christ, it also clearly differentiates between them:

> "The time of Jesus Christ is marked off from their own as not merely present but future, the time which has still to come but is expected and hoped for. And their own time (in and with its retrospective unity with the time of Jesus Christ) becomes to them a time between the times."[90]

The time of Jesus Christ, as a future time and not just a past time and present time, is that which determines the provisional character of the time of the community. The Christian community along with the world in which it continues to exist, has "no option but to participate in and adapt itself" to this Not Yet that has its basis in the Not Yet of Jesus Christ.[91] that the Christian community lives in this time between the times, in this movement from direct vision to direct vision, constitutes both its weakness and its strength.[92] It is strong because it can look back to Easter: it can hear and proclaim this message. It is weak because this hearing and proclaiming is in faith alone; it has no "basis or support in any

---

89) C.D.IV.1.p.319

90) ibid.,p.323

91) ibid.,p.329

92) ibid.,p.725

form of sight".[93] It is strong because it looks forward to the coming of Jesus Christ, to His final revelation. As such it already knows what others do not know; it knows of the verdict of God executed and declared in Jesus Christ. It is strong, because in the recognition of its origin and goal it knows what time is, because it recognizes its time as this time between.[94] But here too it is weak because this recognition is also in faith and not in sight. It knows its goal only in the form of its beginning.[95]

The provisionality of Christian existence therefore coincides with the orientation of the Christian towards the <u>ἔσχατον</u> that is not yet, the future redemption of the Christian that is the consummation and fulfilment of his being in Jesus Christ. This provisionality is both noetic and ontic in character. Noetically it consists in the fact that the final revelation of Jesus Christ and the reconciliation actualized in Him has not yet occurred. Other than in faith and hope the Christian cannot yet see or know his true being in Jesus Christ. Ontically this provisionality of Christian existence consists in the fact that the consummation of redemption in Jesus Christ has not yet occurred; even now the Christian not only exists in the power of the Holy Spirit as the man he is and will be in Jesus Christ, he also exists as the sinful man that he was and still

93) ibid.,p.728

94) ibid.,p.726ff.

95) ibid.,pp.730ff.

is: simul iustus et peccator.[96]

As one would expect, the provisional character of Christian existence is a continuous theme of the third part of Barth's doctrine of Reconciliation, a consequence of the prophetic work of Jesus Christ, the vocation of man, the sending of the Christian community and the hope of the Christian. However, this same conception of Christian provisionality is expounded by Barth throughout the earlier sections of his doctrine of Reconciliation. Justification, Sanctification and Vocation are not ultimate but penultimate words for Barth. They are all qualified not only by an Already and an Even Now but also by a Not Yet. They are reconciliation but they are not yet redemption and glorification.

In relation to the actuality of Man's justification in Jesus Christ the provisionality of Christian existence is ontically identified as the Christian's continuing life as a man who is proud and who has fallen. This is the first sense in which the Christian exists as homo peccator et iustus, as man under the No of God's judgment and the Yes of God's grace.[97] Since this contradiction of Christian existence is known in Jesus Christ rather than in subjective experience it must be understood as the history of God with man and not as a static dualistic being of man; it is the event of

---

96) Note how Barth uses the term "redemption" to refer both to the immediate work of Jesus Christ through the Holy Spirit and to the ultimate consummation of that work C.D.I.1.pp.448ff.

97) C.D.IV.1.pp.358ff.

man's transition from the sphere of God's judgment to the sphere of God's grace.[98] While the Christian's past existence is exclusively under God's No, and while the Christian's future existence is exclusively under God's Yes, the Christian's present existence is under both this No and this Yes:

> "...the man on the left hand is the Whence and the man on the right hand the Whither of the one man, the former being this man as he was and still is, the latter being this man as he will be and to that extent already is."99

Noetically man's justification is his pardon by God that confronts him in the form of a promise, as God's unequivocal affirmation of his future being in Jesus Christ.[100] But this promise is addressed to man in the present as the pardon that has been unconditionally pronounced and is unconditionally valid in Jesus Christ; it relates not only to man's future being but also to his being in the present. Man's future existence cannot be simply equated or identified with his present existence but they must not be considered as mutually exclusive nor must the distinction between them be described in quantitative terms; the Christian in his present existence is not partially peccator and partially iustus, he is simul peccator et iustus:[101]

---

98) ibid.,p.516 & pp.543ff.

99) ibid.,p.543; cf. p.555

100) ibid.,pp.568ff.

101) ibid., pp 595ff.

> "The fact that it is for us something future, that enclosed in the promise of God it can only be hoped and awaited and prayed for, does not in any way limit it or lessen its power. It does not mean that as man lays hold of the promise he cannot receive it here and now with unconditional certainty and unlimited fulness."[102]

The Christian's response to this form of the provisionality of his existence is his faith.[103] Faith is the awakening of the Christian in the power of the Holy Spirit to affirm his objective justification in Jesus Christ as his true being in the present despite his being as homo peccator and, believing the promise of God in Jesus Christ, to recognize his future eschatological existence as his existence in the present.[104] Despite the contradiction of his present existence the Christian "will know the hidden thing in every time as the eternal thing,the depth of every present in which he moves already to the future of the pure present."[105] It is in this affirmation of faith that the Christian within the gathered community of the Church exists as a provisional representation of the justification that has objectively occurred for all men in Jesus Christ.

In relation to the actuality of man's sanctification in Jesus Christ the provisionality of Christian existence is ontically identified

---

102) ibid.,p.598

103) ibid.,pp.608ff.; cf. p.570

104) ibid.,pp.740ff.

105) ibid.,p.604

as the Christian's continuing life as the man who is slothful and miserable. This is the second sense in which the Christian exists as homo peccator et iustus, as the old man of yesterday and the new man of to-morrow.[106] The sanctification of man has objectively occurred in Jesus Christ but the Christian's life is not only in Jesus Christ but also in the flesh,"in the past which is continually present."[107] In the light of the exaltation of Jesus Christ as Son of Man the sanctification of man must be understood in terms of a conversion and a transition, a movement in which the old man and the new man "are simultaneously present in the relationship of a terminus a quo and a terminus ad quem":[108]

> "In Jesus Christ a Christian has already come into being, but in himself and his time he is always in the process of becoming."109

In the transition implied by this penultimate transformation of man the Christian is engaged in warfare,[110] in the conflict of the Spirit against the flesh and the flesh against the Spirit.[111] Yet it is the Christian's being in the flesh, as the old man which he was and is, that is "overwhelmingly and totally compromised" by his being as a "saint", as the new man which he will be and already is, and not vice versa.[112]

---

106) C.D.IV.2.pp.378ff.

107) ibid.,p.496

108) ibid.,p.573

109) ibid.,p.307

110) ibid.,p.570; cf. p.530

111) ibid.,pp.496f.

112) ibid.,p.526

Noetically man's sanctification, as an awakening to conversion, implies the giving and receiving of a new direction in the power of the Holy Spirit.[113] God's determination of man has occurred de jure for the world in Jesus Christ but de facto it is recognized by the Christian.[114] Ultimately this determination issues in man's entry into eternal life, the ending of the contradiction of his existence in the present,[115] but this divine determination confronts man in his present as that which is "eternally resolved and seriously willed and effectively executed by God."[116] In his present existence the Christian is wholly, and not partially, determined by this objective sanctification, he is given total freedom in face of his total bondage,[117] he is simul (totus) iustus, simul (totus) peccator; "the same man, in the simul of to-day, is both the old man of yesterday and the new man of to-morrow".[118]

The Christian's response to this form of the provisionality of his existence is his love.[119] In the power of the Holy Spirit the Christian is given the freedom to correspond to the love in which

---

113) ibid.,p.523; cf. pp.554ff.

114) ibid.,p.511

115) ibid.,pp.598ff.

116) ibid.,p.554

117) ibid.,p.531; cf. p.497

118) ibid.,p.572

119) ibid.,pp.727ff.

God has sanctified him in Jesus Christ, the freedom to correspond to his future being. His acts of love do not annul his existence as a sinner in the present but, as human responsive acts, they are works which praise God and which are praised by Him.[120] It is in the act of love that the Christian within the growing community of the Church exists as a provisional representation of the sanctification that has objectively occurred for all men in Jesus Christ; "a provisional representation of the new humanity in the midst of the old."[121]

In relation to the actuality of man's vocation in Jesus Christ the provisionality of Christian existence is ontically identified as the Christian's continuing life as a man who is false and who is condemned. This is the third sense in which the Christian exists as <u>homo peccator et iustus.</u>[122] The vocation of man in which he is awakened to an active knowledge of the truth and set in the service of the truth has objectively occurred in Jesus Christ exposing man's continuing existence as one who attempts to evade, distort and deny the truth, as one in the sphere of darkness that opposes the Light of Life. In no sense can the liberation of the Christian be considered as complete, his life is that of a pilgrim in transition awaiting the redemption which will be the ultimate revelation of his true being.[123] The vocation of the Christian

---

120) ibid.,pp.584ff.; cf. p.783

121) ibid.,p.642; cf. p.620ff.

122) <u>C.D.</u>IV.3.pp.368ff.

123) ibid.,pp.673ff.

consists in the process of illumination, the turning from falsehood to truth and, as such, it is not only vocatio unica but also vocatio continua.[124]

Noetically man's vocation, as a calling to the service of the prophetic work of Jesus Christ, implies the Christian's ordination to this specific task as a witness of the Truth.[125] The vocation of man certainly includes his liberation, his personal participation in the Truth; the goal of vocation is the union of the Christian with Christ, a union that is concealed hic et nunc but will be revealed illic et tunc.[126] However, this union of the Christian with Jesus Christ is specifically a union in the service of His prophetic work, a summons to the ministerium Verbi divini which confronts the Christian in his present existence.[127] No form of the Not Yet that characterizes Christian existence in the present can detract from the actuality of his vocation in Jesus Christ; his vocation which includes his own liberation, though it is not yet "accomplished",is nonetheless clear, definite and unequivocal.[128]

The Christian's response to this form of provisionality of his existence is his hope, indeed, inasmuch as the Christian's hope

---

124) ibid.,pp.508ff.

125) ibid.,pp.554ff.

126) ibid.,pp.520ff.; cf. pp.647ff.

127) ibid.,pp.594ff.

128) ibid.,p.674; cf. pp.484ff.

is his expectant orientation towards the future parousia of Jesus Christ and the ultimate fulfilment of his own existence as a Christian, Christian hope is that aspect of the Christian's existence which supremely points beyond the provisionality of his present:[129]

> "...in the act of Christian hope the objective becomes subjective. It is affirmed. In the person of the Christian the world of men strives after and seizes the goal and future given to it in Jesus Christ. It waits for it, it hastens towards it, it reaches out for it. In the act of Christian hope that which is promised (as promised and therefore future) is already present. Jesus Christ as the (promised and coming) eternally living One is already present. Not merely virtually and effectively, but actually and actively in the person of the Christian."130

There are a multitude of human hopes and expectations within the world besides the Christian hope, yet all these anthropological hopes are bounded by the same insurmountable barrier, namely that their realization lies in a future that is as yet undisclosed and unknown. Therefore, for all their persuasiveness, such human hopes must always be characterized by an element of uncertainty. Not so the hope of the Christian. The proleptic structure of the Christian's existence determines that the object of his hope lies, not in the unknown future, but in the known past and present. He hopes for the one parousia of Jesus Christ who is the same yesterday and today and for ever. He hopes for a future that is known and not unknown:

---

129) ibid.,pp.902ff. cf. C.D.IV.1.pp.601ff.

130) C.D.IV.1.p.119

> "What the man who hopes as a Christian expects is not twilight. It is not light and also shadow, good and also evil, salvation and also destruction. It is unequivocally and uninterruptedly light and good and salvation. For the One whom he see before him is unequivocally and uninterruptedly God, the living God in His grace and righteousness and mercy and glory, the God towards whom he can go, not with a mixture of confidence and suspicion, but only with confidence."131

No more can there be an anthropological basis for Christian hope than there can be an anthropological basis for Christian faith or Christian love. Any expectation for the future that could be founded upon anthropological considerations would only prove to be a divided hope, an ambivalent hope, and therefore not a Christian hope. The certain hope which is the Christian hope can only be grounded in Jesus Christ. The Christian does not hope for mere abstract blessings such as "the resurrection of the dead, or justification in the day of judgment, or a life of eternal bliss". His only hope is "concentrated upon Him". Any independent hope would be "idle dreaming":132

> "...the world is no longer a world without hope. As it stands under the verdict and direction of God, so too it stands under the promise of God. It is the world set in the light of its future with God. Hence man is the being which exists in this direction, under this determination, with this perspective. And the Christian is the man who for himself and others can know this and therefore hope. His hope derives from Jesus Christ, for Jesus Christ is Himself the divine pledge as such. And He hopes in Jesus Christ, for Jesus Christ is also the content of the divine pledge."133

---

131) <u>C.D.</u>IV.3.pp.907f.

132) <u>C.D.</u>III.2.p.490

133) <u>C.D.</u>IV.1.p.115

Barth concludes the third part of his doctrine of Reconciliation with a discussion of "the Holy Spirit and Christian Hope" in which he considers the response of Christian hope to the specific questions implied by the provisionality of Christian existence in the present.[134]

The Christian exists between the first immediate <u>parousia</u> presence of Jesus Christ and His final <u>parousia</u> presence. In the first place this implies that, though Jesus Christ has spoken and continues to speak, He has not yet spoken of Himself universally in a manner that all men must hear and receive His Word.[135] The Christian exists in the present as one set apart and isolated from the majority of men who have not yet heard the prophetic Word of Jesus Christ. As such the Christian is continually challenged and threatened by the depiction of himself as a member of a dwindling minority within a world of men who do not believe as he believes, love as he loves or hopes as he hopes.[136] Moreover, the world not only passively fails to share the Christian's faith, love and hope, it actively rejects and opposes the Christian. In an earlier section Barth considers the affliction of the Christian, an affliction that derives from the world which misconstrues his witness as an intolerable and insolent presumption, an affliction that cannot be evaded

---

134) <u>C.D.</u>IV.3.pp.902ff.

135) ibid.,p.903

136) ibid.,p.904; cf. p.906

by the Christian without renouncing his vocation as a witness and denying his very existence as a Christian, an affliction which primarily derives from the Christian's participation in Jesus Christ since the world which can no longer afflict Him directly can afflict Him indirectly by afflicting the Christian.[137] The Word of Jesus Christ in the witness of the Christian consists in God's Yes to the world which necessarily includes God's No. The world not only fails to hear this Yes of the Gospel, it also fails to hear this No as God's No and reacts by opposing its own No, rejecting the Word of Jesus Christ in the Christian's witness in the same manner as it previously rejected Jesus Christ Himself.

That the Christian is empowered by the Holy Spirit to hope within this context of isolation and affliction means that, on the objective basis of the death and resurrection of Jesus Christ for all men, he can hope not only for himself but also on behalf of the apparently unreachable majority of men. The Christian's hope cannot be his "private affair" since his expectation is directed towards God's universal act of redemption in Jesus Christ.In the act of hope, not only on his own behalf but as a witness to others, the Christian exists as a provisional representation of the vocation that has objectively occurred in Jesus Christ.[138]The task committed to the Christian community is the Gospel, the great Yes of the goodness of God. Its task is to address this Yes to the man who

---

137) ibid.,pp.614ff.

138) ibid.,pp.917ff. & 930ff.; cf. C.D.IV.1.p.119

lacks the knowledge of the Gospel and who is in supreme need of such knowledge.[139] The ministry of the Christian community is to exist actively for the world: to declare the Gospel; to explain the Gospel; to proclaim and apply the Gospel.[140] The Christian to whom this task and ministry of witness is committed cannot hope merely for himself:

> "...if he really hopes as he can and should as a Christian, he will not let his hands fall and simply wait in idleness for what God will finally do, neglecting his witness to Christ. On the contrary, strengthened and encouraged by the thought of what God will finally do, he will take up his ministry on this side of the frontier. He will thus not allow himself to be disturbed by questions of minorities or majorities, of success or failure, of the probable or more likely improbable progress of Christianity in the world. As a witness of Jesus Christ, He will simply do——and no more is required, though this is indeed required——that which he can do to proclaim the Gospel in his own age and place and circle, doing it with humility and good temper, but also with the resoluteness which corresponds to the great certainty of this hope in Jesus Christ."141

The Christian's existence between the first and the final immediate parousia presence of Jesus Christ implies secondly that, though Jesus Christ has spoken and continues to speak, He has not yet spoken of Himself in such a way "that even those who are awakened by Him to faith and love can hear His voice in perfect purity and to the exclusion of every conceivable contradiction and opposition and above all participation in human falsehood."[142]

---

139) C.D.IV.3.pp.795ff.

140) ibid.,pp.830ff.

141) C.D.IV.3.pp.918f.

142) ibid.,p.903; cf. p.904

Existence as a Christian is continually called into question by factors which apparently contradict the reality of this existence; that which the Christian is by faith is seemingly denied by that which he is by sight. The unremitting presence of such contradictions is the direct consequence of the provisionality of Christian existence in the present. All too clearly the Christian perceives his being as totus peccator while his being as totus iustus remains hidden from his immediate perception.

> "...the Christian can see himself only in his own contradication which has not yet been set aside, in the lasting conflict between his new but not yet exclusive being in the righteousness and holiness of Jesus Christ and his old and rejected but not yet excluded being in the flesh, in his own perishing nature which is also that of the world as a whole. Is not this inevitable, seeing that Jesus Christ has not yet spoken to him the last Word which removes all contradiction?"143

That the Christian is empowered by the Holy Spirit to hope in the context of such contradiction within the history of the world and the Christian's own history means that, on the objective basis of the event of justification, sanctifiation and vocation that has occurred in Jesus Christ, he can move towards the eschatological future and live in hope in spite of these appearances. In the act of hope the Christian is directed towards the final parousia of Jesus Christ in which the contradictions of his present existence and the existence of the world will be finally and completely overcome and his true being in Jesus Christ will be unequivocally clear. Earlier

---

143) ibid.,p.906

in his exposition of this third part of the doctrine of Reconciliation Barth considers the relationship between Jesus Christ as the light (i.e., in the prophetic aspect of His reconciling work) and the surrounding darkness of the world which opposes His light. This relationship is neither dualistic (the equilibrium of opposing forces) nor monistic (the antithesis already removed), rather it is that of "dynamic teleology"; a goal that is not yet attained; a history that is still taking place.[144] This dynamic and teleological character of the prophetic work of Jesus Christ is reflected in Barth's use of the phrase "Jesus is Victor" (a term popularized by J.C.Blumhardt). For this reason the Christian's hope does not issue in mere passivity: in the light of this future the Christian is not called to be victorious since the ultimate victory belongs to Jesus Christ, but he is called to struggle against the unrighteousness and unholiness of his past and present towards the righteousness and holiness of his eschatological future and present.[145] Moreover, the authenticity of the Christian's hope will be demonstrated by his freedom from hopelessness in this present; his ultimate hope will find expression in penultimate hopes, a discerning of the eternally actual in the provisional.[146]

---

144) ibid.,p.168

145) ibid.,pp.919f. & 934ff.

146) ibid.,pp.935ff. cf. C.D.IV.1.pp.120ff.

That the Christian exists between the first and the final immediate parousia presence of Jesus Christ also implies that the final Word of Jesus Christ as the Judge has not yet been spoken.[147] The provisional character of Christian existence means that this ultimate decision of God concerning the Christian and his service has not yet been definitely announced:[148]

> "What is the Christian's hope, and what does it mean, since Jesus Christ has not yet come as Judge of the quick and the dead and has not yet spoken His ultimate Word as such, in face of the mystery whether or not his Christian existence will stand in His judgment, i.e., whether or not that which makes him a Christian, his ministry of witness, will be properly fulfilled by the standard of the One whom he has to attest, whether it will be approved and accepted by Him or repudiated and rejected? This is something which will be manifested to all eyes and therefore to his own in the consummating revelation of Jesus Christ, but which is still completely concealed from him."[149]

The Christian cannot overlook nor overleap this limitation of his provisionality since he is unable to evaluate his own human work of witness by anticipating this ultimate judgment or by usurping this judgment which is the prerogative of God alone. But, confronted by this aspect of his provisionality, the Christian is empowered by the Holy Spirit to hope since the Judge whose ulimate judgment he awaits is not an unknown judge but the Judge who is well known to the Christian, the One who was present in His resurrection and is present even now in the power of the Holy

---

147) C.D.IV.3.pp.903f.

148) ibid.,p.906

149) ibid.,p.920

Spirit. Those who know this gracious Judge already can await His judgment in hope, as the judgment of His grace, "not with hesitant but with assured, unequivocally positive and therefore joyful expectation."[150] Since the Christian's life in hope is a life which derives from God, a life to which he is summoned in election and vocation, the Christian is both liberated to the pursuit of this calling as a witness in confident expectation and liberated from concern regarding his own worthiness and ability.[151]

These three provisional limitations of Christian existence in the present to which Christian hope responds are further compounded by the one event which confronts the Christian and all other men as an absolute certainty, namely the conclusion of temporal existence. Whether that end is reached in man's death or at the final parousia of Jesus Christ its certain occurrence implies that there will be a time when the Christian will no longer have the opportunity to be a more effective witness, no longer have the opportunity to pursue holiness amidst the conflict of his own unholiness, no longer have the opportunity to be other than he has been in the face of God's judgment. Whatever form the Christian's end may take it appears as a bitter "Too Late"; his temporal life is terminated even though he may regard it as the most pitiable of beginnings. Yet the Christian can respond in hope even to this ultimate limitation of his existence since the end which he awaits is not this end in itself but the consummating revelation and judg-

---

150) ibid.,p.922

151) ibid.,pp.939ff.

ment of Jesus Christ. The end expected by the Christian in hope implies not that he has no more opportunities nor possibilities but that no more is expected of him:[152]

> "...the conclusion of Christian existence expected from him can never come too soon, nor give cause for that bitter Too Late. Coming from Him, it can only be an unequivocally welcome, because gracious event."153

The hope in which the Christian response to the provisionality of his existence in the present is an unequivocally positive expectation of the future, it is hope in the form of an unambiguous assurance.[154] Christian hope, like Christian faith, consists of this certain assurance because it is grounded in Jesus Christ and the actual reconciliation that has occurred in Him.[155] This hope is directed towards Jesus Christ in His final parousia but Jesus Christ in this Not Yet is none other than He is in the Already of His resurrection and the Even Now of His presence in the power of the

---

152) ibid.,pp.906 & 924ff.

153) ibid.,p.927

154) ibid.,pp.907ff. Interestingly, Küng's discussion of Barth's doctrine of Justification in which he claims a fundamental agreement between Barth and the teaching of the Roman Catholic Church makes no mention of this doctrine of Assurance (Hans Küng, Justification: The Doctrine of Karl Barth and a Catholic Reflection, trans. by T.Collins, E.E. Tolk and D.Grandskou (London,1966); cf. A.E.McGrath,'Justification: Barth, Trent and Küng', S.J.T.,34 (1981), 517-529 (pp.524ff.).

155) C.D.IV.1.pp.773f. cf. p.96

Holy Spirit.[156] The assurance which is this Christ-centred hope must not be confused with a purely subjective conception of assurance rooted in Christian experience:[157]

> "We are not grasping at more but at less, and ultimately at nothing at all, if in addition to the guarantee which is identical with God Himself we think we must grasp at an unequivocal experience, at a guarantee of the guarantee so to speak, in order that we may then decide for certainty of faith, as though a certainty for which we must first decide could be the certainty of faith.
> ...if we grasp at another, at ourselves, if we seek strength and confirmation in ourselves, we simply show thereby that we are still far from thinking and speaking ἐν πνεύματι, or have long since ceased to do so."158

Neither must this humble assurance of faith be distorted into that arrogant presumption which impertinently boasts of God's grace as if it were a right to be claimed.[159] The Christian may regard himself and all other men as those who are ontologically defined as elect in Jesus Christ but he cannot presume upon this election either for himself or for others, in obedient hope he responds to the promise of God but he neither asserts his own rights nor makes presumptuous claims on the basis of this promise.[160] The source of Christian hope is the grace of God, the electing love of God in which He always remains free, owing nothing to man:[161]

---

156) C.D.IV.3.p.910.

157) Although John Wesley sought to guard against the extremes of subjectivism one is left with the impression that his attempts were largely unsuccessful and that his apparently feeling-centred conception of assurance has vitiated English Evangelicalism. (cf. Arthur S. Yates, The Doctrine of Assurance: with special reference to John Wesley (London, 1952), p.210.

158) C.D.I.1.p.465; cf. C.D.II.1.p.249 & C.D.IV.3.pp.565f.

159) C.D.IV.1.p.539.

160) C.D.II.2.p.416; cf. C.D.III.2.p.190.

161) C.D.IV.3.p.942; cf. p.781.

> "...the fact that He will do this, and does it, is the affair of His sovereign action on which we cannot count, of His unmerited gift, of His free beneficence, of His grace, to which no man, not even the Christian or the Christian community, has any claim, and the receiving of which they cannot take for granted at all times and in all circumstances, as though it were their due. Jesus Christ would not be the true Son of the true God, and His vouching and answering for His people, for His community, for the world which in Him is reconciled to God, would not be the help, deliverance, victory and salvation which has come and is manifested in Him, if we could handle Him with the same assurance and familiarity as we do a bank account. Cheap grace, i.e., the grace which may be counted on in advance, the grace which is disposable, the grace which is waiting to be taken and used by man— this unfree grace is not grace."162

The humble assurance which is the characteristic of Christian faith and Christian hope does not attempt to manipulate the grace of God but neither is it uncertain of this grace.[163] That Christian assurance implies a positive and certain expectation for the future is a consequence of the proleptic structure of Christian existence. The possibility of Christian existence in the eschatological future stands in the light of the Christian's present existence in the resurrection of Jesus Christ and in the power of the Holy Spirit.[164] The reality of Christian existence is determined by its origin in the grace of God which is His essential being because it is His primal and eternal self-determination, it is determined

---

162) <u>C.D.</u>IV.4.pp.208f.

163) ibid.,p.210

164) <u>C.D.</u>IV.3.p.906; cf. <u>C.D.</u>IV.1.pp.40ff.

in the event of God's electing love actualized in Jesus Christ.[165] It is this electing love of God which will be the subject of the remaining chapters of this thesis. The Christian's humble response to the ontic and noetic provisionality of his existence derives from the ontic and noetic actuality of his existence,[166] determined by the Father, actualized in the Son, and realized in the power of the Holy Spirit. The Christian will be he who is because he is who he will be; his authentic life, despite the not yet of his existence in the present, is already and even now "hid with Christ in God".[167]

> "God's revelation stands before us as the goal and end of time. We wait for it even as we look back on its occurrence in the middle of time and grasp it as the Kingdom of God that has drawn near, in the way in which it is possible to grasp this in time, in the way in which it wills to grasp us, and has grasped us in time. After time, in post-temporal eternity, we shall not believe in it. We shall see it. It will be without the concealment which surrounds it in time and as long as time continues. Without deprivation or the danger of deprivation, and without the veil of hope, we shall then have that for which we must now pray, and which we do really receive in its fulness, but in the veil of hope, so that we must continually pray for it again. Post-temporal eternity is free from this fluctuation. It is the same revelation which we have had, but it is now without a veil, whereas in time we may believe in it under the veil of hope and therefore with the fluctuation of praying and receiving and praying again."168

---

165) C.D.II.1.pp.356ff.; cf. C.D.II.2.pp.115f.

166) That J.D.Bettis asserts that, for Barth, the future of all men including the Christian is uncertain may be indicative of his failure to take adequate account of the ontic as well as the noetic nature of Christian existence (J.D.Bettis, 'Is Karl Barth a Universalist?', S.J.T.,20 (1967),423-436(p.433)); cf. pp. 272ff. of this thesis.

167) Colossians 3.3; cf. C.D.IV.3.p.645.

168) C.D.II.1.pp.630f. cf. C.D.IV.3.pp.882ff.

The first three chapters of this thesis have affirmed with Barth that the sole possibility for the task of speaking validly about God is to be located in the actuality of the happening of God in time. This actuality must determine the rationality of the manner and method of theology. Despite a professed concern to be not only rational but also acceptable and relevant, any attempted theology which ignores or refutes the rationality demanded by the actuality of this event of God in favour of an independent rationality must be regarded as itself irrational. If theology persists in the irrationality of ignoring the inherent rationality of its actual subject it condemns itself to effective irrelevance and ultimate oblivion.[169]

Having defined Barth's concept of God's eternity according to the actuality of His happening in time it remains the purpose of the final three chapters of this thesis to examine the manner in which this conception of eternity determines and informs Barth's distinctive understanding of the doctrine of Election. At the very centre of Barth's theology his conception of eternity and his doctrine of Election coincide.[170] Barth conceives of God's eternity as the authentic temporality and constancy of His Triune life. Barth expounds the doctrine of Election as the definition of the identity of this

---

169) cf. Colin E.Gunton, 'Transcendence, Metaphor, and the Knowability of God', J.T.S., 31 (1980), 501-516 (p.516).

170) cf.p. 107 of this thesis.

authentically temporal, constant and Triune living God. The doctrine of Election defines the eternal God as the electing God and a valid conception of God's eternity locates temporally this decision and event of His election.

IV The Doctrine of Election and the Doctrine of God

a) The being of God as event:

The concern of the first part of this thesis has been to establish and expound the principle of the relationship of actuality to rationality in relation to the knowability of God and in particular with reference to the actuality and rationality of His eternity as the authentic temporality of His being. The governing principle of Barth's theological method is that the actuality of this happening of God in time determines the rationality of our knowing Him. Here alone is located the exclusive possibility of valid talk about God, the exclusive possibility of God's knowability:

> "...we can find His knowability only in the readiness of God Himself, which is to be understood as His free good-pleasure. Therefore, in order to assure ourselves of it, and thus of the certainty of our knowledge of God, we must restrict ourselves to the reality of the encroachment carried out by God."1

To use the phrase "God is" in a valid way is to use it solely within the sphere of the event of His Word:

> "What God is as God,...is something which we shall encounter either at the place where God deals with us as Lord and Saviour, or not at all."2

Yet Barth's principal concern, which must also be the principal concern of valid theology, was not to speak merely of the knowability of God but to speak positively of the God who

---

1) C.D. II.1.p.85, cf. pp.79ff.

2) C.D.II.1.p.261.

actually is known. Barth unequivocally denies the reality of any independent knowledge of God in order unequivocally to affirm the reality of the knowledge of God in the event of revelation. He not only claims that we must speak of the being of God exclusively with reference to His self-revelation, he also claims that we may speak of the being of God in this way because God truly is who He actually is in the event of His Word; He is not another in Himself than He is in His works.[3] God is known in the event of revelation because His being is actually to be located in this event; He is identical to His revelation of Himself:

> "God is who He is in the act of His revelation."4

If to speak validly of the knowability of God demands a rationality that is determined by the prior actuality of the event of His revelation in time and space then this actuality itself implies the prior possibility that God is able to actualize Himself in this way; He can be God in this way; He can become the event of His revelation; He can become man in Jesus Christ. Any denial of such a prior possibility in the being of God could only rest upon that supposed independent knowledge of God which Barth rejects:

---

3) <u>C.D</u>.II.1.p.260

4) <u>C.D</u>.II.1.p.257

> "Where God is known He is also in some way or other knowable. Where the actuality exists there is also the corresponding possibility. The question cannot then be posed *in abstracto* but only *in concreto*; not *a priori* but only *a posteriori*. The *in abstracto* and *a priori* question of the possibility of the knowledge of God obviously presupposes the existence of a place outside the knowledge of God itself from which this knowledge can be judged."5

If the epistemological principle that actuality determines rationality is fundamental to Barth's theological method then this complementary ontological principle that actuality implies possibility is fundamental to his theological assertions, a "vital key" to his whole theology.[6] It is this which gives Barth his justification for speaking about God's being in Himself on the basis of His being in the event of revelation. That is to say, it serves as a bridge between the economic Trinity and the immanent Trinity. Yet it is more than just a bridge; it is the means by which Barth asserts the identification of the economic Trinity as the immanent Trinity; who God is in the event of His revelation in Jesus Christ He is beforehand in Himself.

Eberhard Jüngel goes beyond Barth in comprehensively challenging, on the basis of the doctrine of Justification, the

---

5) *C.D.*II.1.p.5; cf. Barth's discussion of God's omnipotence (ibid., pp.522ff.)

6) Colin E. Gunton, 'Karl Barth's Doctrine of Election as part of his Doctrine of God', *J.T.S.*, 25 (1974), 381-392 (p.387)

Aristotelian assumption of the ontological priority of actuality.[7] To apply this assumption to the doctrine of Justification would inevitably produce a doctrine of Justification by works. Rather, the doctrine of Justification by faith implies that Christian existence springs from that which is not yet actual:

> "Because it is absolutely existence out of the creative power of the justifying God Christian existence, in this sense, is existence out of nothing."[8]

Indeed, the doctrine of creation itself as creatio ex nihilo is "out of harmony" with Arostotle's assumption. Man and the world are possibilities existing out of nothing by virtue of God's creative Word. The truth of the language of faith is demonstrated not by its conformity to actuality (i.e., the world as it is) but by its non-conformity to actuality. In this perspective Jüngel considers Karl Barth's Church Dogmatics to be determined throughout by the primacy of actuality; i.e., the actuality of God in His revelation precedes the general question of the possibility of there being any divine revelation at all.[9]

Jüngel's single sentence summary of Barth's adherence to the Aristotelian assumption of the priority of actuality is

---

7) E. Jüngel, 'Die Welt als Möglichkeit und Wirklichkeit: Zum ontologischen Ansatz der Rechtfertigungslehre' in Unterwegs zur Sache: Theologische Bemerkungen, ed. E. Wolf, Beiträge zur evangelischer Theologie, 61 (Munich, 1972), 206-233; cf. E. Jüngel, Gott als Geheimnis der Welt: Zur Begründung der Theologie des Gekreuzigten im Streit zwischen Theismus und Atheismus (Tübingen, 1978), pp.289ff.

8) E. Jüngel, 'Die Welt als Möglichkeit und Wirklichkeit', p.219, my translation.

9) ibid., p.213.

uncharacteristically unfair and superficial. When Barth affirms the priority of actuality he does so epistemologically rather than ontologically; i.e., the possibility of knowing God rests upon the prior actuality of the event of revelation in which He is known. However, ontologically this priority is reversed; i.e., the actuality of the event of revelation implies the prior possibility in God Himself to be God in this event.[10]

It is characteristic of the complexity of Jüngel's writing that it is possible, on the one hand, to read this article and suppose that effectively he is affirming that which Barth also affirms in recognizing the corresponding possibility of God's self-determination behind the actuality of the event of revelation (Wo die Wirklichkeit ist, da ist auch die entsprechende Möglichkeit). Yet, on the other hand, in his concern to establish an ontology of 'speech-event' (Sprachereignis),[11] which he sees as being demanded by Barth's

---

10) This distinction appears to have eluded Robert Brown in his critique of Barth's epistemology. Ontologically God's "noetic absoluteness" certainly derives from His "ontic absoluteness" but epistemologically God's "ontic absoluteness" is the possibility that lies behind His "noetic absoluteness" in the actuality of the event of revelation. Brown assumes the more traditional reversal of the epistemological order and appears to compound the difficulty by failing to grasp the dynamic character of the actual event of revelation as Barth expounds it (Robert Brown, 'On God's Ontic and Noetic Absoluteness: A critique of Barth', S.J.T., 33 (1980), 533-549).

11) This ontological concept of 'speech-event' resting upon the interdependence of being and language is central and foundational to Jüngel's theology.

conception of the Word as event, it is difficult not to conclude that Jüngel introduces into theology an ontological category of which Barth would have been profoundly suspicious. Nonetheless since, despite the introduction of this ontology, Jüngel 'effectively' affirms that which Barth also affirms, his theological thought and particularly his exposition of Barth's theological thought will inform the discussion contained in this chapter.

The concern of the first three chapters of this thesis was to affirm the actuality of the authentically temporal event of God's self-revelation. The concern of this chapter is to recognize that this actuality implies a corresponding possibility in the being of God. Who He is in this event He is beforehand in Himself. The actuality of God's self-revelation as event implies a corresponding possibility of this event as itself the being of God. On the basis of God's self-revelation as act, as event, as happening, we can validly speak of the being of God as the act of God, as event, as happening, as life:

> "The whole being and life of God is an activity, both in eternity and in worldly time, both in Himself as Father, Son and Holy Spirit, and in His relation to man and all creation."12

This is not to say that the being of God is bound to His action:

> "He is the same even in Himself, even before and after and over His works, and without them."13

---

12) *C.D.*IV.1.p.7

13) *C.D.*II.1.p.260

But it is to say that, on the basis of our confrontation with the livingness of God in the event of His revelation in Jesus Christ, we must affirm that God is in Himself the Living God:[14]

> "To its very deepest depths God's Godhead consists in the fact that it is an event——not any event, not events in general, but the event of His action, in which we have a share in God's revelation."15

Colin E. Gunton follows Eberhard Jüngel in suggesting that Barth's contribution to our understanding of the Doctrine of the Trinity is far more radical than is usually realized. It is not just that Barth revises the language of Trinitarian theology but rather that his understanding of the being of God involves a shift from static to dynamic terms.[16] God exists as event, as happening, as dynamic being:

> "Because revelation is God taking place, rational theology is forced to the conclusion that his being consists in his becoming..."17

It is understandable that objections should be raised to talk of God's becoming, especially when it can be expressed in such

---

14) C.D.II.1.p.263

15) ibid.

16) Colin E. Gunton, Becoming and Being: The Doctrine of God in Charles Hartshorne and Karl Barth (Oxford, 1978), pp.142-143; cf. E. Jüngel, The Doctrine of the Trinity: God's Being is in Becoming, trans. by Horton Harris, Monograph Supplements to the Scottish Journal of Theology, eds. T. F. Torrance and J. K. S. Reid (Edinburgh and London, 1976), pp.89ff.

17) Colin E. Gunton, Becoming and Being, p.152.

stark terms:

> "...if these events are God, then God <u>is something that happens.</u>"18

This reference to God as 'something' exposes the principal problem of such language. If on the basis of the actuality of the event of revelation God is to be defined in terms of event how can it be valid to continue to refer to Him in personal terms as 'someone' rather than 'something'. The primary response to this dilemma to which this chapter will return must be that the self-revelation of God is not only in the form of event, it is also personal, the revelation of God as Father, Son and Spirit. The actuality of revelation as both an event and as personal must imply a prior possibility in the being of God. A further response to the dilemma, a response rooted in what has already been affirmed regarding God's relatedness to time, is proposed by Robert Jenson:

> "The difference between an event and a substance is given by the discontinuity of time. What we mean by a substance——a thing or a person or an organisation or whatever——is the something that we posit to provide the continuity of a series of successive and so temporally separated events. <u>As</u> distinct from what I do, "I" am a "something we know not what" that bridges the temporal discontinuities of the various things I do. But precisely the absence of such discontinuities is what distinguishes God from us——and therefore the dichotomy between an event and its agent or sufferer does not apply to God. Why then not drop such words as "he" altogether when talking about God? Because then it would seem that we recognized the applicability of the dichotomy to God, and put God on the one side as against the other."19

---

18) Colin E. Gunton, 'Karl Barth's Doctrine of Election as part of his Doctrine of God', p.387, my emphasis.

19) R. W. Jenson, <u>God after God: the God of the Past and the God of the Future, seen in the work of Karl Barth</u> (Indianapolis and New York, 1969), p.126.

Jüngel also clarifies what is meant by talk of God's becoming when, in the preface to his paraphrase of Barth's doctrine of the Trinity, he states that he is not speaking about a "God who becomes":

> "God's being is not identified with God's becoming; rather, God's being is ontologically localized. ...'Becoming' thus indicates the manner in which God's being exists, and can in so far be understood as the ontological place of God's being"20

In this sense Jüngel's phraseology is an attempt to understand ontologically what is meant by the livingness of God. God is in His essence who He is in the event of His revelation in Jesus Christ. The becoming of God in the event of His Word implies a prior possibility of becoming within the essence of God; He is able to do that which He does; He is able to be God in this way.[21] Thus the being of God in Himself must be affirmed as pure event, as dynamic being.

b) <u>The being of God as decision</u>:

Having established on the basis of the actuality of God's revelation as event that we must speak of the being of God as pure event, as happening, as dynamic being, a further assertion must be made upon the same basis, namely, that we must speak of the

---

20) E. Jüngel, <u>God's Being is in Becoming</u>, p.vii. Because of the possibility of misunderstanding Wilfried Härle prefers to speak of God's being as act; cf. Wilfried Härle, <u>Sein und Gnade: Die Ontologie in Karl Barths Kirchlicher Dogmatik</u> (Berlin and New York, 1975), pp.51f.

21) cf. Colin E. Gunton, <u>Becoming and Being</u>, p.131.

being of God as "being which knows, wills and decides of itself, and is moved by itself"[22]

> "The being of God as we know it from revelation is moved in itself and therefore motivating."23

God exists not only as dynamic being but also as self-moved being and therefore not only as event but also as decision. If God exists as event it is because He may do so, not because it is an *a priori* necessity for Him to do so. That He does so exist is grounded in His own self-determination to so exist. The being of God as act is determined by His decision to be God in this way. God exists, not only as dynamic being, but also as determining being:

> "It is His willed decision, and therefore not an event occurring through external causes or only in an external relationship."24

Barth is hesitant to speak of God's being as necessary being since the Latin *necesse*, the Greek *ἀναγκη* and the German *notwendig*, all imply an external, imposed necessity.[25] God's being is not necessary in this *a priori* manner, it is self-determined. The aseity of God, the absoluteness of God, the hiddenness of God, this is rooted in the self-determination of God, His free decision to exist in this way.

---

22) *C.D.*II.1.p.268

23) ibid.

24) *C.D.*II.1.p.271

25) *C.D.*II.1.p.307, cf. Colin E. Gunton, *Becoming and Being*, pp.196f.

Helmut Gollwitzer has argued against any identification of the being of God with the event of His encounter with men in His Word. Against the concept of God which Gollwitzer accordingly develops Eberhard Jüngel raises two objections.[26] In the first place he questions whether Gollwitzer's understanding of God's existence takes sufficient account of the vulnerability of God centred in the crucifixion of Jesus Christ. In the second place Jüngel objects to Gollwitzer's assertion that it is not possible to argue back from God's being within history to His essence 'in - and - of - itself', according to Gollwitzer it is only possible to argue back from God's being within history to the essence of His will:

> "The fact that 'revelation's mode of being is definable only with reference to persons' has its ground not in the nature of God, but in the will of God, i.e. it is not possible to argue back from it to the nature of God in the sense of how God is constituted, but only to the nature of his will, i.e. from his will as made known in history to his eternal will as the will of his free love."27

Jüngel is surely correct when he suggests that this introduces an erroneous distinction between God's essence and God's will and thereby reintroduces a metaphysical concept of the essence of God hidden behind the will of God that is revealed in history:[28]

---

26) E. Jüngel, God's Being is in Becoming, pp.xii ff. cf. Helmut Gollwitzer, The Existence of God as Confessed by Faith, trans. by James W. Leitch, (London, 1965).

27) Gollwitzer, op.cit.,p.186

28) E. Jüngel, God's Being is in Becoming, pp.xv-xvii

> "Is there not just here a metaphysical background - which is quite indifferent towards God's acts of revelation in history - introduced into the being of God by this distinction between the essence and will of God in the 'essence of God - in the sense of how God is constituted' - which is distinguished from the 'essence of his will'?"29

It is fundamental to Barth's understanding of the Doctrine of God that there is no metaphysical essence of God hidden behind revelation; we cannot investigate behind the livingness of God in act for some other definition of His essence. Such a conception of the hiddenness of God is the denial of the reality of revelation itself and thereby a denial of the Doctrine of the Trinity as a valid exposition, not only of the event of revelation, but also of the being of God in Himself. It is therefore interesting to note that Gollwitzer, in the Preface to the English edition of his book[30] admits to the grave weakness of expounding the reality of God without speaking of the Doctrine of the Trinity. Although he claims that the Doctrine of the Trinity is the "unexpressed, but unfortunately not explicit, background of this book"[31], one cannot avoid believing that it is this "omission" that accounts for his fundamental departure from Barth's understanding of the Doctrine of God.

---

29) ibid., p.xvi

30) Gollwitzer, op.cit., pp.9f.

31) ibid.

Accepting Barth's definition of God as the Lord, we must affirm that His power is not to be understood as an indeterminate, metaphysical omnipotence but is rather to be understood primarily as His power to be in His essence what He is in His will. The will of God determines who He actually is in His essence; God does not exist other than "in the determination of His will".[32] Therefore, both the essence of God and the event of His Word rest upon the choice of God to be God in this way:

> "Here is Barth's final ontological classification of God's being. God is the free event, independent even of his own nature yet nonetheless having a nature, because he decides to be and to be what he is."33

The being of God is identical to His eternal self-determination as the Living God; a being in becoming. The event of God's Word is the actualization of His self-determination as the Living God in history; a being in becoming. God exists as dynamic being because He exists as determining being.

c) The being of God as the event of electing love:

The act of God which is His being is a specific act with a definite content. Prefiguring his exposition of the doctrine of Election[34] Barth expounds the content of this being of God in act in terms of the being of God as the One who loves in freedom.[35]

---

32) C.D.II.2,p.79, quoted by Jüngel, God's Being is in Becoming, p.xvi

33) R. W. Jenson, God after God, p.127

34) C.D.II.2.pp.3ff.

35) C.D.II.1.pp.272ff.

The content of the act with which we are confronted in Jesus Christ is the One who loves us, who seeks us, who creates fellowship between Himself and us:

> "He wills to be ours, and He wills that we should be His. He wills to belong to us and He wills that we should belong to Him. He does not will to be without us, and He does not will that we should be without Him. He wills certainly to be God and He does not will that we should be God. But He does not will to be God for Himself nor as God to be alone with Himself. He wills as God to be for us and with us who are not God."[36]

The question with which we are concerned is the question of the identity and content of the being of God: who and what is God? In answer to this fundamental question Holy Scripture continually directs us to the name of Jesus Christ.[37] In other words, the true question for Christian Theology is not "who and what is God?" but "who and what is God <u>in Jesus Christ</u>?"[38] The meaning of the Godness of the only true God cannot be learned by metaphysical speculations about supreme, absolute being; it can only be learned from what took place in Jesus Christ.[39]

> Who God is and what it is to be divine is something we have to learn where God has revealed Himself and His nature, the essence of the divine. And if He has revealed Himself in Jesus Christ as the God who does this, it is not for us to be wiser than He and to say that it is in contradiction with the divine essence.

---

36) <u>C.D</u>.II. 1.p. 274

37) <u>C.D</u>.II.2.p.53

38) Karl Barth, <u>The Humanity of God</u>, trans. by John Newton Thomas and Thomas Wieser (London and Glasgow, 1961),p.44

39) <u>C.D</u>.IV.1.p.177

> ...We may believe that God can and must only be absolute in contrast to all that is relative, exalted in contrast to all that is lowly, active in contrast to all suffering, inviolable in contrast to all temptation, transcendent in contrast to all immanence, and therefore divine in contrast to everything human, in short that He can and must be only the "Wholly Other." But such beliefs are shown to be quite untenable, and corrupt and pagan, by the fact that God does in fact be and do this in Jesus Christ."40

In the event of God's self-revelation in Jesus Christ we are confronted by the One who creates fellowship with us. His revelation of Himself to us is, at the same time, the revelation of His relatedness to us, His reconciliation of us to Himself:

> "By doing this God proves to us that He can do it, that to do it is within His nature".41

This actuality of the love of His relatedness to us in Jesus Christ implies the prior possibility of the love of His relatedness to Himself:[42]

> "... the God of the Gospel is no lonely God, self-sufficient and self-contained. He is no "absolute" God (in the original sense of absolute, i.e., being detatched from everything that is not himself). To be sure, he has no equal beside himself, since an equal would no doubt limit, influence, and determine him. On the other hand, he is not imprisoned by his own majesty, as though he were bound to be no more than the personal (or impersonal) "wholly other." By definition, the God of Schleiermacher cannot show mercy. The God of the Gospel can and does."43

---

40) C.D.IV.1.p.186

41) ibid.

42) Colin E. Gunton, 'Karl Barth's Doctrine of Election as part of his Doctrine of God', (p.388)

43) Karl Barth, Evangelical Theology: An Introduction, trans. by Grover Foley (London and Glasgow, 1963) p.16

The first implication of the ontological principle that actuality implies possibility was to affirm the being of God as dynamic being; being in becoming. The second implication of this ontological principle was to affirm the being of God as determining being; God is in His essence what He is in His will. The third implication is to affirm the being of God as relational being. This essential relatedness of the being of God is the basis of Barth's understanding of God's Triunity.

> "It is for this reason that although confessions of Jesus of Nazareth's temporal-eternal significance do not presuppose the doctrine of the Trinity, they inevitably lead to it, for they presuppose the reality of a God who is able to become spatio-temporal without loss of his divinity, of an eternal who is able to differentiate himself to become other than he is. It is that which dualistic philosophies of all kinds disallow, for they demand that we choose between temporal and eternal, and between (spatially) finite and infinite. But the impact of the reality of Jesus compels us to say that God is not to be understood as the bare negation of our time and space - as utterly timeless and spaceless - but as being eternally in himself that relatedness to the other which actualizes itself in our history. And that is one of the things meant when we say that God is triune, one in three ways of being."44

For Barth, the doctrine of the Trinity is the necessary exposition of the event of God's self-revelation in Jesus Christ.[45] When we ask the questions: Who is the self-revealing God? What does He do? What does He effect? the identity and distinction of the appropriate answers compells us to reflect on the Triunity of God:[46]

---

44) Colin E. Gunton, Yesterday and Today: A study of continuities in Christology (London, 1983), pp.134f.

45) C.D.I.1.pp.295ff.

46) ibid., p.303

> "If God is triune in his nature, then really to know God means that we must know him in accordance with his triune nature from the start. It is certainly scientifically objectionable to develop a doctrine of the Trinity on ground other than that on which we develop our actual knowledge of God, the One God. But further, if we operate, not with some kind of epistemological dualism between form and being or structure and substance, but with the unity of form and being or of structure and substance, then to know God we must know him in accordance with the form or structure of his own Being——that is, in terms of God's inner divine relations. And that means we must know him as the Triune God who within himself has relations between Father, Son, and Holy Spirit; so that for us to know that God, we must know him in a mode of understanding on our part appropriate to the Trinity of Persons in God. There must be a "trinitarian" character in our knowing of God, corresponding to the trinity of relations in God himself."[47]

In the event of revelation God happens as Father, Son and Holy Spirit and in this manner He relates Himself to us and loves us. Yet this happening of God is not haphazard or arbitrary: actuality implies possibility; who God is in His revelation He is previously in Himself; His relatedness to us in love is the reiteration of His relatedness to Himself in love:[48]

> "The Doctrine of the Trinity is, for this reason, the indispensably difficult expression of the simple truth that God lives because *God lives as love*. That God is living as love is the secret of his being that he has revealed in the life, death and resurrection of Jesus Christ."[49]

Thus, in the event of revelation God interprets Himself to us; God's relatedness to us is His self-interpretation of His relatedness to

---

47) T. F. Torrance, *The Ground and Grammar of Theology* (Belfast, 1980), p.148

48) E. Jüngel, *God's Being is in Becoming*, pp.89ff.

49) E. Jüngel, 'Das Verhältnis von »ökonomischer« und »immanenter« Trinität.' *Zeitschrift für Theologie und Kirche*, 72 (1975) 353 -364(p.354), my translation.

Himself.[50] Not on the basis of any metaphysical speculation, but on the basis of the act of God in Jesus Christ we are compelled to define the being of God as the One who loves, as relational being.

Having established that the being of God is determining being, that God does not exist other than in the determination of His will, the being of God as relational being must be dependent upon the decision of God to be God in this way, as Father, Son and Holy Spirit, as relational being. It is therefore God's determination to be God as the One who loves, both in His revelation (creating fellowship with us) and in His essence (fulfilling fellowship with Himself). Neither in history nor in eternity does God will to be God in solitude - He wills fellowship, He determines to be God as Father, Son and Holy Spirit.

One of the most radical ways in which Barth departs from traditional theology is by placing his exposition of the doctrine of Election within his overall exposition of the doctrine of God and as an essential part of that doctrine.[51] Simply by this arrangement of his Dogmatics Barth affirms that, essentially and primarily, the doctrine of Election is telling us something about God. In the event of God's self-revelation we are confronted by the One who

---

50) ibid. pp.95ff

51) C.D.II.2.pp.76ff.; cf. Colin E. Gunton, 'Karl Barth's Doctrine of Election as part of his Doctrine of God' (p.381)

elects us to fellowship with Himself in Jesus Christ.[52] That God should be the electing God in this event implies the prior possibility that He is in Himself the electing God, and, since God's being is determined by His will, the event of election in Jesus Christ means that it is God's choice to be God in this way, the electing God:[53]

> "Our starting-point must always be that in all His willing and choosing what God ultimately wills is Himself. All God's willing is primarily a determination of the love of the Father and the Son in the fellowship of the Holy Ghost."54

The doctrine of Election thus tells us who the true God is according to His primal decision and it is for this reason that Barth places the doctrine of Election within the doctrine of God:

> "...it belongs to the doctrine of God Himself because God Himself does not will to be God, and is not God, except as the One who elects."55

Moreover, by placing his exposition of Election within the doctrine of God and thus prior to his treatment of the doctrines of Creation, Reconciliation and Redemption, Barth attests that it is this doctrine which tells us first and foremost who the God of Creation, Reconciliation and Redemption is; He is in His essence the electing God and thus everything else which may be said about

---

52) C.D.II.2.p.54

53) ibid.

54) C.D.II.2.p.169

55) C.D.II.2.p.77

Him must be said within the context of this affirmation:[56]

> "In this self-determination and only in this self-determination does God will to be known, to be loved and feared, to be believed in and worshipped as Creator, Reconciler and Redeemer."57

The doctrine of Election, grounded in the event of God's self-revelation in Jesus Christ, informs us that God wills to be God in this way and in no other way, that in His primal decision and therefore both in history and eternity God is gracious and not ungracious,[58] that He does not will to be God other than as the electing God in Jesus Christ:

> "In the beginning it was the choice of the Father Himself to establish this covenant with man by giving up His Son for him, that He Himself might become man in the fulfilment of His grace. In the beginning it was the choice of the Son to be obedient to grace, and therefore to offer up Himself and to become man in order that this covenant might be made a reality. In the beginning it was the resolve of the Holy Spirit that the unity of God, of Father and Son should not be disturbed or rent by this covenant with man, but that it should be made the more glorious, the deity of God, the divinity of His love and freedom, being confirmed and demonstrated by this offering of the Father and this self-offering of the Son."59

No doubt it was passages such as the one quoted that prompted the comment of Heinz Zahrnt that Barth, "instead of seeing into the glass, as is ordained for men, has strayed behind the

---

56) Colin E. Gunton, 'Karl Barth's Doctrine of Election as part of his Doctrine of God' (p.391); E Jüngel, '...keine Menschenlosigkeit Gottes...: Zur Theologie Karl Barths zwischen Theismus und Atheismus', Evangelische Theologie, 31 (1971) 376-390 (pp.382-383)

57) C.D.II.2.p.91

58) C.D.II.2.p.92

59) ibid., pp.101f.

glass. He is peering into the script destined for the persons of the Trinity, and sometimes one even feels that he is prompting them."[60] Such criticisms can only occur through a failure to grasp the central thrust of Barth's thought; a failure to recognize with Barth the inherent 'logic', integrity and veracity of God's self-revelation. Far from being presumptuous speculation Barth's theological affirmations spring from a humble reflection (nachdenkend), a commitment to take the event of God's Word seriously as the event of His self-definition.

The event of God's self-revelation in Jesus Christ therefore consists in God's self-definition of His Godness, the actualization of His eternal decision to be this electing God in Jesus Christ. But Jesus Christ is not only very God, He is also very man;[61] not only is God the electing God in Jesus Christ,[62] He is also the elected man in Jesus Christ.[63] By affirming the doctrine of Election we are not only attesting that God has determined Himself as the electing God, but also that He has determined Himself as the elected man[64] and that God's Godness includes this manness, not only in the event of His self-revelation in Jesus Christ, but (since actuality implies possibility) in His eternal nature.

---

60) Heinz Zahrnt, The Question of God: Protestant Theology in the Twentieth Century, trans. by R. A. Wilson (London, 1969), p.112.

61) C.D.II.2.p.7

62) C.D.II.2.pp.103ff.

63) C.D.II.2.pp.116ff.

64) E. Jüngel, God's Being is in Becoming, p.72.

It is crucial to understand clearly that Barth is not speaking about a man Jesus of Nazareth who pre-existed with God in eternity. He is rather saying that the being of God cannot be otherwise known but can be truly known in Jesus Christ and that therefore, God has determined Himself to be known and to exist solely in this relationship; God has determined Himself to manness in His primal decision to be God in this way and not any other:

> "Barth is not saying that there was a man Jesus who pre-existed as such or was eternal as God is but that, in the light and by the power of election and incarnation, we cannot think of God without or apart from this man through whom alone he is known as God."[65]

That God was not without man in His eternal primal decision of grace, is not dependent upon man previously having been created or previously having become a sinner. Rather Barth is asserting that, in the eternal election of God and prior to the creation and fall of man, man is with the eternal Son of God, the primary object and content of God's eternal decision of grace:[66]

> "He, too, has a basic reality in the counsel of God which is the basis of all reality. At no level or time can we have to do with God without having also to do with this man."[67]

---

65) John Thompson, Christ in Perspective: Christological Perspectives in the Theology of Karl Barth (Edinburgh, 1978), p.99.

66) C.D.IV.2.pp.32ff.; cf. pp.238ff. of this thesis.

67) C.D.IV.2.p.33

Therefore, that God determines man in this eternal decision of grace is not just an event which determines the being of man, it is also an event which determines the being of God:

> "...God in His Godness determines Himself to manness".68

> "It is when we look at Jesus Christ that we know decisively that God's deity does not exclude, but includes His humanity."69

The true Godness of God does not consist in any indeterminate majesty and power, but in His condescension and manness in Jesus Christ as the electing God and the elected man. Hence, Barth considers the true Godness of Jesus Christ in terms of the way of the Son of God into the Far Country.[70] The true Godness of Jesus Christ consists in His obedient humbling of Himself and offering of Himself for the purpose of reconciliation. The true Godness of God is therefore revealed in this history, in the true Godness of Jesus Christ which is His true manness:

> "...God shows Himself to be the great and true God in the fact that He can and will let His grace bear this cost, that He is capable and willing and ready for this condescension, this act of extravagance, this far journey. What marks out God above all false gods is that they are not capable and ready for this."71

---

68) E. Jüngel, '...keine Menschenlosigkeit Gottes...' (p.384), my translation.

69) Karl Barth, The Humanity of God, p.46

70) C.D.IV.1.pp.157-210

71) C.D.IV.1.p.159

If we are to speak of the being of God as dynamic being and as determinative being we must also speak of His being as relational being; it is this relation which is the content of this pure event and this primal, eternal decision. Yet the being of God is not relational being in any general or abstract sense. It is His being as the electing God and the elected man in Jesus Christ. It is His eternal decision to be God in this event, in this relation to man. This and this alone is the true being of God:

> "In this divinely free volition and election, in this sovereign decision (The ancients said, in His decree), God is _human._ His free affirmation of man, His free concern for him, His free substitution for him——this is God's humanity."72

In this expression of the "Humanity of God" we find the true motivation for Barth's categorical and total rejection of any form of analogy of being (_analogia entis_) between God and man. Barth rejects the Roman Catholic concept of _analogia entis,_ not just because it suggests a false unity between God and man by assuming a being which God and man have in common[73] but because it thereby also suggests a false division between God and man by failing to recognize the exclusiveness and depth of the actual correspondence between God and man, expressed by Barth in terms of the _analogia relationis._[74] "God is in relationship, and so too is the man created by Him. This is his divine likeness."[75]

---

72) Karl Barth, _The Humanity of God_ p.48

73) _C.D._I.1.pp.239f.

74) _C.D._III.2.pp.220ff.

75) _C.D._III.2.p.324

The supposed analogy of being, by preserving a metaphysical concept of God as "absolute being", precludes the possibility of God's Godness consisting in His becoming man in Jesus Christ. "The being of the man Jesus is the ground of being and the ground of recognition of all analogy."[76] The actuality of the being of God as man in Jesus Christ identifies the true distinction between God and man: not the distinction between His Godness and our manness but the distinction between His manness and our manness:

> "... the essence of the Christian faith is the correct distinction between God and man, namely between a human God and a man that is always becoming more human."77

By means of the analogia relationis Barth identifies the true imago Dei as God's determination of man, which is the true being of man actualized in Jesus Christ, to be the covenant partner of God, elect in Jesus Christ:

> "If man is ordained to be God's partner in this covenant, and if his nature is a likeness corresponding to this ordination, necessarily it corresponds in this respect to the nature of God Himself. God has created him in this correspondence, as a reflection of Himself. Man is the image of God."78

---

76) E. Jüngel, 'Die Möglichkeit theologischer Anthropologie auf dem Grunde der Analogie: Eine Untersuchung zum Analogieverständnis Karl Barths', Evangelische Theologie, 22(1962), 535-557(p.538), my own translation.

77) E. Jüngel, 'Was ist »das unterscheidend Christliche« ?' in Unterwegs zur Sache: Theologische Bemerkungen, ed. E. Wolf, Beiträge zur evangelischen Theologie, 61, (Munich, 1972) pp.296-299 (p.299).
cf. E. Jüngel, '...keine Menschenlosigkeit Gottes...' (pp.386f.)
cf. also E. Jüngel, Gott als Geheimnis der Welt pp.383ff.

78) C.D.III.2.p.323

Both the being of God and the being of man are determined by the primal decision of God to be the electing God and the elected man in Jesus Christ. There is no other will of God beyond His eternal covenant in Jesus Christ and therefore no other true being of God or true being of man:

> "... in the free decision of His love, God is God in the very fact, and in such a way, that He does stand in this relation, in a definite relationship with the other. We cannot go back on this decision if we would know God and speak accurately of God."79

The doctrine of Election as part of the doctrine of God informs us that the true God is the electing God, the God of the eternal covenant, the God of the Gospel. It is for this reason that Barth speaks of the doctrine of Election as "the sum of the Gospel":

> "... because of all words that can be said or heard it is the best: that God elects man: that God is for man too the One who loves in freedom."80

d) The being of God as the One who loves in freedom:

Although the essential elements of Barth's doctrine of God have been outlined it is nevertheless necessary to emphasize both the manner and the function of Barth's distinction between God's being in Himself and His being for us in revelation. This emphasis is required in view of certain criticisms of Barth's doctrine of God that have been made by Jürgen Moltmann. Like Barth, Moltmann recognizes that we must locate the centre of our knowledge of the being of God in Jesus Christ, in particular in His crucifixion as it is understood in the light of His resurrection:

---

79) *C.D.*II.2.p.6

80) *C.D.*II.2.p.3

> "... a trinitarian theology of the cross no longer interprets the event of the cross in the framework or in the name of a metaphysical or moral concept of God which has already been presupposed ... but develops from this history what is to be understood by 'God'."81

However, Moltmann suggests that Barth's definition of revelation as the self-revelation of God finds its root, not in the event of the crucifixion, but rather in the concept of the Absolute Subject (as in Hegelian Idealism) which Barth has adopted in exchange for the classical concept of Absolute Being. The concept of God as absolute subject as developed by Fichte and Hegel presupposes free will in God in a manner unnecessary within the context of classical theism's conception of God as absolute substance. God is conceived as the subject of His own revelation and, consequently, His revelation can only be 'self-revelation'.[82] Moltmann suggests that this Idealist concept of absolute subject is betrayed as Barth's heritage by his use of the language of reflection "to secure God's subjectivity, sovereignty, self-hood and personality".[83] As in Hegelian Idealism God reveals Himself as the absolute subject through self-distinction and self-recollection. Thus Barth presupposes the divine lordship and uses the doctrine of the Trinity as a means of establishing the subjectivity of that lordship.[84] It is this

---

81) Jürgen Moltmann, The Crucified God: The Cross of Christ as the Foundation and Criticism of Christian Theology, trans. by R. A. Wilson and John Bowden (London 1974),p.247

82) Jürgen Moltmann, The Trinity and the Kingdom of God: The Doctrine of God, trans. by Margaret Kohl (London,1981), p.15

83) ibid., p.142

84) ibid., pp.142ff. Moltmann suggests that, if Barth had stopped here, his theology of God's sovereignty would "only really be an extension of Schleiermacher's anthropology of man's 'absolute dependency'." (ibid., p.144).

equation of God's absolute sovereignty (itself implying personality) with God's nature and divinity that necessitates Barth's identification of Father, Son and Spirit as 'three modes of being' in God; having ascribed subjectivity and personality to God he cannot now ascribe them to Father, Son and Spirit:

> "But to understand God's threefold nature as eternal repetition or as holy tautology does not yet mean thinking in trinitarian terms. The doctrine of the Trinity cannot be a matter of establishing the same thing three times. To view the three Persons merely as a triple repetition of one and the same God would be somewhat empty and futile."[85]

According to Moltmann it is this Idealist conception which gives rise to Barth's problems of pneumatology. There is no need for a third Person in the Trinity merely in order to think of the mutual relationship of love between the Father and the Son:

> "If the Spirit is only termed the unity of what is separated, then he loses every centre of activity. He is then an energy but not a Person. He is then a relationship but not a subject. Basically, the reflection Trinity of the absolute subject is a duality."[86]

Even the Person of the Son is reduced within this scheme to the "self of the divine 'I', the counterpart, the other, in whom God contemplates himself, finds himself, becomes conscious of himself and manifests himself."[87]

---

85) ibid., pp.141f.

86) ibid., p.142

87) ibid.

The validity of such criticisms tends to be jeopardized by overstatement. Certainly there are reminiscences of Hegelian language, particularly in the earlier volumes of the Church Dogmatics but this recognition of itself is insufficient to establish dependence. Rather the (perhaps underestimated) similarities of language and approach could derive from an independent concern to address essentially the same problem.[88] Is the source of Barth's statement that 'God reveals Himself as the Lord' to be located in Idealism's concept of the Absolute Subject or rather in Barth's reflection (nachdenkend) upon the actual event of revelation; i.e., is it a case of 'reading into' or 'reading out of' this event? Is Moltmann's alternative monistic view of revelation in which the tension between veiledness and unveiledness is resolved in the latter's favour, effectively forfeiting God's Lordship in the event, actually a true exposition of the event itself?[89] Certainly it could be said that Barth is 'sailing close to the wind' by expressing the doctrine of the Trinity in terms of three modes of being, but the charge that "Barth took over the concept of 'modes of being' from Dorner"[90] is unsupported. Indeed, Barth astutely (albeit scarcely)

---

88) cf. Lisabeth During, 'Hegel, Barth and the Rationality of the Trinity', King's Theological Review, 2 (1979), 69-81. Note also Barth's own comments with reference to Hegel: "...a great problem and a great disappointment, but perhaps also a great promise." (Karl Barth, Protestant Theology in the Nineteenth Century: Its Background and History, trans. by Brian Cozens and John Bowden (London, 1972), p.421.

89) cf. pp. 229ff. of this thesis.

90) Jürgen Moltmann, The Trinity and the Kingdom of God, p.241

avoids the Sabellian trap into which Dorner appears to fall. Moreover, here is yet another instance of Moltmann's preoccupation with Barth's earlier writings. While Barth never contradicts his earlier statements the later volumes of the Church Dogmatics display a marked preference for speaking of the Father, Son and Spirit in personal terms and the potentially Sabellian language of modes of being wisely recedes to the background of his theological thought. As Moltmann himself implies, Barth did not 'stop here'.[91] Finally it is difficult to understand how anyone can seriously suggest that Barth may underplay the role of the Son, and Barth's pneumatological weakness can be attributed to other causes than that of a dependence upon Hegelian Idealism.[92]

Earlier Moltmann had suggested that it was the adoption of this concept of Absolute Subject which necessitated Barth's distinction between God's being in Himself and His being for us since such a distinction was his only means of avoiding theopaschite language:

> "Remarkably, I see the critical limitation of Barth in the fact that he still thinks too theologically, and that his approach is not sufficiently trinitarian. In stressing constantly and rightly that 'God was in Christ', God humbled himself, God himself was on the cross, he uses a simple concept of God which is not sufficiently developed in a trinitarian direction. For this reason, like Karl Rahner he has to make a distinction in the 'God was in Christ' between the God who proceeds from himself in his primal decision and the God who is previously in himself,

---

91) ibid., p.144

92) cf. pp. 303ff. of this thesis.

> beyond contact with evil. For all his polemic against Luther's distinction between the <u>deus revelatus</u> and the <u>deus absconditus</u>, Barth himself comes very close to the same sort of thing."93

But Barth 'avoids the dangers of theopaschite language', not by employing the classical distinction between the economic and the immanent Trinity but by rejecting any independent metaphysical concept of God that necessarily excludes the possibility of suffering.[94] Moreover, Barth never falls into the theopaschite trap (into which Moltmann appears to fall) of interpreting the crucifixion in the light of any general concept of human suffering; the suffering of Jesus Christ is to be understood in terms of atonement - not in terms of theodicy; the cross is not to be thought of as the justifying of God before suffering man but as the justifying of sinful man before God.

Moltmann acknowledges that Karl Rahner has advanced Barth's concept of God's being as identical with God's act by rejecting any distinction between the economic and the immanent Trinity:[95]

> "...the Trinity of the economy of salvation <u>is</u> the immanent Trinity and vice versa."96

---

93) Jürgen Moltmann, <u>The Crucified God</u>, p.203

94) E. Jüngel, <u>God's Being is in Becoming</u>, p.84
H. P. Owen refers to the notion of divine impassibility as "the most questionable aspect of classical theism" (H. P. Owen, <u>Concepts of Deity</u> (London, 1971), p.24).

95) Jürgen Moltmann, <u>The Crucified God</u>, p.240

96) Karl Rahner, <u>Theological Investigations</u>, IV, trans. by Kevin Smyth (Baltimore and London, 1966), p.87. cf. E. Jüngel, 'Das Verhältnis von »ökonomischer« und »immanenter «Trinität.'

Moltmann considers that Barth continues to maintain a form of distinction between the economic and the immanent Trinity, yet one is compelled to ask whether Moltmann has accurately understood Barth's meaning and the true nature of the distinction which he maintains within his doctrine of God.

Barth certainly rejects Luther's concept of the _deus absconditus_ if this refers to a hidden God behind and beyond His revelation,[97] though it is interesting to note that Eberhard Jüngel has defended Luther's concept of the _deus absconditus:_[98]

> "Luther's distinction between _deus praedicatus_ and _deus absconditus_ ... does not have the function of bringing the hiddenness of God and the revelation of God into a dialectical balance, nor of portraying the revelation of God as continually problematical by its recollection of the hidden God. Luther's doctrine of the hidden God is not simply the continuation of the late nominalistic doctrine of the _deus absolutus_, although in the first place it is correctly understood against the background of this doctrine, namely as the sharpest criticism of this doctrine."99

Jüngel concludes that there is a continuing theological need to distinguish between the hidden God and the revealed God but to distinguish between them in a theologically correct way. He understands Luther's use of the _Dictum Socraticum_ as an instance of this theological correctness by which the hidden God is directly identified with the revealed God since God has hidden Himself in

---

97) _C.D_.II.1.p.210

98) E. Jüngel, 'Quae supra nos, nihil ad nos: Eine Kurzformel der Lehre vom verborgenen Gott - im Anschluss an Luther interpretiert.' _Evangelische Theologie_, 32 (1972), 197-240

99) ibid., p.220 , my translation and my emphases.

the human life, suffering and death of the Son. Thus the majesty and freedom of God are revealed through the hiddenness of God in the Cross.[100]

For Barth also the hiddenness of God is as much the character of His being in His revelation as it is the character of His being in Himself. The event of revelation in Jesus Christ is the revelation of the hidden God, the One who remains Lord in His revelation by veiling Himself in the very act of His unveiling of Himself:

> "He unveils Himself as the One He is by veiling Himself in a form which He Himself is not."101

We cannot get behind the revelation of God, but can only speak of the being of God by attempting to repeat what He alone can tell us in His Word.[102] In the Word of His revelation God remains the hidden God because He remains the free God, He is never wholly at man's disposal:

> "God gives Himself entirely to man in His revelation, but not in such a way as to make Himself man's prisoner, He remains free in His working, in giving Himself."103

The hiddenness of God expounded by Barth is therefore wholly distinct from any form of metaphysical speculative concept of God's absoluteness. The freedom of God's being in Himself, which is His hiddenness, is identical to His freedom in revelation as the hidden God, and the latter is the only basis on which the former can be known.

---

100) ibid., pp.235ff.

101) C.D.II.1.p.52

102) C.D.II.1.p.321

103) C.D.I.1.p.371. cf. C.D.IV.1.p.185

That God exists as the event of electing love in His relatedness _ad extra_, as _Deus pro nobis_, is determined by His free choice to be the electing God in Jesus Christ. God's relatedness to us is not necessitated by any external conditioning, neither is it necessitated by His relatedness to Himself. That God is Father, Son and Holy Spirit independently of any relationship to man means that God is love independently of any relationship to man, i.e., He loves in freedom:

> "He does not have to do it, because in Himself without us, and therefore without this, He has that which He seeks and creates between Himself and us."104

In His Triune life God is wholly self-sufficient; He has no need of us. That this God becomes our God, that He determines to "co-exist with a reality distinct from Himself" is wholly a matter of His grace, His love in freedom.[105] He does not have to will and do this but He does will and do it.

Colin Gunton argues that this is how the divine transcendence should be understood in the light of the actuality of Jesus Christ, not as 'absolute otherness' but as the specific freedom of God to become immanent in this event.[106] The transcendence of God is then not in polarity to His immanence but is itself the

---

104) _C.D._II.1.p.273

105) _C.D._IV.2.p.346

106) Colin E. Gunton, 'Transcendence, Metaphor, and the Knowability of God', _J.T.S._, 31(1980), 501-516 (pp.512ff.)

ground of His immanence. The transcendence of God is "his freedom to happen historically as Father, Son, and Holy Spirit":[107]

> "Transcendence means not only otherness from but also freedom to be for and with that which is other than oneself."[108]

Moreover, that God exists in His relatedness to Himself *ad intra*, as Father, Son and Holy Spirit, is equally determined by His free choice to be God in this way. To speak of the freedom of God's love is not just to speak of a freedom from external conditions, it is rather to assert again that God exists by virtue of His self-determination. He exists as self-moved being, as determining being.[109] That God exists in this internal relatedness is rooted in His free decision to exist in this internal relatedness; i.e., He loves in freedom:[110]

> "God is the free Lord of His inner union."[111]

Given this understanding of God's hiddenness as His free decision to be God in Himself and His equally free decision to be

---

107) ibid., p.513

108) ibid., p.516

109) *C.D.*II.1.p.301

110) *C.D.*II.1.pp.307ff.

111) *C.D.*IV.2.p.345. In this sense it is surely misleading for Colin Gunton to ascribe to Barth a concept of the 'necessary relatedness' of the Father and the Son (Colin E. Gunton, *Becoming and Being*, p.160).

God for us in Jesus Christ it is difficult to see how this form of "dipolarity", expressed by Barth,[112] can be thought of as driving a wedge between the economic and the immanent Trinity. The freedom of God, which is His hiddenness, is as much the characteristic of His being for us as it is the characteristic of His being in Himself. Certainly Barth's form of dipolarity affirms the being of God in His relatedness and His absoluteness, yet the manner in which it does so is clearly not the same as that implied by the classical concept of the deus absolutus. The function of Barth's dipolar concept of God's being is not to distinguish simply between the being of God in Himself and in His revelation but rather to affirm that God's relatedness ad extra, like His relatedness ad intra, is a matter of His freedom:

> " "Dipolar" theism is indeed what both the gospel and our secularity demand. That God is both related and absolute, and that it is exactly his relatedness which is absolute, is exactly what we must learn to understand. But dipolar theism will not work as natural theology. That God is both related and absolute is, as a mere pair of metaphysical assertions, just metaphysical paradox-mongering. But if God's relatedness is first his innertrinitarian relatedness, then it makes sense to say that this relatedness is his absoluteness over against all other being."113

However, although it is impossible to over-emphasize the freedom of God's decision to be Deus pro nobis,[114] it is necessary

---

112) Colin E. Gunton, Becoming and Being, pp.137ff.

113) R. W. Jenson, op,cit., p.151

114) C.D.II.2.p.177

to emphasize equally that this free decision is not an arbitrary decision that is foreign to the nature of God. That God determines Himself to be Deus pro nobis does not imply a 'change' in the being of God. This 'humiliation' is not alien to Him. In this act He is God in 'supreme constancy':[115]

> "The Godhead of the true God is not a prison whose walls have first to be broken through if He is to elect and do what He has elected and done in becoming man. In distinction from that of false gods, and especially the god of Mohammed, His Godhead embraces both height and depth, both sovereignty and humility, both lordship and service." 116

His free decision to be related to us ad extra is a genuine reiteration of His free decision to be related to Himself ad intra. His Triune life ad intra is itself the basis of His will and action ad extra, the basis of man's election, the basis of the Son's determination to become man, the basis of creation, the basis of the atonement with its goal of redemption.[117] The event of revelation in Jesus Christ is the actualizing of God's self-interpretation to us.[118] In His revelation God imparts Himself to us by reiterating Himself. It is in this sense that God's revelation is actually God's self-interpretation. Thus, while man and the world owe their being to this ad extra, God Himself can be ad extra without being dependent upon this extra. In this distinction lies the ontological distinction

---

115) C.D.IV.2.p.84

116) ibid.

117) ibid., p.345

118) E. Jüngel, God's Being is in Becoming, pp.89ff.

between God and the world:[119]

> "In that we called God's being a being in becoming we understood that God can reveal himself. But that God does what he can, that he has reiterated himself in his revelation, this rests on no necessity. That is much more grace. Yet this grace is not strange to God's being. How otherwise would it be distinguished from necessity? God's grace is rather the reiteration of God's Yes to himself (which constitutes God's being) in relation to something other."120

God's freedom is not God's prison, it is His specific freedom to be the One who loves. The absoluteness of the hidden God is not just His freedom to transcend that which is external to Himself but also the freedom to be immanent within it:[121]

> "...when in the presence and action of Jesus Christ in the world created by Him and characterised in malam partem by the sin of man He chooses to go into the far country, to conceal His form of lordship in the form of this world and therefore in the form of a servant, He is not untrue to Himself but genuinely true to Himself, to the freedom which is that of His love. He does not have to choose and do this. He is free in relation to it. We are therefore dealing with the genuine article when He does choose and do this."122

That God's specific freedom is to be the One who loves determines that Barth, in his exposition of the "perfections" of God, speaks of the perfections of God's loving prior to speaking of the

---

119) ibid., p.104; cf. R. D. Williams, 'Barth on the Triune God' in Karl Barth: Studies of his Theological Method, ed. S. W. Sykes (Oxford, 1979), pp.147-193 (p.168)

120) E. Jüngel, God's Being is in Becoming, p.107

121) C.D.II.1.p.313

122) C.D.IV.1.pp.192f.

perfections of God's freedom.[123] Although Barth does not intend to imply any subordination of the latter to the former it is easy to infer an element of necessity in God's relatedness _ad extra_ implied by this order of Barth's exposition. Is there not a sense in which God's freedom is compromised by His love? In what sense is it valid to speak of grace and mercy as dispositions of God's being? Is it sufficient to dismiss this latter question by reference to the incomprehensibility of God?:[124]

> "...Barth sometimes hovers on the brink of bringing necessity into God's relationship with the world, so insistent is he on the reality of that relationship. ...It is only the dominant theme of freedom that avoids the necessitation..."125

Barth certainly excludes any possibility of an _a priori_ necessity in relation to the being of God; God is God in this way solely because of His free self-determination. But it is surely possible, and in fact correct, to speak of God's being in terms of an _a posteriori_ necessity.[126] In the case of an _a priori_ necessity the self-determination of God would be a deduction from an external necessity, whereas, in the case of an _a posteriori_ necessity an internal necessity would be a deduction from the self-determination of God.[127]

---

123) _C.D._II.1.pp.351-677

124) _C.D._II.1.p.357

125) Colin E. Gunton, _Becoming and Being_, p.159

126) For the distinction between these two forms of necessity see John McIntyre, _St. Anselm and his critics: a re-interpretation of the Cur Deus Homo_ (Edinburgh and London, 1954), pp.162ff.; cf. pp.117-121

127) ibid., pp.162f.

Such an a posteriori necessity in no sense threatens but, in fact, simply reaffirms the aseity of God:[128]

> "...the necessity which it imposes upon Him, the necessity of consistency, ...is, in other words, the necessity of self-determination."129

Hence, God is not constrained by any external a priori necessity to be God in the living relatedness of Father, Son and Holy Spirit, but, having freely decided so to exist, it is necessary a posteriori for God to exist in this way in order to be consistent with His self-determination. Thus Barth can speak of the inner-relatedness of the Trinity as a "free but also necessary fellowship", even an "ontological necessity".[130] Similarly, God is not constrained by any a priori necessity, whether external or arising from His relatedness ad intra, to be Deus pro nobis, but, having freely decided in Jesus Christ to be this God, it is necessary a posteriori for this eternal covenant to be actualized in Jesus Christ in order to be consistent with this decision:

> "...God 'can' no more contract out of space and time than He 'can' go back on the Incarnation of His Son or retreat from the love in which He made the world, with which He loves it, through which He redeems it, and by which He is pledged to uphold it——pledged, that is, by the very love that God Himself is and which He has once and for all embodied in our existence in the person and being of Jesus Christ. That is the infinite freedom and the unique kind of necessity that hold between God and the world, which not only preserve its contingence but which so ground it in the being and rationality of God as to provide for us in our creaturely existence an intelligible medium

---

128) ibid., p.165

129) ibid., p.119

130) C.D.IV.1.p.209

> and an objective basis for all our relations with God. Therefore, now that the Incarnation has taken place we must think of it as the decisive action of God in Christ which invalidates all other possibilities and makes all other conceivable roads within space and time to God actually unthinkable."131

God has limited Himself to be this God and no other; through His Son He has bound Himself in eternal covenant with man. But He Himself has done this; He was under no external obligation. It must be understood as God's free decision of grace, but it must also be understood, since it has actually occurred, as a 'necessary' decree and act of God.[132] On the basis of the actuality of this eternal decision and act of grace, and on the basis of the constancy of the eternal God "the proposition 'God is in-and-for-himself' in concreto is just as false as the proposition 'God is God only as the God of man'":[133]

> "...it is a relation which is irrevocable, so that once God has willed to enter into it, and has in fact entered into it, He could not be God without it."134

> "...we have to do with a divine commission and its divine execution, with a divine order and divine obedience. What takes place is the divine fulfilment of a divine decree. It takes place in the freedom of God, but in the inner necessity of the freedom of God and not in the play of a sovereign liberum arbitrium. There is no possibility of something quite different happening."135

---

131) T. F. Torrance, Space, Time and Incarnation (Oxford, 1969) pp.67f.

132) C.D.II.1.p.518

133) E. Jüngel, God's Being is in Becoming, p.104

134) C.D.II.2.p.7

135) C.D.IV.1.p.195

This same form of necessity occurs again in Barth's section entitled "The Judge Judged in Our Place".[136] Once more Barth stresses the freedom of God's love; the lack of any a priori necessity, be it external or arising from His own being, that He should be this "Judge Judged in Our Place" in Jesus Christ. Nonetheless, Barth does refer to an inner necessity based, not upon the being of God, but upon His eternal decision to be Deus pro nobis:

> "If we can speak of a necessity of any kind here, it can only be the necessity of the decision which God did in fact make and execute, the necessity of the fact that the being of God, the omnipotence of His free love, has this concrete determination and no other, that God wills to magnify and does in fact magnify His own glory in this way and not in any other, and therefore to the inclusion of the redemption and salvation of the world. This fact we have to recognise to be divinely necessary because it derives from and is posited by God."137

The "possibilities of equivocation" inherent in the concept of freedom prompt Prof. George Hendry to question Barth's use of the concept.[138] Hendry suggests that Barth has failed to recognize the different senses of the word, that he "glides silently, and perhaps unconsciously, from one sense to another."[139] In particular Hendry raises two question regarding Barth's use of the concept:

Firstly, does God's election of Himself involve the same kind of freedom, in the sense of 'choice', as does His election of

---

136) C.D.IV.1.pp.211-283

137) C.D.IV.1.p.213

138) George S. Hendry, 'The Freedom of God in the Theology of Karl Barth', S.J.T., 31 (1978), 229-244 (p.244).

139) ibid., p.233

sinful humanity? Here Hendry believes that Barth has confused two distinct meanings of the word freedom; i.e., freedom as 'self-determination' and freedom as 'choice':

> "God is certainly not constrained to be God——but as certainly he does not choose to be God."140

But surely 'self-determination' does imply 'choice', not the choice to be God but the choice to be God in this particular way, the choice to be this God.

Secondly Hendry questions the sense in which creation can be conceived as an act of God's freedom. In particular how is this freedom of God in creation to be related to the freedom of God in the generation of the Son? Like Moltmann, Hendry suggests an indebtedness of Barth to Hegel, particularly in the use of the word _Übergriff_ (which Hendry interprets as the 'over-reaching' of a concept to posit an other than itself).[141] Whereas Hegel is often indicted as having equated the creation of the world and the generation of the Son by logical necessity Barth equates them analogically; i.e., there is a correspondence that is different but not dissimilar. This is regarded by Hendry as an attempt to maintain Hegel's conclusion while rejecting his premise. Hendry also seems to regard the Prologue to the Fourth Gospel as implying a logical connection between the two acts:

---

140) ibid., p.237

141) ibid., pp.239ff.

> "If there is a 'correspondence' between 'God and his Word' and 'God and his creature', that is only an esthetic link, and it is not strong enough to bind them together. Hegel saw (as did the Fourth Evangelist) that unless creation is referred to the divine Logos, there can be no doctrine of creation; creation becomes the contingent effect of a contingent act of God, as Florovsky has expressed it, and the confession of faith in God the Creator becomes a meaningless shot in the dark."[142]

Why? Why should not the creation of the world and the generation of the Son be analogically related acts of God's freedom? Hendry's fundamental criticism is that Barth has used an ambiguous term in too general a way. But Barth does not refer to God's freedom in this general manner; consistently he refers to God's specific freedom and its inherent inner necessity. While Hendry acknowledges Barth's rejection of caprice or arbitrariness[143] he fails to recognize the _a posteriori_ or contingent necessity which is implicit in Barth's specific conception of God's freedom in the sum of its references.

As with Barth's concept of God's eternity, one must not just affirm the freedom of God, one must at the same time affirm His constancy, i.e., the inner necessity which constrains Him to be self-consistent with His self-determination to be this God. That God _is_ gracious to us is the outcome of this _a posteriori_ necessity for Him to be true to His free decision in Jesus Christ to be _Deus pro nobis._ That God is _gracious_ to us is the outcome of this

---

142) ibid., p.244

143) ibid., p.236

decision remaining a free decision, unconstrained by any a priori necessity. To jettison Barth's dipolar concept of God's being is to make God's relatedness ad extra the necessary a priori consequence of His relatedness ad intra, thereby forfeiting the grace of God by forfeiting the freedom of God since love which is necessary is not grace.

The significance of Barth's 'dipolar' conception of God in Himself and in His revelation appears to have eluded Jürgen Moltmann:[144]

> "If God is the truth in that he corresponds entirely to himself, then his revelation can only be true if he entirely corresponds to himself in that revelation. That is to say, not to reveal himself and to be contented with his untouched glory would be a contradiction of himself. And if he himself determines not to be sufficient for himself (although he could be so), then there is after all a contradiction between his nature before and after this decision; and this would mean a contradiction between his nature and his revelation."145

That Moltmann fails to grasp the concept of an a posteriori necessity is demonstrated by his dismissal as 'inappropriate' any reasoning concerning prior possibilities for God such as 'God could' or 'God could have'.[146] Neither is Moltmann content with Barth's definition of God as 'the One who loves in freedom': Either God loves as the one who is free, in which case his love is arbitrary and nominalistic, or else God is free as the one who loves, which is mere tautology.[147]

---

144) Jürgen Moltmann, The Trinity and the Kingdom of God, pp.52ff.

145) ibid., p.53

146) ibid.

147) ibid., p.55

Moreover, Moltmann's assertion that talk of an eternal decision necessitates a 'beforehand - afterwards' structure being carried over into eternity[148] reveals that he also has failed to grasp Barth's conception of God's eternity as pure simultaneity, the compresence of 'beforehand' and 'afterwards'.

It may well be that, despite his criticisms of Luther, a 'nominalist fringe' lingers on in Barth's doctrine of God's primordial decision,[149] but theological issues are not resolved by the affixing of labels. Barth's criticisms of nominalism and 'partial nominalism' centre upon his rejection of the Occamistic view that statements about God's being "have no other value than that of purely subjective ideas and descriptions...to which there is no corresponding reality in God, who is pure simplicity."[150] Therefore Barth's concern in these criticisms is to maintain positively 'objectivity' and validity in speaking of God's attributes.[151] He certainly rejects the view that such descriptions of God's being have no existence but as names or words, the actuality of the event of God's Word is the basis for meaningful (not subjective or meaningless) reflection. Yet he does define God's being as 'self-determined' and prefers to speak of the divine 'perfections' rather than of the divine 'attributes'.

---

148) ibid., p.53

149) ibid., p.52

150) C.D.II.1.p.327

151) ibid., pp.327ff.; cf. pp.335ff.

However, although Moltmann certainly wants to reaffirm God's love in the form of grace he has surely forfeited the logical requirements for doing so by his rejection of Barth's dipolar concept of God in favour of a monistic Trinitarian understanding of the crucifixion. If grace is to be grace it must derive from the free decision of God, it must be free from any form of external or a priori necessity. But such grace need not be considered as arbitrary. If revelation is truly revelation then God's grace is an authentic reiteration of God's eternal decision to be gracious, the outcome of an a posteriori necessity. Moreover, if revelation is truly revelation then God's self-motivated being ad extra is a genuine reiteration of His self-motivated being ad intra. Finally, if this eternal decision is authentically eternal, a decision to which every 'beforehand' and every 'afterwards' is compresent, it implies no temporal 'change' in the eternal being of God; there is no God other than or beyond the God of this eternal, self-motivated, and therefore free and gracious, decision. Moltmann's effective forfeiture of God's grace gives substance to Barth's comment on the relative poverty of Moltmann's 'God':[152]

> "God's free and gracious choice of relation with reality that is other than himself is what makes it possible for him to be both fully related and yet ontologically distinct. By contrast a doctrine of necessary relatedness produces a virtual pantheism,..."153

---

152) Karl Barth, 'An Prof. Dr. Jürgen Moltmann, 17 November 1964', Gesamtausgabe V: Briefe 1961-1968 (Zürich, 1975), p.276

153) Colin E. Gunton, Becoming and Being, pp.162f.; cf. R. D. Williams, 'Barth on the Triune God', p.168

God actually exists, both in Himself and in the event of His revelation, as dynamic being, as determinative being, as relational being. His relatedness ad extra is His genuine self-interpretation of His relatedness ad intra. Neither in His being ad extra nor in His being ad intra is God governed by any external a priori necessity. His relatedness ad extra and ad intra is wholly self-determined, governed by the a posteriori necessity of His eternal decision to be God in this way. He who confronts us in the event of revelation as the One who loves in freedom is actually God as He exists in Himself:

> "For Barth, the freedom of God's love does not consist in the ability to do what He chooses with men. To retain the option of actualising alternative possibilities is not necessarily freedom. The element of freedom in God's love refers to the fact that no external factor figures necessarily in determining His activity. The freedom of God is His ability to act solely on His own internal motivation. God's freedom is not the freedom to act in any one of an infinite number of ways, but the freedom from all external considerations in determining His action."154

---

154) J. D. Bettis, 'Is Karl Barth a Universalist?', S.J.T., 20, (1967), 423-436 (p.428)

V The Doctrine of Election - the determination of man in Jesus Christ

a) Jesus Christ as the electing God:

In the Preface to the second part of the Church Dogmatics volume II Karl Barth confesses that he would have preferred to have more closely followed Calvin's doctrine of predestination instead of so radically departing from it.[1] He also claims that he was "driven irresistibly to reconstruction" in his exposition of this doctrine by the constraint of what the Bible actually says.[2] Certainly the prominence which the doctrine of Election had for the Reformers is not sacrificed by Barth's reconstruction. On the contrary, Barth could not grant any greater importance to the doctrine than by placing it within the doctrine of God, yet it is precisely this which fundamentally distinguishes Barth's exposition of the doctrine from its usual expression within the Reformed tradition.

Barth refuses to locate the source of the doctrine of Election anywhere other than in the event of God's self-revelation. A theologically correct expression of Election will not be formulated by allowing any Reformed tradition to dictate its theme,[3] nor by

---

1) C.D.II.2.p.x

2) ibid.

3) C.D.II.2.pp.35f

substituting the didactic usefulness of the doctrine for its foundation,[4] nor by founding the doctrine upon a datum of experience,[5] nor by attempting to derive the doctrine from a general concept of God as omnipotent will, thereby considering predestination to be one aspect of a general providence.[6] The God to whom Scripture testifies is not to be defined _in abstracto_ as omnipotent will but is to be defined as He has defined Himself in His Word. His power and His will are not indeterminate but self-determined.[7] God exists as He has determined Himself to exist and as He Himself has revealed His self-determined existence in Jesus Christ.[8] The doctrine of Election must not be derived from any concept of God in general but from the self-revelation of God in this particular. The corrective which Barth brings to the Reformed understanding of Election is the identification of Jesus Christ as both the electing God and the elected man:[9]

> "In its simplest and most comprehensive form the dogma of predestination consists, then, in the assertion that the divine predestination is the election of Jesus Christ. But the concept of election has a double reference—to the elector and to the elected. And so, too, the name of Jesus Christ has within itself the double reference: the One called by this name is both very God and very man. Thus the simplest form of the dogma may be divided at once into the two assertions that Jesus Christ is the electing God, and that He is also elected man."10

---

4) _C.D._II.2.pp.37f

5) _C.D._II.2.pp.38ff

6) _C.D._II.2.pp.44ff

7) _C.D._II.2.p.50

8) _C.D._II.2.p.54

9) _C.D._II.2.p.59

10) _C.D._II.2.p.103

This identification of Jesus Christ as the electing God immediately excludes the concept of a decretum absolutum since the latter identifies the electing God by not identifying Him, by proposing a gracious decision of God that is wholly unknown and unknowable to man, a decree of election that remains essentially hidden.[11] But that which is hidden cannot possibly be the ground of faith and assurance:[12]

> "How can we have assurance in respect of our own election except by the Word of God? And how can even the Word of God give us assurance on this point if this Word, if Jesus Christ, is not really the electing God, not the election itself, not our election, but only an elected means whereby the electing God——electing elsewhere and in some other way——executes that which He has decreed concerning those whom He has——elsewhere and in some other way——elected?"13

In practice this concept of a decretum absolutum, by forfeiting any objective basis for faith in the God who is known, opens the very flood-gates of subjective introspection which the Reformed tradition ought to have been anxious to close. When the assurance of election cannot be securely grounded in Jesus Christ the temptation arises to ground that assurance in the actuality of one's own faith or to examine one's own life for evidences of election. The event of faith, instead of being recognized as that which makes election concretely actual and visible, comes to be considered as the cause, or a co-efficient cause, of election.[14] Similarly the individual's

---

11) ibid.,

12) C.D.II.2.p.168

13) C.D.II.2.p.111

14) C.D.II.2.pp.326-328

own testimony to his own works comes to be considered as the evidence of his own election; a correspondence is assumed between the hidden counsel of God and the piety and morality of the individual.[15]

If Calvin maintains a Christ-centred understanding of assurance he can only do so by ignoring the dilemma of his own position, the apparent contradiction of grounding the assurance of election in Christ when election itself is grounded in the hidden counsel of God. The followers of Calvin could not ignore this dilemma but attempted to resolve it by effectively grounding the assurance of election in the individual's testimony of works:[16]

> "...can we really expect this man...to hold primarily to Christ? If Christ is only the means of grace of the God who secretly elects or rejects, then how can He be the crown witness for his election? If he himself is the one elected by the hidden God, why cannot he himself rather be the crown witness, and the consideratio operum be no mere adminiculum inferius, but the first and decisive stage of his assurance of election?"17

Thus the Reformed tradition, by clinging to the concept of a hidden decree and thereby forfeiting a Christ-centred assurance, smuggled

---

15) C.D.II.2.pp.333ff.

16) ibid.

17) C.D.II.2.p.338

Pelagianism in through the back door by means of the syllogismus practicus.[18]

The only valid correction to this doctrine of Election must be the total exclusion of any decretum absolutum. The object of Trinitarian theology is not the unknown God of any hidden decree but the God who is known in the event of His Word. That the being of God is identical both with His determination to exist in this way and with His self-revelation in Jesus Christ means that there is "no such thing as a will of God apart from the will of Jesus Christ";[19]

> "In the very foreground of our existence in history we can and should cleave wholly and with full assurance to Him because in the eternal background of history, in the beginning with God, the only decree which was passed, the only Word which was spoken and which prevails, was the decision which was executed by Him."20

Jesus Christ Himself rightfully occupies the place usurped by the decretum absolutum. Certainly there have been continued attempts

---

18) R. T. Kendall argues that it was the doctrine of 'limited atonement' as taught by Theodore Beza (Kendall maintains that Calvin himself did not teach 'limited atonement') and enshrined within the Westminster Confession that became the source of this 'syllogismus practicus' (R. T. Kendall, Calvin and English Calvinism to 1649 (Oxford, 1979). While Kendall may be correct in his analysis of this distinction between Calvin and Beza, and also correct in the way that he traces subsequent Reformed tradition, Barth's logic here is compelling: The ultimate source of any 'testimony of works' must be located in Calvin's view of the 'hiddenness' of the decree of election.

19) C.D.II.2.p.115

20) ibid.

to affirm the Christ-centredness of the doctrine of Election, yet these attempts have either, like that of Luther, referred equally definitely to a divine decision apart from Christ alongside the reference to Christ[21] or, like that of the later Lutherans and Arminians, have jeopardized the doctrine of Election itself in the attempt to remove the blemish of a hidden decree.[22] The essence of Barth's amendment of the doctrine of Election is the substitution of Jesus Christ for the decretum absolutum.[23] The event of Jesus Christ is the actualization of the eternal decision of God to be God in this way, to be the electing God and the elected man in Jesus Christ:

> "What takes place in Jesus Christ, in the historical event of the atonement accomplished by Him in time, is not simply one history among others and not simply the reaction of God against human sin. It stands at the heart of the Christian message and the Christian faith because here God maintains and fulfils His Word as it was spoken at the very first. He affirms to us and sets among us His original promise and His original command in the concrete reality and actuality of His own being as man."[24]

Similarly for Colin Gunton the pivotal statement of the focal chapter of his study of Christology is that "Jesus of Nazareth is the logic of divine love, logic in the sense of spelling out and making present in earthly actuality its eternal reality."[25]

---

21) C.D.II.2.pp.63ff.

22) C.D.II.2.pp.67ff.

23) C.D.II.2.p.161

24) C.D.IV.1.p.47

25) Colin E. Gunton, Yesterday and Today: A study of continuities in Christology (London, 1983), p.133

Barth's exclusive identification of the eternal will of God with the event of Jesus Christ attests that the Incarnation is God's first thought, not His second. While the event of creation may come first in the series of the works of God its purpose is to make possible the actualization of God's eternal covenant with man in Jesus Christ. It is this covenant of grace which is the aim and goal of God's act of creation:[26]

> "...if Jesus Christ is the content and form of the first and eternal Word of God, then that means further that the beginning of all things, of the being of all men and of the whole world, even the divine willing of creation, is preceded by God's covenant with man as its basis and purpose: His promise, in which He binds and pledges Himself to man, and His command by which He pledges and binds man to Himself. At the beginning of all things in God there is the Gospel and the Law, the gracious address of God and the gracious claim of God, both directed to man, both the one Word of the *Deus pro nobis* who is the one God and beside whom there is no other."27

Therefore the Incarnation cannot merely be God's answer to the fall of man; it is rather God's original determination both for man and for Himself:

> "The point being made is that God's electing grace is not an afterthought, hastily improvised after the catastrophe that overtook the first and independent order of creation. God, as essentially the electing God, makes the universe in order that it may be the arena on which his gracious purposes may come to pass."28

This necessarily raises the question of the relationship of the Incarnation to man's sin, not just the hypothetical question of

---

26) *C.D.*III.1.pp.42ff.

27) *C.D.*IV.1.p.53

28) Colin E. Gunton, 'Karl Barth's Doctrine of Election as part of his Doctrine of God.' *J.T.S.*,25 (1974), 381-392 (p.384)

whether the Incarnation would have been necessary apart from man's sin, but the more serious question of whether the Incarnation is primarily propter nos homines and only secondarily propter nostram salutem, and whether the true significance of the Incarnation could have been located in the former even without reference to the latter.[29]

That Barth refuses to understand man's fall, co-ordinated with grace, as that which instigates election is demonstrated by his discussion of the Supralapsarian-Infralapsarian controversy;[30] i.e., the discussion of whether the object of election is man not yet created or fallen, homo creabilis et labilis (the Supralapsarian position) or whether the object of election is man already created and fallen, homo creatus et lapsus (the Infralapsarian position). The function of the Supralapsarian view-point is to affirm election as the primal and basic purpose of God, quite apart from His purpose to create man and to permit the fall of man. Thus the creation and fall of man are necessary means to fulfil the end of God's primal election. The function of the Infralapsarian view-point is to affirm created and fallen man as the object of election and thereby both to deny the possibility of knowing the content of God's

---

29) John Thompson, Christ in Perspective: Christological Perspectives in the Theology of Karl Barth (Edinburgh, 1978) p.23;
cf; J. L. Scott, 'The Covenant in the Theology of Karl Barth', S.J.T.,17(1964), 182-198

30) C.D.II.2.pp.127ff.

primal election and to deny that the purpose of the creation and fall of man can be deduced from that primal decree. Although Barth's rejection of any <u>decretum absolutum</u> (and its inherent implications) obviously distinguishes him from both traditional view-points in the controversy, and although he also acknowledges the disadvantages of the Supralapsarian position[31] and certain advantages of the Infralapsarian position (namely that, in the context of the original debate, it appeared to do greater justice to the moral difficulties of the concept of predestination which both view-points held in common),[32] he clearly expresses his preference for the former point of view. Once the idolatrious concept of a <u>decretum absolutum</u> has been totally expunged from the debate,[33] once the object of election is identified as Jesus Christ rather than some individuals as opposed to others,[34] once the subject of election is identified as Jesus Christ rather than the unknown God of the hidden decree, then this wholly untraditional Supralapsarian view-point affirms this God's election of this man as the first and only will of God. Since the Infralapsarian position posits a second divine decree of creation, providence and fall alongside the decree of election it cannot be corrected in this Christological manner.[35]

---

31) <u>C.D</u>.II.2.pp.130f.

32) <u>C.D</u>.II.2.pp.131 & 136ff.

33) <u>C.D</u>.II.2.p.143

34) <u>C.D</u>.II.2.pp.140f.

35) <u>C.D</u>.II.2.pp.143ff.

In eternity Jesus Christ is the homo creabilis et labilis elected by God, He is not, in eternity, the homo creatus et lapsus:

> "God wills homo labilis, not in order that he may fall, but in order that when he has fallen he may testify to the fulness of God's glory."36

The purpose of reconciliation in Jesus Christ is not to actualize God's afterthought in response to human sin, not merely to restore the status quo of man's being as a creature, not merely to obviate the effects of man's fall, but to actualize God's eternal covenant with man in Jesus Christ and thus to open up the possibility of man's true being, man's true humanity, man's eschaton.[37] The atonement is not just God's counter to man's sin but the accomplishment of His original will, His eternal covenant in Jesus Christ:[38]

> "...we must continue with Barth and reject the view that reconciliation is only God's reaction to sin. If God's will to rescue and exalt us in Christ is really to be God's last secret, then it must be His eternal will as He is eternal. It cannot be merely His reaction to anything."39

Certainly the fulfilment of this covenant, in the light of man's breaking of the covenant, takes the form of the overcoming of an obstruction, the form of atonement. Yet the atonement finds its eternal basis, not in the creation and fall of man, but in the eternal

---

36) C.D.II.2.pp.141f.

37) C.D.IV.1.pp.13f.

38) C.D.IV.1.pp.47ff.

39) R. W. Jenson, Alpha and Omega: A study in the Theology of Karl Barth, (New York, 1963) p.150

decision of God;[40] that the Incarnation is propter nostram salutem is grounded in the eternal decision of God to be propter nos homines.[41]

In the second place, Barth's identification of the eternal will of God with the event of Jesus Christ raises again the far deeper question of the validity of the temporal in the light of the eternal; is the Incarnation the actualization (i.e., the actual event) of God's eternal decision or is it merely the temporal accomplishment of a decision located elsewhere in God's eternity? Is the ontic basis of election to be located in the primal history of God's decision or is it to be located in the event of Jesus Christ? If this ontic basis is not truly temporal then does not Barth's theology become an 'ahistorical ideological illusion'?[42] Is the temporal history of Jesus Christ merely the knowledge of His eternal history and not the fact of His eternal history?:[43]

---

40) C.D.IV.1.pp.67ff.

41) cf. John Thompson, op.cit., pp.24 & 146

42) cf. R. H Roberts, 'Eternity and Time in the Theology of Karl Barth: An essay in Dogmatic and Philosophical Theology.' (dissertation, Edinburgh, 1975), pp.180ff.

43) R. W. Jenson, Alpha and Omega, p.162

"Jesus Christ is the eternal decree of God before all time. Jesus Christ is the history in Palestine which reveals this decree. Barth does not separate these two; his concept of revelation and knowledge is far too rich. But we must still ask: which is the prior definition? Barth defines the history in time as the revelation and analogy of eternal history and so gives his answer. And with this answer he puts himself in danger of removing reconciliation itself, the inner reality of Jesus' life, from our history."44

The significance of temporal history is surely jeopardized if temporal history in its entirety is comprehended within a pretemporal decision of God:[45]

"Henceforth Barth remains captive within this triune circle. Consequently everything is anticipated, has already happened in this original perfect tense, which one is tempted to call a pluperfect tense. Everything is not merely decreed in eternity, but already perfected; what takes place in time is merely the carrying out of the original divine decree, a repetition of the original and eternal pattern. Reduced to a formula, we might say that the divine Trinity devised a drama in eternity, and gave its first performance within itself, played by the three persons. Now this drama is to be re-enacted on earth, as it has been in heaven. To this end the world is created as the stage, and man as the spectator."46

It would be inappropriate here to repeat in full the complex discussion of time and eternity, rather it should be sufficient to refer again to the two poles of the irreducible tension

---

44) ibid., pp.162f.; cf. R. W. Jenson, God after God: the God of the Past and the God of the Future, seen in the work of Karl Barth (Indianapolis and New York, 1969), pp.151-153.

45) ibid., p.151; cf. Colin E. Gunton, Becoming and Being: The Doctrine of God in Charles Hartshorne and Karl Barth (Oxford, 1978), p.182.

46) Heinz Zahrnt, The Question of God: Protestant Theology in the Twentieth Century, trans. by R. A. Wilson (London, 1969), p.113; cf. A. Brandenburg, 'Der Zeit- und Geschichtsbegriff bei Karl Barth', Theologie und Glaube, 45 (1955), 357-378 (pp.377f.)

which is Barth's conception of God's time. Understanding the resurrection of Jesus Christ as the occurrence of God's time in our time, Barth affirms God's eternity both (in identity with our time) as His true temporality and (in distinction from our time) as His pure simultaneity:[47]

> "The ambivalence of Barth's position is intrinsic and methodologically deliberate; Jesus Christ is both a concrete person and the decision of the eternally living God. The temporal basis of this lies in the doctrine of the pre-, supra- and post-temporality of eternity which in turn is built upon the doctrine of God's dynamic being."48

What Barth understands as an irreducible tension may appear to others to be an illogical ambiguity, yet this tension can only be avoided effectively by either reverting to an abstract concept of timelessness or by denying any distinction between God's time and man's time. Moreover, the motive for avoiding this tension may perhaps be located in the irrational resolve to comprehend all actuality within a preconceived rationality instead of allowing rationality to be determined by actuality.

On the one side of the tension the true temporality of God must be affirmed. God's eternity is not His timelessness but His authentic temporality.[49] It must be admitted that there certainly are passages, especially in volume IV of the Church

---

47) C.D.II.1.pp.608ff.

48) R. H. Roberts, 'Eternity and Time in the Theology of Karl Barth', p.200

49) C.D.III.2.p.437

Dogmatics, where Barth does refer to the temporal history of Jesus Christ as the realization, the revelation or the accomplishment of God's eternal covenant:

> "...this actualisation, ...is characterised as an act of faithfulness, of constancy, of self-affirmation on the part of God, as the consequence of a presupposition already laid down by Him, as the fulfilment of a decision which underlies and therefore precedes that actualisation, an "earlier" divine decision, as the successful continuation of an act which God had already begun, from the very beginning."[50]

Such references must be considered in the context of Barth's central affirmation of the true temporality of God's time as His living history. In the light of the fundamental structure of Barth's doctrine of revelation, that God is who He is in the event of His revelation, it is surely reasonable to assume that, despite an evident equivocality of phraseology, it was Barth's intention to maintain an identification of the temporal history of Jesus Christ as the eternal decision of God.[51] Even if it may be unreasonable to speculate concerning Barth's intentions it is not unreasonable to affirm that which is the logical implication of Barth's concept of revelation:

> "We wish to speak of God's decision and, in so doing, speak more unequivocally than Barth of the life of Jesus Christ in our history, of His life in created time and space. Jesus Christ is God's great decision about us, and not as an event in a "third" level between time and eternity. In our history God makes His eternal decision."[52]

---

50) C.D.IV.1.p.36

51) cf. R. W. Jenson, God after God, p.152

52) R. W. Jenson, Alpha and Omega, p.163

However, the other side of the tension, the aspect which some of Barth's critics may be in danger of losing,[53] must be affirmed equally unequivocally: in the pure simultaneity of His time God is identical to this event in His past, His present and His future; God is in this event who He is previously in Himself. The term "previously", as with the reference to God's "primal" decision, is not to be simplistically understood as referring to the infinite past of an everlastingness of God, nor as referring to the otherness of an abstract timelessness of God, but as referring to the pure simultaneity of God's time in which this decision is both absolutely previous, absolutely contemporary, and absolutely future. It is this pure simultaneity which distinguishes God's authentic temporality from man's fallen temporality. God's eternity is His living history, His past, present and future, in which He is simultaneously constant to the decision which is His being. To jettison this other side of the tension is to risk the evaporation of God's true time into man's fallen time by failing to distinguish adequately between God's time and man's time. The understanding of God's eternity within this tension does not answer the question of the validity of the temporal in the light of the eternal, it renders the question meaningless. It is to refuse to be caught in the dilemma of a false "either-or"; the ontic basis of election is to be simultaneously located in both the primal history of God's decision and the temporal event of Jesus Christ.

---

53) cf. R. W. Jenson, Alpha and Omega, pp.161ff.; R.W. Jenson, God after God, pp.153ff.; Colin E. Gunton, Becoming and Being, pp.179ff.

b) Jesus Christ as the elected man:

Until now this treatment of the doctrine of Election has been wholly concerned with the doctrine of God, with the identification of the true God as the electing God in Jesus Christ and, therefore, with the rejection of any independent definition of a supposed God beyond and other than the event of Jesus Christ, the rejection of any hidden decision or election of God beyond and other than this specific determination. But this is not the whole scope of the doctrine. The doctrine of Election informs us that God, who has determined Himself to be the electing God in Jesus Christ, has determined Himself also to be the elected man in Jesus Christ.[54] In Jesus Christ God has determined Himself as both the subject and the object of His election. The object of the doctrine of Election is not any abstract concept of man in general, nor the totality of the human race, nor even particular men and their individual destiny.[55]

The object of the doctrine of Election is not any general concept of man. Barth certainly wishes to preserve the distinction between Christology and Anthropology; the distinction which comprises of both the mystery of man's sin and the mystery of Jesus

---

54) C.D.II.2.pp.116ff.; cf. E. Jüngel, The Doctrine of the Trinity: God's Being is in Becoming, trans. by Horton Harris, Monograph Supplements to the Scottish Journal of Theology, eds. T. F. Torrance and J. K. S. Reid (Edinburgh and London, 1976), p.72

55) C.D.II.2.p.55

Christ's identity with God.[56] There is a non-theological knowledge of man which is not only possible and justified but also genuine and necessary, yet such a knowledge of man, while it may not be false or worthless, cannot, of itself, lead to a knowledge of real man, it may only presuppose that real man is knowable and known exclusively in the light of God's revelation.[57] The real man who is the object of theological anthropology is the creature of God, the man whose relationship to God is both revealed and established in the Word of God.[58] Jesus Christ is the exclusive source for our knowledge of this real man who is the creature of God,[59] the object of God's election.[60] In Jesus Christ alone that which constitutes true humanity is revealed[61] because Jesus Christ is Himself both the source and the actualization of God's ontological determination of man.[62] Our knowledge of ourselves is "included and enclosed in the knowledge of Jesus".[63] We must now reckon

---

56) C.D.III.2.p.71; cf. p.222

57) C.D.III.2.p.202

58) C.D.III.2.p.19

59) C.D.III.2.p.41

60) C.D.III.2.pp.142ff.

61) C.D.III.2.p.50

62) C.D.III.2.p.132

63) C.D.IV.2.p.268.

with an anthropologocal sphere that is dominated by Him as the Lord. The more we concentrate upon Him the better will be our knowledge of ourselves. Moreover, His history is not just the basis for our knowledge of ourselves, it is the history in which we participate. Our humanity is elevated and exalted in His humanity. We are what we are in Him:[64]

> "There is no one who is not raised and exalted with Him to true humanity."65

Just as God's true Godness is actually defined in the event of Jesus Christ, so also man's true manness is defined in this event. Jesus Christ is the "pre-requisite of the possibility for the recognition of the being of man in general."[66] Exclusively in Jesus Christ the true God is revealed as the electing God, and, exclusively in Jesus Christ the true man is revealed as the elected man. The testimony of scripture never permits us to blur the name of Jesus Christ with abstract presuppositions concerning either God or man:[67]

---

64) C.D.IV.2.pp.268ff.

65) ibid., p.271

66) E. Jüngel, 'Die Möglichkeit theologischer Anthropologie auf dem Grunde der Analogie: Eine Untersuchung zum Analogieverständnis Karl Barths', Evangelische Theologie, 22 (1962), 535-557 (p.537), my translation; cf. E. Jüngel, 'Was ist » das unterscheidend Christliche « ?' in Unterwegs zur Sache: Theologische Bemerkungen, ed. E. Wolf, Beiträge zur evangelischen Theologie, 61 (Munich, 1972), pp.296-299 (p.298)

67) C.D.II.2.p.59

> "Barth turns anthropology on what we have previously supposed to be its head by saying that the incarnation is not the Son of God assuming a "human nature" already defined by our lives, but that rather the Son defines human nature by assuming it."68

The object of the doctrine of Election is not the totality of the human race. There is no such thing as a predestined humanity, there are no predestined families or nations.[69] The election of the "many" as the mediate and mediating community, giving testimony to election in the world is not independent of the election of Jesus Christ but is actually included in His election.[70] Even in his discussion of the election of the community in Jesus Christ Barth never equates this elected community with an abstract totality of individuals.[71] The "fulness of the Gentiles" must not be construed to refer to the sum total of all Gentile individuals, nor "all Israel" to refer to the sum total of Jewish individuals; the Scriptures never reckon with the unqualified totalities that normally form the basis of a supposed apokatastasis.[72] To speak of such totalities as the object of God's election and thereby to imply the salvation of all men to be in some way "necessary" is to deny

---

68) R. W. Jenson, God after God, p.73; cf. D. F. Ford, 'Barth's interpretation of the Bible' in Karl Barth: Studies of his Theological Method, ed. by S. W. Sykes (Oxford, 1979), pp.55-87 (p.74)

69) C.D.II.2.pp.313ff.

70) C.D.II.2.pp.195ff.

71) C.D.II.2.p.300; cf. p.295

72) C.D.II.2.pp.267-305

election as an event of God's grace.[73] God is love in Himself without having to love any man and certainly without having to love all men. The problem of the doctrine of apokatastasis is not that it ties God to all men but that it ties God to man at all. That God is related ad extra as well as ad intra, that He loves man in Jesus Christ as a reiteration of His self-relatedness, is an outcome of the a posteriori necessity of His grace, not any a priori necessity constrained by the external object of His love.[74] God is not to be defined in terms of any supposed relationship to totalities of men but in terms of His actual relationship to man in Jesus Christ, the true object of God's electing love.

The object of the doctrine of Election is not particular men and their individual destiny. Certainly the election of Jesus Christ is not exclusive but inclusive, establishing the election of individuals as valid, as that which is genuinely at issue in His election.[75] Certainly the election of Jesus Christ is the revelation of the election of those who are elected in Him; the revelation of God's eternal covenant with man in Jesus Christ.[76] But the election of individuals is not independent of the election of Jesus Christ, it is rather actually included in His election and can only

---

73) C.D.II.2.pp.417-418; cf. C.D.IV.3.pp.477-478

74) C.D.II.1.pp.280ff.

75) C.D.II.2.pp.310ff.

76) C.D.II.2.pp.116f.

be truly considered in the light of His election:[77]

> "Those whom God elects He elects "in Him," not merely "like Him," but in His person, by His will, and by His election."78

Just as the traditional doctrine of predestination, by referring to a supposed hidden decree of God, failed to attest Jesus Christ as the true subject of election, so also, by referring to a supposed private and independent relationship between God and some individuals,[79] and by the tendency to set election and rejection side by side as the hidden will of this hidden God, it failed to attest Jesus Christ as the true object of election:

> "The problem began to be obscured when the "book of life" came to be spoken of as though it had in it a death-column; when the divine election and the divine rejection came to be spoken of as inter-connected divine acts similar in character and determination; when they came to be regarded and understood as though they could both be grouped under the one over-ruling concept."80

The devastating consequence of this combination was to effectively deny that the election of Jesus Christ could be considered as the ground of assurance for the election of individuals; "the election of Jesus Christ may possibly mean something for them, but it may equally well mean nothing."[81] Only when Jesus Christ is attested as both the subject and the object of election, only when the election of the individual is exclusively considered as included in

---

77) C.D.II.2.pp.309ff.

78) C.D.II.2.p.121

79) C.D.II.2.pp.306ff.

80) C.D.II.2.p.16

81) C.D.II.2.p.325

His election, only then is the doctrine of Election the valid ground for Christian assurance,[82] only then is the doctrine of Election unequivocally good-news, the sum of the Gospel, the divine Yes which includes but overwhelms the divine No.[83]

In distinction to such fallacious objects of election the true object of election is Jesus Christ, _the_ elect man, and the elect people who are united in Him and represented by Him:[84]

> "If we would know what election is, what it is to be elected by God, then we must look away from all others, and excluding all side-glances or secondary thoughts we must look only upon the name of Jesus Christ and upon the actual existence and history of the people whose beginning and end are enclosed in the mystery of His name."[85]

Barth's rejection of any _decretum absolutum_ involves not only the denial of any hidden subject of election but also the denial of any hidden object of election; Jesus Christ Himself is both the electing God and the elected man.[86] In the event of Jesus Christ God actualizes, and thereby reveals, His eternal affirmation of this man as the object of His love, as His covenant partner, as the external cause and object of His glory.[87] This positive aspect of God's

---

82) _C.D._II.2.pp.333ff.

83) _C.D._II.2.pp.3-34

84) _C.D._II.2.p.58

85) _C.D._II.2.pp.58f.

86) _C.D._II.2.p.146

87) _C.D._II.2.p.169

election certainly involves the negative aspect of God's rejection of man as a sinful creature, yet the latter is overwhelmed by the former since, by electing Himself to become this lost Son of Man in Jesus Christ,[88] God has elected this rejection to Himself and made it His own;[89] in Jesus Christ He is the "Judge Judged in Our Place":[90]

> "Because He was a man like us, He was able to be judged like us. Because He was the Son of God and Himself God, He had the competence and power to allow this to happen to Him. Because He was the divine Judge come amongst us, He had the authority in this way——by this giving up of Himself to judgement in our place——to exercise the divine justice of grace, to pronounce us righteous on the ground of what happened to Him, to free us therefore from the accusation and condemnation and punishment, to save us from the impending loss and destruction. And because in divine freedom He was on the way of obedience, He did not refuse to accept the will of the Father as His will in this self-giving."91

Indeed, it is only in the light of that rejection which God has elected for Himself that the reality of God's rejection of this man is revealed;[92] "In that He takes our place it is decided what our place is."[93]

That God has elected this rejection for Himself in Jesus Christ means that rejection "cannot again become the portion or

---

88) C.D.II.2.p.157

89) C.D.II.2.pp.161ff.

90) C.D.IV.1.pp.211ff.

91) C.D.IV.1.pp.222f.

92) C.D.II.2.p.165

93) C.D.IV.1.p.240

affair of man";[94] Jesus Christ alone bears this rejection:

> "No one outside or alongside Him is elected. All who are elected are elected in Him. And similarly——since no one outside or alongside Him is elected as the bearer of divine rejection——no one outside or alongside Him is rejected."95

The No of God which fell upon us in the death of Jesus Christ has "no autonomous or definitive or absolute significance";[96] this divine No has been totally and utterly overwhelmed by the divine Yes inasmuch as Jesus Christ has Himself borne this divine No totally and utterly. For any individual to choose to reject this gracious election and live under the rejection of God which God has, in actuality, elected for Himself, is to choose for himself the possibility that God, by choosing it for Himself, has determined to be impossible. Such a man chooses what, in the light of God's choice, he cannot choose, he chooses the possibility which God has excluded and, therefore, his choice is defined as null and void:[97]

> "We are summoned to accept our life on this presupposition, as those who are liberated, whose sin is cancelled and forgiven in Him: in the genuine confidence that our being in sin (as our own) belongs to God and not to us, that the responsibility which we owe Him in this matter has been borne by Him."98

Barth determines to understand predestination unequivocally as God's affirmation of man in Jesus Christ; not as a Yes and a

---

94) *C.D.*II.2.p.167

95) *C.D.*II.2.p.421

96) *C.D.*IV.1.p.350

97) *C.D.*II.2.pp.315ff.; cf. pp.237 & 349

98) *C.D.*IV.1.p.242

No of equal and opposing force but as the Yes which, although it cannot be heard apart from the No, totally overwhelms the No.[99] For this reason Barth refuses to consider the existence of the "rejected" man, the man who resists his election in Jesus Christ, as being determined by any positive will of God;[100] there is no covenant of wrath in correspondence to the covenant of grace. The godlessness of man cannot make God a "manless" God. God does not allow the sin of man to divert Him from the Yes of His grace. There is therefore no such thing as an ontological godlessness of fallen man.[101] The man who resists his election in Jesus Christ can only live as one who is not-willed by God; the determination of his existence is that of God's non-willing:

> "He does not will him as rejected. Only in His non-willing does He will him as such."102

The man who resists his election in Jesus Christ is the man who refuses his pardon by attempting to turn it into judgment and condemnation. God still says Yes to him but he can only hear this Yes as a destructive No. He hates and despises the grace of God, he will not live by it, he only receives it as non-grace, as wrath and as judgment:

---

99) C.D.II.2.p.13; cf. C.D.IV.1.pp.591ff.

100) C.D.II.2.pp.449ff.

101) C.D.IV.1.pp.480ff.

102) C.D.II.2.p.458.

> "A "rejected" man is one who isolates himself from God by resisting his election as it has taken place in Jesus Christ. God is for him; but he is against God. God is gracious to him; but he is ungrateful to God. God receives him; but he withdraws himself from God. God forgives him his sins; but he repeats them as though they were not forgiven. God releases him from the guilt and punishment of his defection; but he goes on living as Satan's prisoner. God determines him for blessedness, and His service; but he chooses the joylessness of an existence that accords with his own pride and aims at his own honour."103

Such a man falls under the threat that he will be taken seriously in this his lie, "that he will be granted and finally assigned to a life by an in untruth as the portion which he himself has chosen, a life which as such can only be a lost life."[104] His lie is the attempt to substitute a rejection which is not God's will in the place of the election which is God's will. As such he stands under the threat of condemnation even though that condemnation is not yet pronounced.[105] But the threat is nonetheless real. It is the threat of divine rejection. It is the threat of the unwillingness of God for everything that He does not positively will. It is the wrath of God which is the form His love assumes when it is ignored and rejected by man.[106]

Yet this lie of man has no power to alter the truth of God and man in Jesus Christ. Despite his attempt man cannot

---

103) C.D.II.2.pp.449f.

104) C.D.IV.3.p.462; cf. C.D.IV.1.pp.482f.

105) C.D.IV.3.p.465

106) C.D.IV.1.p.489; cf. J. D. Bettis, 'Is Karl Barth a Universalist?', S.J.T., 20 (1967), 423-436 (p.432).

change the truth into untruth:

> "Man can stand on his own head, but he cannot make the truth do so."107

This man has no autonomous existence apart from the positive electing will of God; the grace which, apart from God's wisdom and patience, would totally consume him and annihilate him without ceasing to be grace.[108] As such this man lives unwillingly as a continuing witness, albeit a shadowy witness, of the positive electing will of God. He is the witness on behalf of the elect to the rejection which has been borne by Jesus Christ, the rejection from which the elect have been delivered. He thereby offers the same service to the Church as that of Israel, a witness to the non-willing of God and, therefore, a witness to election.[109] That God has defined man as elect in Jesus Christ means that such a man's existence must be understood as a denial of this election and not as a separate and distinct definition of the being of man.[110]

Just as the doctrine of Creation must be understood in the context of the doctrine of Election so also evil must be understood in the light of this non-willing of God. Evil can have no autonomous existence; it can only exist as an impossible possibility, as the shadow of God's primal decision, as that which God rejects.[111]

---

107) <u>C.D</u>.IV.3.p.475

108) <u>C.D</u>.II.2.pp.450f.

109) <u>C.D</u>.II.2.p.458; cf. pp.195ff.

110) <u>C.D</u>.II.2.p.349

111) <u>C.D</u>.II.2.p.170; cf. <u>C.D</u>.III.3.pp.289ff.

What God rejects by His decision to elect is not merely nothing, it is nothingness.[112] This nothingness is a reality, it must not be demythologized, overlooked or forgotten,[113] but it can only "exist" on the basis of its rejection by God, as that which He does not will, as the chaos which resists and refuses grace:[114]

> "God elects, and therefore rejects what He does not elect. God wills, and therefore opposes what He does not will. He says Yes, and therefore says No to that to which He has not said Yes. He works according to His purpose, and in so doing rejects and dismisses all that gainsays it. Both of these activities, grounded in His election and decision, are necessary elements in His sovereign action. He is Lord both on the right hand and on the left. It is only on this basis that nothingness "is," but on this basis it really "is." As God is Lord on the left hand as well, He is the basis and Lord of nothingness too."115

Because this nothingness was not created or willed by God it has no perpetuity,[116] it reaches its end in the consummation of God's positive will in Jesus Christ;[117] though the final revelation of the destruction of nothingness lies in the future it is now, in Jesus Christ, objectively overcome.[118] Only in the light of the actuality of God's decision of election in Jesus Christ is the true knowledge of nothingness and of its absolute defeat revealed:[119]

---

112) C.D.III.3.p.352

113) C.D.III.3.p.300

114) C.D.III.3.p.353

115) C.D.III.3.p.351

116) C.D.III.3.p.360

117) C.D.III.3.p.363

118) C.D.III.3.p.367; cf. E. Jüngel, God's Being is in Becoming, pp.107f.

119) C.D.III.3.pp.302ff.

"...we can achieve a true and relatively clear definition of evil only as we pursue thinking which is controlled by the living person of Jesus Christ in His self-disclosure and which is thus consistently "christological,"..."120

In the event of Jesus Christ God has actualized His ontological definition of Himself as the electing God; God has determined that He should exist eternally according to this primal decision. In the event of Jesus Christ God has also actualized His ontological definition of Himself as the elected man; God has determined that man should exist according to this primal decision and, therefore, any other "existence" of man is an existence according to God's non-willing, an ontological impossibility.[121] There is no God other than the God of the covenant, but also there is no man other than the man of the covenant:[122]

"Godlessness is not, therefore, a possibility, but an ontological impossibility for man. Man is not without, but with God. This is not to say, of course, that godless men do not exist. Sin is undoubtedly committed and exists. Yet sin itself is not a possibility but an ontological impossibility for man."123

For man to sin, for man to continue to live under the rejection which God has elected for Himself, is a denial of God's ontological definition of man actualized in Jesus Christ. Jesus Christ is Himself the decision of God that determines the existence of all

---

120) C.D.IV.3.p.177

121) C.D.II.2.p.316

122) C.D.IV.1.p.43

123) C.D.III.2.p.136

men;[124] His exaltation as the "Royal Man" is God's affirmation of man in Him.[125] The being of man is not an autonomous state, neither is it determined by human decisions and actions, it is determined by the gracious decision of God in election, only here is the being of real man actually defined:[126]

> "From the thesis that there is no manlessness of God and, for this reason, no ontological godlessness of man, one may infer that man is defined theologically precisely by the fact that God is closer to him than he is to himself. To formulate this in other words: man is defined theologically through the justification of the godless by God. If there is no divine "Above, in which man is not found", then neither is there a human Below in which God himself is not found."127

The Christian community consists of those who recognize this decision of God which is His ontological definition of man, those who know that in Jesus Christ He has elected their rejection for Himself and that they are elect in Him.[128] But, in recognizing this divine definition of man for themselves, this elect community are compelled to recognize it for all men, for those who, like them, have recognized it but also for those who, unlike them, have not recognized it.[129] The content of this community's testimony will therefore be the declaration of this divine determination of man:

---

124) C.D.IV.2.p.36; cf. pp.280ff.

125) C.D.IV.2.pp.154ff.

126) cf. B. C. Hanson, 'Hope and Participation in Christ: A Study in the Theology of Barth and Pannenberg' (dissertation, Princeton, 1970), pp.49ff.

127) E. Jüngel, '...keine Menschenlosigkeit Gottes...: Zur Theologie Karl Barths zwischen Theismus und Atheismus' Evangelische Theologie, 31 (1971), 376-390 (p.389), my translation.

128) C.D.II.2.pp.318ff.

129) ibid.; cf. pp.414ff.

> "The content of the promise when it is rightly delivered in and with the message of Jesus Christ is as follows: In Jesus Christ thou, too, art not rejected—for He has borne thy rejection—but elected. A decision has been made, in Jesus Christ, concerning the futility of thy desire and attempt to live that life; and it has been decided that thou canst live only this other life. This is the promise which the community has to deliver to the godless man, and which he may receive and hear and believe. To hear means to be aware that in Jesus Christ this decision has been made concerning him. To believe means to accept the situation which has been created by this decision."130

Thus the distinction between the Christian and the non-Christian is noetic and not ontological. Ontologically both the Christian and the non-Christian are defined as elect in Jesus Christ; their election is that which has happened "to" rather than "in" their human nature and history.[131] While the Christian is one who has recognized this the non-Christian is one who has not yet, or no longer, recognizes it.[132]

This noetic distinction between the Christian and the non-Christian is maintained and clarified in Barth's treatment of the doctrine of Reconciliation.[133] The being of man is that of man as reconciled to God in Jesus Christ; that which makes a man a Christian is his knowledge of his being as a reconciled man, but, while knowledge and obedience are that which make a man a Christian they are not that which make him reconciled to God. The Christian's knowledge of His being in Jesus Christ is the presupposition and theme of Barth's understanding of the Christian's

---

130) C.D.II.2.p.322

131) C.D.II.2.p.321

132) ibid.

133) C.D.IV.1.pp.90ff.

faith, love and hope. Barth therefore defines the call to faith as a call "to acknowledge" (anerkennen), "to know" (erkennen), and "to confess" (bekennen); each a form of the German verb "to know":[134]

> "As this human act it has no creative but only a cognitive character. It does not alter anything. As a human act it is simply the confirmation of a change which has already taken place, the change in the whole human situation which took place in the death of Jesus Christ and was revealed in His resurrection and attested by the Christian community."135

Similarly, the Christian has the freedom to love because he knows that he belongs to Jesus Christ and may therefore live in a different manner from those without this knowledge.[136] The Christian is one who has been "awakened to conversion" and is thus distinguished from those who still sleep:[137]

> "The people of God in the world are those to whom it is revealed, and who may live in and by the knowledge, that their being as sinners is one which is assailed by God, and therefore basically and definitively; that the ground on which they are sinners has been taken away from them, even though they are still sinners. This is what distinguishes the recipients of the direction of the Son of God from the world which does not share this knowledge —although the ground has already been cut from under its sinful being as well."138

Finally, that the Christian may live in hope, in the confident expectation of the future consummation of God's primal decision, rests upon the enlightening power of the Holy Spirit by which the

---

134) C.D.IV.1.pp.740ff.

135) ibid., p.751; cf. pp.630ff.

136) C.D.IV.2.pp.727ff.

137) C.D.IV.2.pp.553ff.

138) C.D.IV.2.p.526

Christian recognizes the actuality of this decision in Jesus Christ.[139] The Christian exists as one who has been awakened to an active knowledge of the truth,[140] who has been called because he has been illuminated.[141] But, while the Christian recognizes Jesus Christ as the ground of his hope and the non-Christian does not recognize this, Jesus Christ is, nonetheless, objectively the hope of both.[142]

Whether Barth understands Christian existence in purely noetic terms, how the Christian comes to this knowledge, and what is the precise meaning of "knowledge", are all questions which must be reserved for the next chapter. The purpose at present is to affirm unequivocally the ontological definition of man in Jesus Christ and thereby to reject the tendency of formulating the doctrine of Election as a means of explaining the phenomena of faith and disbelief, the tendency of interpreting faith and disbelief in terms of election and rejection.[143] According to His primal decision, actualized in Jesus Christ, God has borne the rejection of all men; irrespective of their attitude, they are ontologically defined as elect in Him.[144]

---

139) *C.D.*IV.3.pp.902ff.

140) *C.D.*IV.3.p.481

141) *C.D.*IV.3.pp.508ff.

142) *C.D.*IV.3.pp.345ff.

143) *C.D.*II.2.pp.38ff.; cf. pp.329 & 333

144) cf. *C.D.*IV.3.p295

VI The Doctrine of Election - The realization of man's determination in the Holy Spirit

a) The ontological definition of man in Jesus Christ:

Nothing is more understandable than that logical implications should be drawn from a theological formulation which is as logically coherent as that of Karl Barth. On this basis there certainly are further implications to be identified by those committed to the study of theology after Barth. On this basis also it is, in one sense, understandable that an implicit universalism (apokatastasis) should be identified within the logical structure of Barth's doctrine of Election. If all men are defined ontologically in Jesus Christ as elect, if the rejection of man is that which God elects to Himself, if a man's choice to live other than by this divine definition is null and void, an impossible possibility, an ontological contradiction, then is it not reasonable to suggest that the ultimate salvation of all men is the logically necessary consequence of this exclusive ontological definition of man?

The apparent logic of Barth's doctrine of Election must, however, be contrasted with the two complementary assertions which he continually makes concerning the possibility of an apokatastasis.[1] In the first place, as already noted, Barth rejects universalism as a doctrine because it limits the freedom of God by tying God to man, by implying that God's love for all men is

1) C.D.II.2.pp.417ff.; cf. C.D.IV.3.pp.461ff.

an a priori necessity if God is to be considered as love in Himself. God is not constrained by any "ism" to give salvation to men:

> "It is His concern what is to be the final extent of the circle. If we are to respect the freedom of divine grace, we cannot venture the statement that it must and will finally be coincident with the world of man as such (as in the doctrine of the so-called apokatastasis). No such right or necessity can legitimately be deduced. Just as the gracious God does not need to elect or call any single man, so He does not need to elect or call all mankind."[2]

God's love cannot be presumed upon in this way and remain love in the form of grace, love in freedom. Even though "theological consistency" may appear to lead in this direction salvation as a free gift must not be cheapened into an obligatory right.[3]

In the second place Barth, while refusing to accept universalism as an a priori necessity for God, presumptively limiting God's freedom, refuses with equal emphasis to reject universal salvation as a possibility for God, presumptively limiting God's grace.[4] Such a divine possibility that the final circle of God's people may prove to be "greater than was previously visible" would be entirely consistent with the loving-kindness of God revealed in Jesus Christ.[5] On this basis, while we are forbidden to count on universal salvation as a claimed right or tenet of faith, we are

---

2) C.D.II.2.p.417

3) C.D.IV.3.p.477

4) C.D.II.2.p.418

5) ibid.; cf. Karl Barth, The Humanity of God, trans. by John Newton Thomas and Thomas Wieser (London and Glasgow, 1961), pp.59-60.

certainly constrained, not only to be open to this divine possibility but to hope and pray for it.[6] This refusal to reject the possibility of the ultimate salvation of any man is highlighted by Barth's discussion of Judas Iscariot as the "character in which the problem of the rejected is concentrated and developed in the New Testament".[7] David Ford is somewhat unfair when he suggests that Barth's concern to understand all rejection as enclosed and overcome in the death and resurrection of Jesus Christ has led him to press "the typology of Judas with Paul so as to support the possibility of an ultimately favourable verdict on Judas."[8] Neither in his discussion of Judas nor in his discussion of Israel as a form of the one community of God (a discussion based upon the letter to the Romans chs.9-11 which accompanies Barth's treatment of the Election of the Community[9]) does Barth affirm any more nor any less than he is compelled to affirm for every man in the light of Jesus Christ. On the basis of God's ontological definition of man as elect in Jesus Christ such a "favourable verdict" must be at least a possibility, even for Judas:

> "This is the open contrast of which the Church and every member of the Church must think when the question of the final and definitive rejection of men is raised. The Church will not then preach an apokatastasis, nor will it preach a powerless grace of Jesus Christ or a wickedness

---

6) *C.D*.IV.3.pp.477f.

7) *C.D*.II.2.pp.458ff.

8) David Ford, 'Barth's interpretation of the Bible' in *Karl Barth: Studies of his Theological Method*, ed. by S. W. Sykes (Oxford, 1979), pp.55-87 (p.85)

9) *C.D*.II.2.pp.195ff.

> of men which is too powerful for it. But without any weakening of the contrast, and also without any arbitrary dualism, it will preach the overwhelming power of grace and the weakness of human wickedness in face of it. For this is how the "for" of Jesus and the "against" of Judas undoubtedly confront one another. We may not know whether it led to the conversion of Judas or not, but this is how it always is in the situation of proclamation."10

The orientation of the above quotation identifies the true context of every assertion concerning the possibility of an ultimate universal salvation in the Dogmatics. Barth is referring to God's ontological definition of man in Jesus Christ, to the Word of God and therefore to the witness of the Christian community, the content of the Church's proclamation. Barth's acceptance of the possibility of an apokatastasis is wholly misunderstood when it is not recognized that such assertions belong exclusively to the context of the Christian witness to election. In his discussion of the Election of the Individual[11] it is not Barth's purpose to speculate concerning the ultimate destiny of every individual man but rather to affirm the inclusiveness of the community's witness to every individual man. The Christian community does not possess the power to make any man one of the elect nor even to make it clear to any man that he is elected, this is the prerogative of God alone.[12] But the Christian community does possess the commission to declare to every man that which it knows and other men do not, the election of Jesus Christ by which man's existence is defined. This

---

10) C.D.II.2.p.477

11) C.D.II.2.pp.306ff.

12) C.D.II.2.p.320; cf. pp.410ff.

testimony of the Church must remain unequivocal; though it certainly knows the reality of a threatened rejection, though it can exercise no control over the outcome of its proclamation, it is not at liberty to reverse the ordained relationship between election and rejection, promise and threat. Its proclamation to every individual man must be that Jesus Christ died and rose for him also,[13] that his existence too is defined by the election of Jesus Christ:

> "It is, therefore, impossible for him to regard any of them as if they were not elect, as if God's love for men did not apply to them too, as if His covenant of grace had not been sealed for them, as if the godlessness in which they deny their real status were to be seriously taken as conclusive, as if it were therefore senseless and futile to witness to them too of the divine election of grace that has taken place in Jesus Christ."14

Just as there is no question of any hidden decree of God, independent of the election of Jesus Christ, so also there is no question of an equivocal proclamation by the Church in the light of which men may regard themselves as neutral.[15] The Church is called to proclaim the Gospel, good-news, the divine election that overcomes rejection, the Yes that overwhelms the No:

> "On the basis of the eternal will of God we have to think of every human being, even the oddest, most villainous or miserable, as one to whom Jesus Christ is Brother and God is Father; and we have to deal with him on this assumption. If the other person knows that already, then we have to strengthen him in the knowledge. If he does not know it yet or no longer knows it, our business is to transmit this knowledge to him. On the basis of the knowledge of the humanity of God no other attitude to any kind of fellow man is possible."16

---

13) C.D.II.2.p.320

14) C.D.II.2.p.416

15) C.D.II.2.p.325

16) Karl Barth, The Humanity of God, p.50

Interpreters of Barth are confronted with the enigma of how Barth's explicit rejection of universalism can be harmonized with the apparent logic of his doctrine of Election, the universal scope of God's ontological definition of man and the universal scope of the Church's proclamation of this ontological definition. G. C. Berkouwer suggests that these two strands of Barth's theology are indicative of an unresolved dilemma in his thinking; the crossroads between either reflecting anew on the seriousness of the human decision of faith or embracing universalism.[17]

> "There is no alternative to concluding that Barth's refusal to accept the apokatastasis cannot be harmonized with the fundamental structure of his doctrine of election."18

It is one thing to admit suspicions of a "fundamental ambiguity in Barth's thought",[19] it is another matter entirely to imply that he remained blissfully oblivious to the most obvious implication of the most fundamental tenet of his theology. The alternative to the assumption that Barth is an idiot would be the suggestion that there must be some factor in his doctrine of Election that has been overlooked by Berkouwer and others who criticize Barth in this way.

In defence of Karl Barth, J. D. Bettis observes that the accusation of universalism arises as a logical deduction from Barth's

---

17) G. C. Berkouwer, The Triumph of Grace in the Theology of Karl Barth, trans. by Harry R. Boer (Grand Rapids, 1956), p.290

18) ibid., p.116

19) Colin E. Gunton Becoming and Being: The Doctrine of God in Charles Hartshorne and Karl Barth (Oxford, 1978), p.182

rejection of Arminianism and double predestination; the supposition that there is no other choice besides these three logical alternatives.[20] He supports this observation by outlining the criticisms of Barth expressed by Emil Brunner[21] and G. C. Berkouwer.[22] While Brunner argues that Barth's understanding of election denies the effective value of the human decision of faith, Berkouwer, while agreeing with this analysis, dismisses Brunner's alternative as "Arminian"[23] and re-affirms the Reformed conception of a double decree with its "correlation between the faith-unfaith distinction and the saved-rejected distinction".[24] Neither critic recognizes any other logical option besides the three alternatives of a double-decree, universalism and Arminianism.

The dominant element of Berkouwer's critique of Barth, however, rests upon his dismissal of Barth's appeal to the freedom of God in election as a means of avoiding universalism on the basis that Barth himself has excluded the possibility of such an appeal by his definition of God's freedom as the positive freedom to elect rather than as the arbitrary freedom to elect or not to elect which

---

20) J. D. Bettis, 'Is Karl Barth a Universalist?', S.J.T.,20 (1967), 423-436.

21) E. Brunner, The Christian Doctrine of God, Dogmatics vol.I, trans. by Olive Wyon (London,1949),pp.346ff.

22) G. C. Berkouwer, op.cit.

23) ibid.,p.264

24) J. D. Bettis, op.cit.,p.426

25) G. C. Berkouwer, op.cit.,p.295

was enshrined in the Reformed tradition's conception of the hidden God.[25] Berkouwer is not confusing the inner a posteriori necessity of God's grace with an external a priori necessity, rather his objection is that this a posteriori necessity of grace, by limiting God's freedom in terms of the self-consistency of His self-determination, confirms the orientation of Barth's doctrine of Election towards universalism. It may be true that Berkouwer, in his alternative to Barth's understanding of election, falls into the trap of defining God's love in terms of His love ad extra,[26] but this of itself does not weaken the force of Berkouwer's objection to Barth, it merely invalidates Berkouwer's alternative. It is not that universalism is an apparent logical consequence of God's love ad intra but that universalism is an apparent logical consequence of God's free but constant decision to be love ad extra.

The crux of Bettis's defence of Barth against the onslaught of this devastating and compelling criticism, is the contention that Barth's understanding of the free but constant love of God ad extra does not necessarily exclude the possibility of reprobation.[27] For Berkouwer, who reaffirms the double decree of the Reformed tradition, reprobation is not a manifestation of the love of God but of the freedom of God's justice, His freedom to choose which

---

25) G. C. Berkouwer, op.cit.,p.295

26) J. D. Bettis, op.cit.,pp.428f.

27) ibid., pp.429ff.

men He will as objects of His love. For Barth reprobation is itself a manifestation of the love of God, the love by which He allows man's disobedience to be real but ineffective, the love which therefore never banishes the threat of ultimate rejection. Even the goodness of God's love ad extra in the election of Jesus Christ as the elected man is not dependent upon the ultimate salvation of any man, man's sin remains real and the threat of reprobation remains real. According to Bettis, universalism rests upon the mistaken substitution of Jesus Christ for the decretum absolutum of the Reformed tradition whereby the work of Jesus Christ is conceived as the cosmological or ontological reorganization of the universe through the knowledge of which men may live anew:[28]

> "The work of Christ is not some ontological reorganisation or historical reorientation which men are called on to acknowledge."29

However, this defence of Barth, taken in isolation, may not be as persuasive as it at first appears. How can Barth's location of the ontological definition of man in Jesus Christ, the principal content of Christian proclamation, be reconciled to the denial that the work of Jesus Christ represents an ontological reorganization of the universe? Moreover, how can Bettis's contention that men are saved by faith and not by knowledge be reconciled to Barth's predominantly noetic conception of Christian faith? Bettis's defence of Barth crumbles if faith is understood in "purely" noetic terms and if an ontological definition is indistinguishable from

---

28) ibid., p.435f

29) ibid., p.434

an ontic (rather than ontological) reorganization of the universe.[30] Instead of resolving the ambiguity in Barth's doctrine of Election Bettis's article actually compounds that ambiguity by failing to take adequate account of that other element of Barth's teaching: that the being of man is actually defined ontologically in Jesus Christ and that to be a Christian is to be one who acknowledges, recognizes and confesses this ontological definition. Attention has already been drawn to the criticisms of other interpreters of Barth concerning his apparent tendency to affirm precisely what Bettis denies, to consider Jesus Christ as occupying the place previously held by the decretum absolutum and thereby to conceive of the totality of temporal history and the totality of human existence as enclosed and completed either in the event of Jesus Christ or in the primal decision of God.[31] Barth's conception of Jesus Christ as the ontological definition of man's existence, taken in isolation, could be considered as indicative of a monistic conception of God

30) John Macquarrie draws attention to this distinction between that which is ontological and that which is ontic(al) during his discussion of Heidegger's thought:
"It follows that we can make two kinds of statement about anything. A statement may be ontological (ontologisch), that is to say, it will tell us about the being of something and its range of possibilities. Or a statement may be ontical (ontisch), that is to say, it will tell us about some entity in its actual relations with other entities. But every ontical statement carries ontological implications, for to say that A is, in fact, B implies that A has the possibility of being B. This is a statement about the being of A, namely, that its being is such that A can be B."
(John Macquarrie, An Existentialist Theology: A Comparison of Heidegger and Bultmann (London, 1955), p.30).

31) Colin E. Gunton, Becoming and Being, p.182; cf. R. W. Jenson, Alpha and Omega: A Study in the Theology of Karl Barth (New York, 1963), pp.161ff.; & R. H. Roberts, 'Eternity and Time in the Theology of Karl Barth: An essay in Dogmatic and Philosophical Theology' (dissertation, Edinburgh, 1975), pp.180ff.

and his relatedness to men, but it would be wholly unfair to interpret Barth in this one-sided way. To this extent at least Bettis is correct in drawing attention to that other strand which is certainly present in Barth's thinking, though he has not really identified any means by which Barth is able to affirm both elements without self-contradiction.

It is the purpose of the final chapter of this thesis to identify that facet of Barth's doctrine of Election which may preserve him from such an obvious contradiction if not from an element of ambiguity. Barth clearly prohibits too simplistic a relationship between the ontological definition of man as elect in Jesus Christ and the actual election of individual men. The Church is called to proclaim this ontological definition to all men (there is no other authentic definition of real man which it could proclaim) but it does not possess the authority to make any man one of the elect, only God can do this;[32] the Church cannot presume that any man is one of the elect.[33] The Church must proclaim the election of Jesus Christ that has occurred on behalf of the whole world but this does not imply the ultimate salvation of the whole world as a necessary consequence.[34] Such passages must signify that the actuality of the ontic inclusion of any man in the election of Jesus Christ cannot be considered as an a priori necessary consequence

---

32) C.D.II.2.p.320

33) ibid., cf. p.416

34) ibid., p.423

of the actuality of the ontological definition of man as elect in Jesus Christ; that the election of any individual man only becomes an actuality through the continuing but self-consistent activity of God Himself:

> "It is always the concern of God to decide what is the world and the human totality for which the man Jesus Christ is elected, and which is itself elected in and with Him. It is enough for us to know and remember that at all events it is the omnipotent loving-kindness of God which continually decides this. For the fact that Jesus Christ is the reality and revelation of the omnipotent loving-kindness of God towards the whole world and every man is an enduring event which is continually fulfilled in new encounters and transactions, in which God the Father lives and works through the Son, in which the Son of God Himself, and the Holy Spirit of the Father and the Son, lives and works at this or that place or time, in which He rouses and finds faith in this or that man, in which He is recognized and apprehended by this and that man in the promise and in their election——by one here and one there, and therefore by many men!"35

It is the contention of this thesis that the acknowledgement of this continuing free activity of God in the ontic inclusion of individual men in the election of Jesus Christ can only be reconciled logically with an ontological definition of all men as elect by considering Barth's doctrine of Election in the light of his distinctive conception of God's eternity.

b) The noetic and ontic participation of man in Jesus Christ:

In a comparative study of the manner of man's participation in Jesus Christ in the theologies of Karl Barth and Wolfhart Pannenberg, B. C. Hanson concentrates atention on that aspect of

---

35) C.D.II.2.p.422

Barth's teaching which emphasizes the objective actuality of the participation of all men in Christ by virtue of God's primal decision:[36]

> "We died: the totality of all sinful men, those living, those long dead, and those still to be born, Christians who necessarily know and proclaim it, but also Jews and heathen, whether they hear and receive the news or whether they tried and still try to escape it. His death was the death of all: quite independently of their attitude or response to this event..."37

Hanson concurs with Dorothee Sölle that this conception of Christ implies not merely His representation of all other men but His substitution in the place of all other men: Jesus Christ replaces other men by occupying their place and positing them in another sphere.[38] Hanson compares this thorough objectification of man's participation in Christ with the notion of a Platonic form, a perfect "already" which is to be acknowledged and to which nothing significant can be added: the true being of all men has already been decided and actualized in the primal decision of God.[39] But if man's inclusion in Christ has already been actualized how can man's present or future response in faith or unbelief retain any significance?[40] Hanson admits that Sölle's criticism rests upon a

---

36) B. C. Hanson, 'Hope and Participation in Christ: A study in the Theology of Barth and Pannenberg.' (dissertation, Princeton, 1970)

37) C.D.IV.1.p.295; cf. C.D.IV.2.pp.269ff.

38) B. C. Hanson, op.cit., p.98; cf. Dorothee Sölle, Christ the Representative: An Essay in Theology after the 'Death of God', trans. by David Lewis (London, 1967), pp.88ff.

39) B. C. Hanson, op.cit., pp.54, 98ff. & 108

40) ibid., pp.40f.; 52 & 97ff.

one-sided reading of Barth[41] and he acknowledges the existence of that other aspect of Barth's teaching which affirms the history and decisions of men, a teleological direction for man that corresponds to the direction of Christ,[42] yet Hanson, like Berkouwer, appears to maintain that these two poles of Barth's thinking are logically irreconcilable. On this basis Hanson refuses to accept that Barth's emphasis upon man's history and decisions, man's belief or unbelief, can bear any reference to man's ultimate salvation.[43] Despite Barth's protests against an apokatastasis Hanson maintains that the ultimate salvation of all men must be the inevitable consequence of the cosmic and objective inclusiveness of Christ:[44]

> To end up elsewhere than universalism would require a change in the original decision, so that Jesus Christ would not take the wrath of God for all men."45

Such an extreme interpretation of Barth's conception of participation in Christ in terms of the absoluteness of God's primal decision, its self-contained otherness to the history and responsive decisions of men in a manner comparable with a Platonic form, not only confirms the utterly one-sided character of such interpretations, it also indicates, by the nature of its deficiency, the manner by which the tension in Barth's doctrine of Election may

---

41) ibid., p.98

42) ibid., p.107

43) ibid., pp.95f.

44) ibid., p.53

45) ibid., p.151

be resolved without logical contradiction. Barth's fundamental definition of the being of God clearly testifies against such misinterpretations. God's being is not to be defined in terms of a supposed absolute otherness to the world and the history of men. God's being is to be defined where He has defined Himself: in the event of His electing love. God's being is not to be conceived in static terms comparable with the notion of a Platonic form - God exists as dynamic being, as this pure event of electing love, as being in this becoming. Since God's being is identified as this event of His election, since the doctrine of Election is intrinsically part of the doctrine of God, then the doctrine of Election, like the doctrine of God, must necessarily be considered in dynamic and not static terms. God's primal decision to be the electing God in Jesus Christ is itself an event and not a static form.[46] Predestination is a movement from the electing God to the elected man and back again.[47] In this movement God is self-consistent with His self-determination to be this electing God; He is unchangeable but not immovable:[48]

> "...we must remember that praedestinatio, like creatio and reconciliatio like vocatio, iustificatio, sanctificatio and glorificatio, describes a divine activity, and that there is no reason whatever why we should suddenly substitute for this concept a concept of isolated and static being."49

---

46) C.D.II.2.pp.175ff.

47) ibid., p.186

48) ibid., p.185

49) ibid., p.184

Barth refers to a paper read at the Congres international de theologie calvaniste in Geneva in which his brother, Peter Barth (a Calvin scholar) proposed an activist correction of Calvin's Doctrine of Predestination.[50] Karl Barth maintains that this activist interpretation (which was met partly with obvious evasion and partly with open opposition in Geneva) can only be accepted when it is understood Christologically; the only possible basis for an activist understanding of predestination is the event of the person and work of Jesus Christ.[51] Without the provision of this necessary basis Peter Barth's activist conception of predestination remains purely formal and subject to the same threat of determinism and synergism as the traditional static formulation. Inasmuch as the decision of God has been actualized in Jesus Christ it is an active but not an arbitrary decision, a freely living but also a constant decision.[52] But this decision of God is not to be identified as a static, timeless decretum absolutum, it is rather to be identified as the living event of Jesus Christ.

Therefore the primal decision of God, as an event of God's eternity, must not be considered in a way that precludes

---

50) ibid., pp.188ff.; cf. Peter Barth, 'Die biblische Grundlage der Praedestinationslehre bei Calvin' in De l'election eternelle de Dieu (Geneva, 1936) pp.21ff.

51) C.D.II.2.p.187

52) ibid., It is in this sense that Barth refuses to press the dynamic case against the static.

the reality of man's history and decisions - this is not the manner in which Barth understands eternity; God's time does not deny but affirms man's time:

> "Election is not therefore some dead predestination in the past or some still point in a timeless eternity, but a living act that enters time and confronts us face to face in Jesus Christ the living Word of God."53

The primal decision of God is prior, not simply in a chronological sense as that which has always been from the very beginning, but in an ontological sense as the basis of the actualization of man's election in Jesus Christ.[54] God's election is in time as well as before time, it cannot remain beyond time,[55] His primal decision would not be eternal if it ceased as an event at the beginning of time:[56]

> "What meaning can there be in the word "then" when we are speaking of God's eternity? It is true, of course, that in that eternity there can be an "earlier" as there can be a "now" and a "later," for eternity is certainly not the negation but the boundary of time as such. But for this very reason "then" cannot mean only "earlier." When we speak of God's eternity we must recognise and accept what is "earlier" as something also present and future."57

Similarly, the actualization of God's eternal decree in the event of Jesus Christ ontologically comprehends the real event of

---

53) T. F. Torrance, 'Universalism or Election?', S.J.T., 2 (1949), 310-318 (p.315)

54) cf. B. C. Hanson, op.cit., pp.108f.: Hanson appears to interpret "primal" in the chronological rather than the ontological sense.

55) C.D.II.2.p.188

56) ibid., p.184

57) ibid., p.183

man's participation in Jesus Christ and is not simply chronologically prior to it. God's decision includes the history in which it is made visible and becomes operative as the Word of God proclaimed and received; it includes the event of the calling, justification, sanctification and glorification of man; it includes the event of man's faith, hope and love.[58] The single event of God's election genuinely occurs in the history of men because it occurs in Jesus Christ and because it occurs in the eternal determination of God: in the pure simultaneity of God's time the event of man's actual participation in the election of Jesus Christ is authentically comprehended within the event of the primal decision of God that has been actualized in the event of Jesus Christ. The event of man's participation in Jesus Christ is a reality but never an independent reality; the eternal will of God <u>is</u> Jesus Christ, <u>is</u> man's participation in the election of Jesus Christ:

> "The fact that from all eternity God has predestinated, elected and decided has, of course, all the weightiness of the eternal <u>perfectum</u>. It is something isolated and complete. It is the foreordination which precedes all creaturely life. It stands as hard as steel or granite before and above all things and all events. But in so doing, it has and is the life of God. It has really been predetermined from all eternity. It has the character not only of an unparalleled "perfect" but also of an unparalleled "present" and "future." And it remains because it is eternally before time. It is not left behind by time, but as that which is above time (for there is only one eternity with God) it accompanies time, and as that which is beyond time it outlasts it. It not only was but is and will be. It happened: never by any subversion can we weaken the fact that it happened, and happened once and for all. But it not only happened; it does happen and will happen. For it is the principle and essence of all happening everywhere."59

---

58) ibid., p.185

59) ibid., p.183

Inasmuch as God has ontologically defined Himself as the electing God and the elected man in Jesus Christ, and, inasmuch as there can be no other authentic definition of true God or true man beyond that which has been actualized in Jesus Christ, there is an ontological relationship between Jesus Christ and all men. But this ontological definition of man as elect which is the primal decision of God in eternity must not be considered in terms of a static Platonic form, invalidating the genuine history and decisions of men. The election of each individual man, while it is comprehended within the election of Jesus Christ as the primal decision of God, actually enlarges "the (in itself) closed circle of the election of Jesus Christ and His community".[60] Just as God's eternity includes, and does not preclude, man's time, just as God's eternal decision includes, and does not preclude, the actualization of that decision in the event of Jesus Christ, so the ontological definition of man in Jesus Christ includes, and does not preclude, the actual participation of man in that election. The relationship between Jesus Christ and other men is not just ontological, it is also authentically dynamic, though the dynamic is never independent of the ontological. The participation of man in the election of Jesus Christ is an event of God's Triunity: it occurs in the primal decision of the Father, it occurs in the actualization of that decision in the Son, and it occurs in the realization of that decision in the Holy Spirit. In the Holy Spirit this ontological definition is present for man as the living event of God's Word in Jesus

---

60) C.D.II.2.p.417

Christ.[61] The work of the Holy Spirit is no more of an addendum to the completed work of the Son than the work of the Son is an addendum to the eternal decision of the Father, rather the Holy Spirit makes this completed work subjectively known and real (because objectively known and real) in the life of the individual.[62] The Holy Spirit is God Himself in His freedom to correspond to His primal decision in relationship to individual men:

> "The Spirit constitutes the subjective condition which is necessary for the apprehension and recognition of the objective self-manifestation of God in Christ; for the Spirit is God knowing himself, and to receive the Spirit is to participate in that knowledge."63

Only when the doctrine of Election is understood in dynamic and not static terms, only when the primal decision of God is understood as an event of His eternity which includes human history and not as a timeless abstraction, only when election is understood as a Trinitarian event and not as a unitarian or binitarian event that excludes its subjective realization in the Holy Spirit and thereby invalidates the authentic futurity of God's eternity, only then can universalism be avoided without logical contradiction. Because the participation of individual men in the election of Jesus Christ is an event of the Holy Spirit it is an event of God's freedom, an event in which He remains the free Lord in respect

---

61) C.D.IV.1.p.158

62) cf. John Thompson, Christ in Perspective: Christological Perspectives in the Theology of Karl Barth (Edinburgh, 1978), p.43

63) George Hendry, The Holy Spirit in Christian Theology (London, 1957), p.34; cf. p.25

of the actual realization of His ontological definition of man in the existence of individual men. God is constant: He is self-consistent with His self-determination in Jesus Christ, but His primal decision is not His prison because it is not a decision of the infinite past which binds Him in the present and the future but a decision of eternity in which past, present and future, in their distinction, are simultaneously comprehended and included. For this reason a man may be assured of his participation in the election of Jesus Christ since it rests upon an ontological definition that has been objectively actualized in the Son, but he may not arrogantly presume upon this inclusion since its actual subjective realization remains a free event of the Holy Spirit:[64]

> "The fundamental significance of the character of predestination as act ought to be clear without further discussion. If it is unchanged and unchangeably the history, encounter and decision between God and man, there is in time an electing by God and an election of man, as there is also a rejecting by God and a rejection of man, but not in the sense that God Himself is bound and imprisoned by it, not as though God's decree, the first step which He took, committed Him to take a corresponding second step, and the second a third. If it is true that the predestinating God not only is free but remains free, that He does not cease to make use of His freedom but continues to decide, then in the course of God's eternal deciding we have constantly to reckon with new decisions in time. As the Bible itself presents the matter, there is no election which cannot be followed by rejection, no rejection which cannot be followed by election. God continues always the Lord of all His works and ways. He is consistent with Himself. He is also consistent with the prearranged order of election and rejection. But He is always the living God."65

---

64) C.D.II.2.p.416

65) C.D.II.2.pp.186f.

On the basis of this conception of election as a free divine activity Barth can continue to speak in terms of the elect and other men[66] he can refer to the work of the Holy Spirit in the "calling" of the elect as "the objective difference" (die objective Unterscheidung)[67] which "corresponds objectively" (entspricht objektiv)[68] to the distinction which is peculiar to the elect. Barth does not mean that men become the elect because of their calling. Rather the calling of men "discloses and confirms the fact that they already are the elect";[69] the work of the Holy Spirit in the calling of men is that by which "their election is accomplished in their life" (zur Vollstreckung ihrer Erwählung in ihrem Leben).[70] Neither does Barth mean that those men who are uncalled are necessarily not among the elect. The calling of the elect and the work of the Holy Spirit is the "actualisation" (Verwirklichung) and the "objectively necessary expression of their election" (objectiv notwendige Entsprechung ihrer Erwählung):[71] "How could those whom God has chosen in His Son lack the gift of His Holy Spirit"?[72] But there is no antithetical ontological definition of man

---

66) C.D.II.2.p.345; my emphasis

67) ibid.; cf. Karl Barth, Die Kirchliche Dogmatik, II: Die Lehre von Gott, 2 (Zurich, 1942) p.380

68) ibid.

69) C.D.II.2.p.341

70) ibid., p.348; cf., Karl Barth, Die Kirchliche Dogmatik, II.2, p.383

71) ibid.

72) C.D.II.2.p.345

to which the godlessness of the uncalled can correspond,[73] they, as much as those who are called, are defined ontologically in Jesus Christ. They do not possess the Holy Spirit but their godlessness is an ontologically impossible possibility, a futile attempt to live under the rejection which God has elected for Himself in Jesus Christ.[74] The uncalled man who lives a godless life may be described as "apparently rejected"[75] but, in the light of his solidarity with the elect in the free grace of God, no more and certainly no less can be asserted about him. The determination of this godless man is that of God's non-willing; he has no autonomous existence apart from God's positive election in Jesus Christ and only continues to exist because God is patient.[76]

Conversely, the man who is called through the work of the Holy Spirit is distinguished from other men by the twofold possibility of proclamation and faith.[77] The elect are those who, in their calling, are assured in faith of their participation in the election of Jesus Christ, but they cannot possess this faith for themselves without proclaiming it to other men; that which they recognize and other men fail to recognize is the election of God in Jesus Christ and therefore that ontological definition of man

---

73) ibid., p.349

74) ibid.

75) ibid., p.351

76) C.D.II.2.pp.449ff.

77) C.D.II.2.p.345

which must be heard and proclaimed both by themselves and by other men. In their calling and in the gift of the Holy Spirit, the elect recognize their solidarity with the godless: in Jesus Christ they recognize the rejection that is real for them and for other men apart from Him, in Jesus Christ they recognize the election that is true for them and for other men in Him. Therefore the expectation of the elect for the godless must be that this distinction will become theirs also, that their election also will be fulfilled in their calling and the gift of the Holy Spirit.[78] The work of the Holy Spirit in the calling which is the fulfilment of a man's election is to open that life to the definite goal and content which is God's determination of the elect: that he is elect in and with Jesus Christ, that he is elect in and with the community of Jesus Christ, that he is elect to participation in the ministry of that community as a witness to the election of Jesus Christ.[79]

This conception of the work of the Holy Spirit in terms of the Christian's actual participation in the election of Jesus Christ is confirmed in the course of Barth's treatment of the doctrine of Reconciliation. Reconciliation is an act of God, not a state but an event.[80] It is an event that is objectively realized, actualized and accomplished in Jesus Christ as the Word of God, the Word in which God makes known His covenant will to be God

---

78) ibid., pp.349f.

79) C.D.II.2.p.410

80) C.D.IV.1.p.6

with us in the act of reconciliation,[81] but it is subjectively apprehended, accepted and appropriated in the work of the Holy Spirit.[82] The work of the Holy Spirit is that which makes a man a Christian and thereby distinguishes him from the non-Christian.[83] Objectively the ontological definition of man which is God's primal decision has been pronounced over all men in Jesus Christ and, to that extent, all men are ontologically defined as those reconciled in Him. But subjectively the presence and activity of the Holy Spirit has not touched and seized all men in such a way that they can perceive, accept and receive that objective reconciliation.[84] God gives His Spirit to whom He will and, in this sense, it is only Christians who are "converted to Him",[85] it is only in the work of the Holy Spirit that reconciliation is an event not only as _de iure_ but also as _de facto_:[86]

> "The Holy Spirit is the one eternal God in His particular power and will so to be present to the creature in His being and activity, so to give Himself to it, that it can recognise and embrace and experience Himself and His work and therefore the actuality and truth of its own situation, that its eyes and ears and senses and reason and heart are open to Him and willing and ready for Him."87

---

81) ibid., pp.34ff.

82) ibid.,p.147

83) ibid., p.93; cf. p.148

84) ibid., p.148

85) ibid.

86) _C.D._IV.2.p.511; cf. _C.D._I.1.pp.448ff. where Barth refers to the Holy Spirit as "the subjective side in the event of revelation".

87) _C.D._IV.1.p.148

The Holy Spirit is the awakening power in which man is summoned to believe in the justification that has been actualized in Jesus Christ, to acknowledge, to recognize and to confess Him.[88] No man is himself capable of this faith, nor can the Spirit of God in whom man is awakened for this faith ever be possessed or controlled by man.[89] The knowledge of justification is itself an event of the free grace of God;[90] man only has the freedom for this knowledge when Jesus Christ makes him free through the awakening power of the Holy Spirit:[91]

> "The Holy Spirit is the power in which Jesus Christ the Son of God makes a man free, makes him genuinely free for this choice and therefore for faith."92

The atonement, the single event of man's justification in Jesus Christ, therefore has both an objective and a subjective aspect that must not be confused or separated.[93] The work of the Holy Spirit is to awaken man to the subjective realization of the objective realization of this atonement in Jesus Christ; the Holy Spirit is "God in this His self-attestation".[94] As a human act, faith has a cognitive rather than a creative character, faith is not self-justification but is the subjective confirmation of a change that

---

88) C.D.IV.1.p.740

89) ibid.,p.646

90) ibid.,p.538

91) ibid.,p.745

92) ibid.,p.748

93) ibid.,p.643

94) ibid.,p.646

has already occured objectively in Jesus Christ.[95] But since this confirmation actually occurs in the power of the Holy Spirit, since faith is in Jesus Christ and effected by Him, the event of faith is not only a cognitive human act but also a creative event, the positing of a new being, a new creation, a new birth, a total change in man's whole situation.[96]

Similarly, the Holy Spirit is the quickening power in which man is given the freedom to correspond to the sanctification that has been actualized in Jesus Christ, to the love of God that overcomes his sinfulness.[97] Man himself is not capable of this, he cannot sanctify himself,[98] he can only become free for it through the work of the Holy Spirit, but thus he becomes genuinely free for it. The event of man's sanctification includes both the objective event of God's love actualized in Jesus Christ, His holiness and exaltation, and the subjective realization of this event through the enlightening and quickening power of the Holy Spirit by which the Christian is awakened to obedience, to holiness, to love. To be so enlightened and to live in this knowledge is actually to live in communion with Jesus Christ,[99] to participate in the sanctification of Jesus Christ that is already the objective sanctification of

---

95) ibid., p.751; cf. pp.615ff.

96) ibid.,pp.752f.; cf. p.769

97) C.D.IV.2.p.727ff.

98) ibid., p.777; cf. p.517

99) ibid., p.727

man in Him.[100] Thus the objective truth of the sanctification of man actualized in Jesus Christ "includes our own reality" and "presses in upon us, from its objectivity to our subjectivity, in order that there should be in us a correspondence";[101] the being of God Himself, His primal decision to be the electing God in Jesus Christ, is repeated, represented and expressed in the being and work of His Holy Spirit in human history.[102] Certainly the Christian's love for his neighbour as a witness to and a proclamation of the love of God is a free human act,[103] the Holy Spirit does not usurp man's proper activity but liberates him for it.[104] But, in the Holy Spirit, Jesus Christ does not only demand but also calls and transposes conversion and discipleship.[105] As the presence and action of Jesus Christ Himself, the power of His resurrection and His revelation, the Holy Spirit effects a new creation and a new birth.[106] The creative love of God creates within men a correspondingly free act of genuine love and genuine obedience.[107] The work of the Holy Spirit in the sanctification of man is certainly to be described

---

100) ibid., pp.516f.; cf. p.530 & pp.581ff.

101) ibid., p.303

102) ibid., p.341

103) cf. pp.811ff.

104) ibid., p.785

105) ibid., p.729

106) ibid., pp.319ff.; cf.p.778

107) ibid., p.800

as the giving and receiving of a direction but this new direction radically alters man's actual existence,[108] it does not just consist of a new possibility but the new actuality in which man is genuinely liberated from the bondage of his sinful being.[109] The Holy Spirit is the power by which God makes possible and actual the existence of a people who participate in the sanctification of Jesus Christ. Despite the provisionality of the Christian's existence as _simul iustus, simul peccator_ there is a genuine "praise of works" both in the sense that God praises the works of those sanctified by His Spirit and in His Son, and in the sense that these good works (which themselves do not have the power to justify men before God) are acts of praise to God:[110]

> "In this sense, and on all these presuppositions, we must say of man's sanctification that it already takes place here and now in works which are really good, i.e., which are praised by God and praise Him."[111]

Finally, the Holy Spirit is the enlightening power of man's vocation, the power of the creative call of Jesus Christ by which man is awakened to a knowledge of the truth as one who hopes

---

108) ibid., pp.522f.

109) ibid., pp.530f.

110) ibid., pp.584ff.

111) ibid., p.596; such passages surely refute Hugo Meynell's over-statement that "for Barth, justification is an alteration so heavenly that it makes no earthly difference." (Hugo Meynell, _Grace versus Nature: studies in Karl Barth's Church Dogmatics_ (London and Melbourne, 1965), p.261)

in Jesus Christ and by which man is thrust into the service of the prophetic work of Jesus Christ.[112] The vocation of man is therefore the event of the Christian's actual participation in the specific prophetic action of Jesus Christ,[113] the event in which man is "set and instituted in actual fellowship with Jesus Christ, namely, in the service of His prophecy".[114] The vocation of man is the specific prophetic action of Jesus Christ in His own history but while this action is complete in itself it is still moving towards its fulfilment. The event of vocation is the action of Jesus Christ as the "Contemporary of all men", as the Prophet who is among men in His Word and His Spirit.[115] Certainly the Spirit by whose action this vocation is an event in man's own history must not be conceived as independent of Jesus Christ; He is the Spirit of the prophetic Word of Jesus Christ, the immediate parousia presence of Jesus Christ Himself.[116] Certainly the vocation of man, like his justification and sanctification, does not acquire significance only when it occurs in man's own history; it has its true basis in the election of man in Jesus Christ.[117] But as an event of man's own history the goal of vocation is that man should become a Christian: that he should live as one who hopes in Jesus Christ,[118]

---

112) *C.D.*IV.3.p.902; cf. p.481

113) ibid., p.903

114) ibid., p.482

115) ibid., p.497; cf. pp.504 & 903

116) ibid., pp.502ff.; cf. pp.292ff.

117) ibid., pp.483ff.

118) ibid., pp.902ff.

that he should live as a witness of Jesus Christ, as a proclaimer of the reconciliation accomplished in Him,[119] that Jesus Christ should live in him by the Holy Spirit.[120] This life of hope which is at issue in man's vocation cannot derive from man himself, it can only derive from God: "What derives and proceeds from man can never be Christian faith, nor Christian love, nor Christian hope."[121] It is the Holy Spirit who awakens man to live in hope and therefore He does so in the manner that establishes man as a free subject, He genuinely awakens man to freedom, "He wills his hope as his own spontaneous act".[122] But He is the Holy Spirit and thus remains the free Lord of this action; He never becomes the spirit of man but remains the Spirit of God: "...He does not fall into the power of the Christian, nor does He become superfluous when He makes him a free man and sets him on his own feet."[123] The event of vocation as it actually occurs in the power of the Holy Spirit is correctly understood in terms of illumination but as such it is a seeing of which man was incapable previous to this event, an event of new creation:

---

119) ibid., pp.554ff.

120) ibid., p.594

121) ibid., p.939

122) ibid., p.942

123) ibid.

> "It is certainly illumination, and therefore the event of divine revelation and knowledge. Yet it is not restricted to a special sphere of the noetic which the being of man can confront neutrally and without being really affected. Rather it is an event of revelation and knowledge by which the being of man is not only affected but seized and refashioned so that it becomes his new being."124

The event of man's vocation therefore implies and creates not merely a subjective but an objective distinction and alteration of the being of the man who is called.[125]

In the light of the foregoing summary of his conception of the work of the Holy Spirit it is surely clear that Barth is seriously misrepresented by interpretations which imply that he has a "purely noetic" understanding of this work in the event of election and reconciliation.[126] It is beyond question that Barth represents this event in terms of man's knowing, a realization in the power of the Holy Spirit of an ontological and objective reality, but it is crucial to discern the precise nature and significance of this "knowing". The ontological basis of man's election is the election of Jesus Christ, an election that has happened _to_ man rather than _in_ man's history;[127] all men are ontologically elect in Jesus Christ though this event has not yet been realized in the power of the Holy Spirit in the history of all men. But the objective event of

---

124) ibid., p.519

125) ibid., pp.650f.

126) Philip J. Rosato, S. J., _The Spirit as Lord: The Pneumatology of Karl Barth_ (Edinburgh, 1981) p.161; cf. pp.299ff. of this thesis.

127) _C.D._II.2.p.321

reconciliation that has occurred ἐφ' ἅπαξ in Jesus Christ is an event of His history and therefore an eternal event, it does not merely occur in the past, it is not left behind by the present and the future.[128] Throughout Barth's exposition of the doctrine of Reconciliation it is evident that the distinction between the Christian and the non-Christian consists in the knowledge and obedience of the former with regard to this ontological status of man in Jesus Christ.[129] But, as in the language of Scripture so in the language of Barth's Dogmatics, knowledge does not mean "the acquisition of neutral information" nor merely a subjective attitude of acceptance or reflection but the process in which the object of knowledge comes to man and transforms man as the acting subject so that the event of the knowledge of salvation is itself an event of salvation:[130]

> "According to the speech and thought-forms of the Bible, concepts such as light, illumination, revelation and knowledge do not have, either alone or in their interrelationships, the more narrowly intellectual or noetic significance which here as elsewhere we usually give them. ...
> In making Himself known, God acts on the whole man. Hence the knowledge of God given to man through his illumination is no mere apprehension and understanding of God's being and action, nor as such a kind of intuitive contemplation. It is the claiming not only of his thinking but also of his willing and work, of the whole man, for God. ...
> Illumination and therefore vocation is the total alteration of the one whom it befalls."131

---

128) C.D.IV.3.p.223

129) C.D.IV.1.pp.92ff.

130) C.D.IV.3.pp.183ff. & 218ff.

131) C.D.IV.3.p.510

The calling of man, as an event of the Holy Spirit, is more than an enlightenment to knowledge, it actually creates a "distinction and alteration" of man's being,[132] it is a knowledge that is both noetic and ontic in character,[133] it is a knowledge in which the event of reconciliation actually occurs:[134]

> "Baptism with the Spirit is effective, causative, even creative action on man and in man. It is, indeed, divinely effective, divinely causative, divinely creative. Here, if anywhere, one might speak of a sacramental happening in the current sense of the term. It cleanses, renews and changes man truly and totally. Whatever may be his attitude to it, whatever he himself may make of it, it is (we recall the New Testament descriptions) his being clothed upon with a new garment which is Jesus Christ Himself, his endowment with a new heart controlled by Jesus Christ, his new generation and birth in brotherhood with Jesus Christ, his saving death in the presence of the death which Jesus Christ suffered for him. All this is to be taken realistically, not just significantly and figuratively. As this divine change takes place in his life, as he is baptised with the Holy Ghost, he is to be claimed in all seriousness for this change which has come upon him. In the light of it, he is in truth a man who has been changed by God's act on him and in him.135

Hans Küng, commenting upon Barth's conception of Christian faith, recognizes the cognitive character of this faith but recognizes also that this faith involves the creation of a new man:

> "The just man, despite the _simul peccator,_ is ontologically different from the sinner. This clear teaching of Barth must not be overlooked."136

---

132) _C.D_.IV.3.pp.650ff.

133) _C.D_.IV.1.p.538

134) _C.D_.IV.3.p.218

135) _C.D_.IV.4.p.34

136) Hans Küng, _Justification: The Doctrine of Karl Barth and a Catholic Reflection,_ trans. by T. Collins, E. E. Tolk and D. Grandskou (London, 1966), p.82 (commenting upon _C.D_.IV.1.pp.749ff.); cf. p.67.

Similarly, in his exposition of the text of the Church Dogmatics, Philip Rosato recognizes that, for Barth, the Holy Spirit is the "divine Noetic which has all the force of a divine Ontic".[137] For the Spirit to cause what is ontic in Jesus Christ to become noetic in man involves the actualizing in man of "what was already an actuality both in the historical existence and eternal election of Jesus Christ".[138] He "makes real in man what was and still is real in Jesus Christ".[139] As such He is the subjective reality of the objective revelation in Jesus Christ;[140] the means by which that which is already extra nos is made effective in nobis.[141] Rosato affirms that this implies an alteration of man's being,[142] an "ontic renewing" in the experience of Christians,[143] whereby the ontological connection between the being of Jesus Christ and that of all men is made "an existential reality".[144]

---

137) Philip J. Rosato, S. J., op.cit., p.126

138) ibid., p.67

139) ibid., p.69

140) ibid., p.70

141) ibid., p.86

142) ibid., p.112

143) ibid., p.123

144) ibid., p.126

In the light of such statements it is all the more surprising that Rosato should later conclude that within Barth's theology the Spirit "is purposely conceptualized as possessing from eternity a purely noetic function".[145] This strange assertion can only be indicative of yet another attempt to resolve in a one-sided manner the inherent tension of Barth's theology. The indications of such a resolution are already observable in Rosato's earlier exposition. For example, having referred to the Holy Spirit as achieving "the creation of a new being", albeit a being "already assured ontically by the eternal Son of God", Rosato summarizes this creative rôle of the Spirit as making "noetic the ontic freedom man always enjoys in Jesus Christ" and, in a corresponding footnote suggests that the "Spirit's role is more corroborative than creative in Barth's system".[146] More fundamentally, throughout his thesis Rosato tends to confuse the terms 'ontic' and 'ontological'.[147] It is the contention of this present thesis that Barth considers that the ontological definition of man, itself ontically actual in Jesus Christ, only becomes ontically actual in the being of man through the action of the Holy Spirit. Yet in some passages Rosato seems to imply that, for Barth, this ontological definition of man's being which becomes ontically actual in Jesus Christ Himself (through the Holy Spirit's "pivotal task of actualizing the Son's eternal decision to become man"[148]) includes the being of all

---

145) ibid., p.161

146) ibid., pp.74f. and footnote 17, p.198

147) see p.273 of this thesis

148) Philip J. Rosato S.J., op.cit., pp.82f.

men not only ontologically but also ontically. Perhaps the very fact that Rosato can interpret Barth in this way is symptomatic of Barth's infuriating reticence in this matter.

In the course of his paraphrase of Barth's Dogmatics Eberhard Jüngel (in a manner that is perhaps characteristically Lutheran) proposes the suggestion that, since the election of Jesus Christ is a concrete event of the Spirit and since the event of faith is itself a work of the Holy Spirit, faith should be "spoken of along with the election of Jesus Christ". Jüngel does not intend to reintroduce the Lutheran concept of the fides praevisa which Barth rejects, rather he is seeking to understand God's being in the act of the Spirit as the One who makes faith possible, as a 'being-in-act' which is already present in the election of Jesus Christ, thus precluding a Pelagian conception of faith.[149] Jüngel elaborates (and to some extent clarifies) this proposition in a consideration of the Reformation doctrine of justification which occurs in an article written as a response to Wolfhart Pannenberg on the subject of natural theology:

> "If man becomes defined theologically through the event of iustificatio sola fide then it is in the sense that the defining event itself belongs to the thing defined. But in that case the theologically defined nature of man would be to be justified by God and to submit to this justification.

---

149) E. Jüngel, The Doctrine of the Trinity: God's Being is in Becoming, trans. by Horton Harris, Monograph Supplements to the Scottish Journal of Theology, eds. T. F. Torrance and J. K. S. Reid (Edinburgh and London, 1976), pp.82f.

> That is to say: ontologically man already derives from his justification by God which has happened in Christ and ontically he both proceeds from it and also moves towards it to the extent that he believes. In faith man _is in his existence_ (_existiert_) what he already _is_ (_ist_) in Christ. But what he _is_ already in Christ, namely one acknowledged by God despite his actual sinful existence, implies the feasibility of the _existence_ and the summons to the _existence_ which corresponds to this being, so that the _demand_ of the existential consummation of this being belongs to the full theological definition of man's being. Man is defined theologically precisely through justification _by faith alone_."150

Despite the complexities of the above passages (both in German and in English) it is clear that Jüngel is venturing three propositions of pertinence to the character of election as event: (1) that in the event of faith the ontological definition of man in Jesus Christ is ontically realized in man's existence. (2) that by implication the event of faith as an event in the power of the Holy Spirit is an ontic and not merely a noetic occurrence. (3) that this ontic event in man's existence is itself inherent in the ontological definition of man's being in Jesus Christ and not in any way independent of it.[151]

The character of this ontic event of faith is enhanced by Jüngel's use of the term _Geistesgegenwart_ with reference to

---

150) E. Jüngel, 'Das Dilemma der natürlichen Theologie und die Wahrheit ihres Problems: Überlegungen für ein Gespräch mit Wolfhart Pannenberg' in _Denken im Schatten des Nihilsmus: Festschrift für Wilhelm Weischedel zum 70 Geburtstag_; ed. A. Schwan (Darmstadt, 1975), pp.419-440 (p.429) my translation.

151 cf. Philip J. Rosato, S. J., op.cit., pp.124 & 126

Christian proclamation.[152] Christian proclamation is language which claims to be the presence of God - Geistesgegenwart occurs when this claimed presence is an actuality.[153] It is not Jüngel's intention simply to spiritualize this somewhat ambiguous German construct,[154] rather he seems to refer to an awareness of an eschatological now through the presence of God's Spirit which itself involves an awareness of an existential now through a resultant presence of mind. The Word of Christian proclamation, because it is an event in the power of the Holy Spirit, creates within man a sensitivity to the future and thus to eternity, as such it not only imparts to man the capacity of surpassing his being in the here and now, it actually enhances and intensifies man's being in this present. Jüngel therefore considers that the continuity of the human self in past, present and future is grounded in this Word which addresses man.[155]

---

152) cf. Jüngel's conception of a "speech-event" (Sprachereignis) - Eberhard Jüngel, Gott als Geheimnis der Welt: Zur Begründung der Theologie des Gekreuzigten im Streit zwischen Theismus und Atheismus (Tübingen, 1978), pp.12ff.

153) Eberhard Jüngel, Geistesgegenwart: Predigten I/II (München, 1979), p.3

154) The German word Geist can mean the Spirit of God but can also refer to the human spirit or the human mind - similarly, the German word Gegenwart can mean present in the locational sense (i.e., presence; being here) and can also mean present in the temporal sense (i.e., present rather than past or future; being now).

155) Eberhard Jüngel, Gott als Geheimnis der Welt, pp.234ff.; cf. Geistesgegenwart, pp.3f.

In this way Jüngel makes explicit what is surely implicit in Barth's Dogmatics: that the event of Christian faith which is the event of Christian proclamation is an authentically ontic event because it is an authentically noetic event, a genuine subjective realization of the objective and ontological event of election and reconciliation actualized in Jesus Christ, a genuine participation in His eternal life and therefore a genuine anticipation of an eschatological future. However, any distinction between Jüngel and Barth at this point is indicative not only of the originality and complexity of Jüngel's own theological thought but also of an apparent reticence in Barth concerning the doctrine of the Holy Spirit. This observable hesitation could easily be overstated. It is hardly fair to suggest that Barth failed to commence volume five of the Church Dogmatics for anything other than chronological reasons,[156] nor would it be fair to ignore the explicit and thorough emphasis upon the work of the Holy Spirit in all three completed parts of volume four. However, the tendencies to criticize Barth in this manner cannot be ignored. With regard to Barth's discussions of the Holy Spirit in relation to the Father and the Son Jenson states:

---

156) R. W. Jenson, God after God: the God of the Past and the God of the Future, seen in the work of Karl Barth (Indianapolis and New York, 1969). pp.173f.

> "Without the Father there would be no Son or Spirit—but it is not said that without the Spirit the Father and the Son would not occur. In every nuance of his formulations, Barth displays the doctrine that the Father is "the fount of the Trinity." But that the Trinity also has a goal in the Spirit remains a mere occasional assertion. This gathering to the past, to the Beginning in which all has already been decided, pervades all Barth's thinking."157

Colin E. Gunton concurs with Jenson's criticism of Barth at this crucial point and acknowledges the debilitating effect of this partial failure for a "satisfactory expression of the eschatological dimension of Christian theology".[158] However, Gunton refuses to view this as more than a "partial failure",[159] an ambiguity rather than a logical contradiction, albeit an ambiguity at the most fundamental and crucial point of Barth's Trinitarian understanding.[160] This caution of Barth with regard to the doctrine of the Holy Spirit is the valid root of those criticisms which expose Barth's tendency, despite his own characteristic understanding of eternity, to locate the being and activity of God in the completed past. This same reticence is also the root of the persistent charges of incipient universalism. Despite Barth's expressed concern for the actuality

---

157) ibid., p.173. Note however that Jenson's proposed alternative tends towards the inverse of Barth's supposed deficiency instead of an intended Trinitarian corrective.

158) Colin E. Gunton, Becoming and Being, pp.163 & 182; for similar criticisms of Barth with reference to the doctrine of the Holy Spirit cf. Jürgen Moltmann, Theology of Hope: On the Ground and the Implications of a Christian Eschatology trans. by James W. Leitch (London,1967), pp.37ff. & R. D. Williams, 'Barth on the Triune God' in Karl Barth: Studies of his Theological Method, ed. S. W. Sykes (Oxford, 1979), pp.147-193 (pp.169ff.)

159) op. cit., p.218

160) ibid., pp.182 & 218

of the event of election this event still carries with it the lingering aroma of an eternity of God which, while it is unambiguously inclusive of its actualization in Jesus Christ and identified within it, is not so unambiguously inclusive of its realization in the power of the Holy Spirit nor identified within it. Perhaps even "ambiguity" is too strong an accusation and "observable reticence" should be preferred; the relationship between Barth's conception of eternity and his doctrine of Election and the ensuing character of election as event explicitly safeguard Barth from such charges. Moreover, the very fact that Philip Rosato can write of Barth's pneumatology, can describe Barth as a pneumatocentric theologian, and can recognize the person and work of the Holy Spirit as the "dominant theme" of Barth's exposition of the doctrine of Reconciliation (despite the merits or demerits of Rosato's thesis), militates against any exaggeration of this ambiguity or of Barth's so-called 'Christomonism'.[161]

Barth's hesitation concerning the doctrine of the Holy Spirit should perhaps be understood in the light of the subjectivism of 19th century Liberalism and Pietism as the theological inheritance of Barth against which he reacted.[162] Barth's reticence at this

---

161) Philip J. Rosato, S.J., op.cit., p.109

162) Not only this reaction of Barth to the Liberalism of the 19th century but also his suspicion of the theological stance of many of his contemporaries is noted by Rosato as a contributory cause of Barth's apparent limitation of the Spirit's rôle (Philip J. Rosato, S.J. op.cit., pp.160f & 185ff.)

point can be interpreted as a refusal to allow any supposed doctrine of the Spirit to open again the flood-gates of subjectivism which pervaded the theology of the 19th century. Such a motive fully justifies Barth's meticulous concern to relate the work of the Holy Spirit inextricably to the work of Jesus Christ. The event of man's justification, sanctification and vocation is itself an event of the living Jesus Christ acting immediately and directly by the power of the Holy Spirit, a second form of His immediate parousia presence, the subjective aspect of the single event of revelation and reconciliation in Him:

> "It is crucial that the Holy Spirit should not in any sense be understood as a relatively or absolutely independent and independently operative force intervening between Jesus Christ and the man who is called by Him, but as His Spirit, as the power of His presence, work and Word, as the shining of the life of which He is the fulness."163

Towards the end of his life Barth elaborated this same caution in a postscript to a selection of Schleiermacher's writings.[164] After an irenical review of his own lifelong relationship to Schleiermacher's thought Barth ponders the question of whether a theology of the Holy Spirit might have been "the legitimate concern of Schleiermacher's theological activity, the concern of which he was hardly conscious yet which was effectively dominating him."[165] Although Barth finally appears to dismiss this favourable conjecture (which, for the sake of consistency, would have to

---

163) C.D.IV.3.p.503

164) Karl Barth, 'Nachwort' in Schleiermacher - Auswahl mit einem Nachwort von Karl Barth, ed. Heinz Bolli (München und Hamburg, 1968), pp.290-312

165) ibid., p.311, my translation

be extended beyond Schleiermacher to every area of subjectivism in the history of Theology) he acknowledges the Christological domination of his own Church Dogmatics and admits to dreaming of the development of a theology dominated by and determined by the 3rd Article of the Creed, a theology of the Holy Spirit.[166] Yet here again Barth urges caution lest such a development should, in reality, take man rather than the Holy Spirit as its starting point, exchange Pneumatology for Anthropology and evaporate into a mere continuation of Schleiermacher's own direction.[167]

While acknowledging the justification for Barth's caution in the face of subjectivizing tendencies in Theology, and, while refusing to exaggerate any possible ambiguity implied by his reticence into a logical contradiction, the debilitating effect of this hesitation must not be ignored. Certainly the Holy Spirit must never be considered independently of Jesus Christ, He is the Spirit of the Word, but neither must His person and work be subsumed under the person and work of Jesus Christ. As Philip Rosato also observes, the work of the Spirit tends to be conceived by Barth in terms of the "ongoing action of the risen Christ";[168] there is a "dangerous confusion of the second and third articles of the creed":[169]

---

166) ibid., pp.310ff.

167) ibid., p.312

168) Philip J Rosato, S.J., op.cit., p.160

169) ibid., p.168

> "....the person and activity of Jesus Christ so dominates Barth's dogmatics that pneumatology virtually becomes a subordinate function of christology."170

Is it really sufficient to equate the person and work of the Spirit with Christ's own "spiritual being and work"?[171] The deepest insights of Barth's conception of the relationship between time and eternity and of his Christ-centred and dynamic understanding of election are jeopardized by this hesitation concerning the Holy Spirit. The most disappointing aspect of this reticence is that it is entirely unnecessary, a misleading intrusion in an otherwise thoroughly Trinitarian theology.

---

170) ibid., p.160

171) C.D.IV.1.p.147

Conclusion: Towards a theology 'after' Barth

Rather than summarizing again the preceding analysis it is fitting to conclude this thesis by raising the general question of the appropriate direction for theology 'after' Barth and the specific question of the manner of corrective which may be brought to Barth's reticence concerning the Holy Spirit. It would be hard not to conclude that this reticence underlies and weakens the entire scheme of thought that has been the theme of this analysis. Not only does it obviously undermine Barth's highly original treatment of the doctrine of Election, it also seriously affects his account of the relationship between the actuality and the provisionality both of the event of God's revelation and of the manner of Christian existence. Any hesitation concerning the Holy Spirit can only debilitate an understanding of the manner in which the revelation of God and the reconciliation of men are already actual and the manner in which they remain provisional.

It would therefore be hardly surprising if theology 'after' Barth either sought to 'improvise' a doctrine of the Spirit and superimpose it upon Barth's thought or, abandoning Barth's effort, returned to the predominant manner in which the work of theology was attempted in the 19th century, prior to Barth's resounding protest. In may ways Philip Rosato's thesis represents both tendencies. While the first two parts of his thesis consist of meticulous exposition and analysis of Barth's pneumatology, leading Rosato to conclusions regarding Barth's reticence similar to those referred to at the conclusion of the last chapter.[1] Rosato follows this interpretation in the final part of his thesis with his own suggested "improvisations on Barth's Spirit Theology".[2]

Rosato's first suggested "improvisation" of Barth's Spirit Theology is to conceive the Spirit not only as Spiritus Redemptor but also explicitly as Spiritus Creator as the basis for introducing an interaction of God's Spirit and man's nature that is "missing in Barth's theology".[3] This would lead to a view of the Spirit in which man's role in salvation would not be pre-empted; in which respect could be given to Man's "free intellectual power as the means which the Holy Spirit wisely uses to create the full manifestation of divine truth which is most intense in Jesus Christ, while it still seeks for ontic reinforcement until Christ returns".[4] Similar criticisms of Barth's 'totalitarianism of the sovereignty of grace' are made previously by George Hendry who also calls for a theological view of man other than that of Barth's Christological anthropology, a theological view of man that springs from an understanding of the Spirit's work in creation.[5] Rosato

---

1) pp.303ff. of this thesis

2) Philip J. Rosato, S.J., The Spirit as Lord: The Pneumatology of Karl Barth (Edinburgh, 1981), pp.129ff

3) ibid., p.139, cf. pp.131ff.

4) ibid., p.152

5) George S. Hendry, The Holy Spirit in Christian Theology (London, 1957), pp.109ff.; cf. also Hendry's discussion of Barth's defence of the filioque clause (ibid., pp.42ff.)

may be right in the belief that such an emphasis upon the Spiritus Creator could have ended Barth's isolation from such thinkers as Karl Rahner and Paul Tillich.[6] He is certainly right in the belief that Barth would have considered such an improvisation to be a speculative and non-christological Spirit theology.[7]

Rosato's second and related "improvisation" centres upon his view that the Holy Spirit plays an inadequate part in Barth's theology of Christ and the Church;[8] that, because of its dominant transcendental overtones, Barth's Christology is incompatible with a "pneumatic understanding of salvation and eschatology":[9]

> "Either the Spirit prepares man's mind for Christ or conforms man's mind to Him. There is little attention paid to the possibility that the Holy Spirit could bring about new salvific events and that His definition as Revealedness and Historicity could be interpreted to mean that the Spirit supplements the revelation of the Word or that the Church, because of the Spirit's presence, can make up what is wanting in Christ."[10]

Thus Rosato envisages the possibility of a conception of the Spirit in which His identity as the Spirit of Christ does not necessitate his working in "an exclusively Christ-centered capacity".[11] As a basis for such a conception of the Spirit Rosato offers his own

---

6) Philip J. Rosato, S.J., op.cit., p.155

7) ibid., p.141

8) ibid., pp.157ff.

9) ibid., p.159

10) ibid., p.163

11) ibid., p.165

outline of a Spirit Christology as an alternative to Barth's "Logos Christology".[12] Barth may tend to subsume the work of the Spirit under the work of Christ but rather than correct that tendency Rosato appears to reverse it to the degree of being in danger of subsuming the person and work of Christ under the person and work of the Spirit.

Rosato is well aware of the pitfalls of his enterprise, that his second improvision is "pursuing a direction which Barth judges to be possible but dangerous",[13] that his thoughts may represent precisely that form of speculation that Barth so purposefully avoided:[14]

> "Certainly the main lines of the two improvisations sketched in the last part of this study would be judged intellectually hazardous by Barth. By advocating a theology of Spiritus Creator active everywhere in the universe and by affixing to it a theology of Spiritus Redemptor at work in Christ and in His community, one would seem to fragment the Spirit and deprive Him of His essential relationship to the eternal Word. Furthermore, to suggest that man be awarded an ontic part in the salvific mission of the Holy Spirit, even beyond those who explicitly confess Jesus Christ as Lord, would be deemed an excessively dangerous concession to an innocuous philosophy of spirit which leaves the very identity of this so-called "Holy" Spirit in question. In a real sense, therefore, the issues raised here place this study in the camp of Barth's rivals: Is this really a theology of the Holy Spirit?"15

---

12) ibid., pp.173ff.

13) ibid., p.159

14) ibid., p.171

15) ibid., p.188

In this sense Rosato is his own leading critic yet he feels compelled to such revision for pastoral as well as dogmatic reasons:

> "The cultural and religious climate in which Barth fashioned his christology and pneumatology was considerably different from that prevailing at this writing. Though on the one hand the forces opposed to transcendent faith may have increased, so that the theologian is constantly constructing his thought with an eye to the practical atheism even within the Church, on the other the rise of biblical fundamentalism, the widespread existence of lively charismatic groups and the growing socio-political consciousness of many leading believers compel the theologian to develop a christology which is both apologetical in tone, pneumatic in character and socio-political in intent. Thus the advantages of a charismatic and liberational christology are not purely academic but predominantly pastoral."16

The inherent problems of any attempted theology of the Spirit are simply that it is an attempted theology of the Spirit. Just as the problems of any attempted theology of the Son or of the Father are that it is an attempted theology of the Son or of the Father. No valid Christian theology can be constructed from the perspective of the third article of the creed any more than from the perspective of the second article of the creed. The Spirit is always and only the Spirit of the Father and the Son; only thus is He the Spirit:

> ὅταν δὲ ἔλθῃ ἐκεῖνος, τὸ πνεῦμα τῆς ἀληθείας, ὁδηγήσει ὑμᾶς ἐν τῇ ἀληθείᾳ πάσῃ· οὐ γαρ λαλήσει ἀφ' ἑαυτοῦ, ἀλλ' ὅσα ἀκούσει λαλήσει, καὶ τὰ ἐρχόμενα ἀναγγελεῖ ὑμῖν. ἐκεῖνος ἐμὲ δοξάσει, ὅτι ἐκ τοῦ ἐμοῦ λήμψεται καὶ ἀναγγελεῖ ὑμῖν. πάντα ὅσα ἔχει ὁ πατὴρ ἐμά ἐστιν· διὰ τοῦτο εἶπον ὅτι ἐκ τοῦ ἐμοῦ λαμβάνει καὶ ἀναγγελεῖ ὑμῖν. 17

---

16) ibid., pp.177f.

17) John ch. 16 vv. 13-14.

In this sense Rosato's thesis is no more but also no less misconceived than those that comprehend Barth's theology as a form of Christomonism. It is at least to Rosato's credit that he admits this:

> "A Christian theology that is worthy of its name must be neither christomonistic or anthropomonistic, nor must it be either totally objective or totally subjective; it must contain both a christology and a pneumatology, or, as the structure and content of the Church Dogmatics suggests, a pneumatology which is rooted in Jesus Christ and a christology which is fulfilled by the Holy Spirit."18

More than once Rosato refers to Barth's 'Nachwort' to the Schleiermacher - Auswahl. The closing paragraph begins with advice which all would do well to heed:

> "But do not let any talented young man - who is of the opinion that he is called for the purpose - immediately rush across the street and into the market with a superficially written booklet 'On the Theology of the Holy Spirit' or anything like that. And how my beautiful dream would have been misunderstood if someone thought that it was only a matter of repeating once again 'the same thing now with man as the starting point.'"19

Any approach to theology from the perspective of the third article of the creed will inevitably produce distortion and particularly will be in danger of propounding Anthropology dressed up in pneumatological clothes. But to fail to allow a proper Pneumatology to develop within the framework of a thoroughly

---

18) Philip J. Rosato, S.J., op.cit., p.127

19) Karl Barth, 'Nachwort', Schleiermacher - Auswahl mit einem Nachwort von Karl Barth (München und Hamburg, 1968), pp.290-312 (p.312)

Trinitarian theology will produce a distortion which, while it may be more popularly acceptable simply because it is more common (at least within the Reformed tradition), is just as serious and dangerous. It is the suspicion that Barth may be guilty of such a 'failure' that gives rise to the unease of so many of his critics[20] but Rosato's "improvisations" are unlikely to go very far in relieving that unease; what is needed is not "improvisation".

The present requirement is to do the work of theology 'after' Barth; neither ignoring him nor mindlessly repeating him but moving beyond him, with particular attention to any discernable weakness in his account, to address our present context. This present context may inform the manner in which the work of theology is done, its emphases, and perhaps even its priorities; but this context does not have the authority to affect the object and the content of that work. The task of theology in this context, just as also in the context within which Barth worked, is to attempt to speak with clarity of its proper object, the living and gracious God who confronts us in the actuality of the event of election.

Theology 'after' Barth must continue to speak unequivocally of God as the electing God, taking its rationality from the actuality of the event of His Word. In particular theology 'after' Barth

---

20) cf. pp.303f. of this thesis

must speak of election as the dynamic event of God's eternity; before all time but in all time, not 'left behind' by time; actualized in Jesus Christ but also noetically realized, and therefore authentically ontically realized, in the power of the Holy Spirit. In this latter respect theology 'after' Barth must attempt to speak with even greater clarity than Barth himself, without ambiguity or reticence but with humble confidence in its method and Triune structure.

But in dispensing with Barth's reticence theology 'after' Barth ought not to dispense with Barth's caution lest it embrace a doctrine of the Spirit that is not a doctrine of <u>the</u> Spirit, a Pneumatology that can be expressed other than in terms of the relatedness of God's Triunity, other than in terms of the constancy of God's authentic temporality, other than in terms of the event of election which according to its actuality is the only true will and being and Word of God. The alternative is for the work of theology not to be effectively 'after' Barth at all but to undertake its task as if he had never existed or spoken. The alternative is for theology to continue to speak of God independently of the event in which He is actually known, to 'speak of man in exalted tones' under the delusion that it is speaking of God. The alternative is for theology not to be authentically theology at all.

Bibliography

a) Works by Karl Barth

The Epistle to the Romans, translated from the sixth edition by Edwyn C. Hoskyns (Oxford, 1933).

The Resurrection of the Dead, trans. by H. J. Stenning (London, 1933).

Church Dogmatics, vols. I - IV, Eng. trans. eds. G. W. Bromiley and T. F. Torrance (Edinburgh, 1956-1975).

'Evangelical Theology in the 19th Century' in God, Grace and Gospel, trans. by J. S. McNab, Scottish Journal of Theology Occasional Papers, No. 8, ed. T. F. Torrance and J. K. S. Reid (Edinburgh and London, 1959), pp. 55-74.

Anselm: Fides Quaerens Intellectum: Anselm's Proof of the Existence of God in the Context of his Theological Scheme, trans. by Ian W. Robertson (London, 1960).

The Humanity of God, trans. by John Newton Thomas and Thomas Wieser (London and Glasgow, 1961).

'Rudolf Bultmann—An Attempt to Understand Him' in Kerygma and Myth: A Theological Debate, vol. II, ed. H. W. Bartsch, trans. by R. H. Fuller (London, 1962), pp.83-132.

Evangelical Theology: An Introduction, trans. by Grover Foley (London and Glasgow, 1963).

Karl Barth's Table Talk, recorded and edited by John D. Godsey, Scottish Journal of Theology Occasional Papers, No. 10, (Edinburgh and London, 1963).

'Nachwort' in Schleiermacher - Auswahl mit einem Nachwort von Karl Barth, ed. Heinz Bolli (München u. Hamburg, 1968), pp.290-312.

Protestant Theology in the Nineteenth Century: Its Background and History, trans. by Brian Cozens and John Bowden (London, 1972).

Gesamtausgabe V: Briefe 1961-1968, ed. by Jürgen Fangmeier u. Hinrich Stoevesandt (Zürich, 1975).

Ethics, ed. Dietrich Braun, trans. by Geoffrey W. Bromiley (Edinburgh, 1981).

b) Works by other authors

P. C. Almond, 'Karl Barth and Anthropocentric Theology', S.J.T., 31 (1978), 435-447.

Ray Sherman Anderson, Historical Transcendence and the Reality of God: A Christological Critique (London, 1975).

Hans Urs von Balthasar, Karl Barth: Darstellung und Deutung seiner Theologie (Köln, 1951).

R. Bauckham, 'Moltmann's Eschatology of the Cross', S.J.T., 30 (1977), 301-311.

G. C. Berkouwer, The Triumph of Grace in the Theology of Karl Barth, trans. by Harry R. Boer (Grand Rapids, 1956).

J. D. Bettis, 'Is Karl Barth a Universalist?', S.J.T., 20 (1967), 423-436.

H. Bouillard, Karl Barth. vol.I: Genèse et évolution de la théologie dialectique; vols.II & III: Parole de Dieu et existence humaine, (Paris, 1957).

A. Brandenburg, 'Der Zeit- und Geschichtsbegriff bei Karl Barth', Theologie und Glaube, 45 (1955), 357-378.

G. W. Bromiley, 'Karl Barth' in Creative Minds in Contemporary Theology, ed. P. E. Hughes (Grand Rapids, 1966), pp.27-62.

G. W. Bromiley, An Introduction to the Theology of Karl Barth (Edinburgh, 1979).

Colin Brown, Karl Barth and the Christian Message (London, 1967).

Robert F. Brown, 'On God's Ontic and Noetic Absoluteness: A critique of Barth', S.J.T., 33 (1980), 533-549.

E. Brunner, The Christian Doctrine of God, Dogmatics vol. I, trans. by Olive Wyon (London, 1949).

Eberhard Busch, Karl Barth: His life from letters and autobiographical texts, trans. by John Bowden (London, 1976).

Eberhard Busch, Karl Barth und die Pietisten: Die Pietismuskritik des jungen Karl Barth und ihre Erwiderung (München, 1978).

Oscar Cullmann, *Christ and Time: The Primitive Christian Conception of Time and History*, trans. by Floyd V. Filson, 3rd edition (London, 1962).

H. Diem, 'Die Christologie Karl Barths in der Sicht von Friedrich Wilhelm Marquardt', *Kerygma und Dogma*, 20 (1974), 138-157.

Lisabeth During, 'Hegel, Barth and the Rationality of the Trinity', *King's Theological Review*, 2 (1979), 69-81.

Grover Foley, 'The Catholic Critics of Karl Barth: in Outline and Analysis', *S.J.T.*, 14 (1961), 136-155.

David F. Ford, 'Biblical Narrative and the Theological Method of Karl Barth in the Church Dogmatics' (dissertation, Cambridge, 1977).

David F. Ford, 'Barth's interpretation of the Bible' in *Karl Barth: Studies of his Theological Method*, ed. S. W. Sykes (Oxford, 1979), pp.55-87.

E. H. Friedmann, *Christologie und Anthropologie: Methode und Bedeutung der Lehre vom Menschen in der Theologie Karl Barths* (Münsterschwarzach, 1972).

Allan D. Galloway, 'The New Hegelians', *Rel. St.*, 8 (1972), 367-371.

Helmut Gollwitzer, *The Existence of God as Confessed by Faith*, trans. by James W. Leitch (London, 1965).

Colin E. Gunton, 'Karl Barth's Doctrine of Election as part of his Doctrine of God', *J.T.S.*, 25 (1974), 381-392.

Colin E. Gunton, *Becoming and Being: The Doctrine of God in Charles Hartshorne and Karl Barth* (Oxford, 1978).

Colin E. Gunton, 'Transcendence, Metaphor, and the Knowability of God', *J.T.S.*, 31 (1980), 501-516.

Colin E. Gunton, *Yesterday and Today: A study of continuities in Christology* (London, 1983).

B. C. Hanson, 'Hope and Participation in Christ: A study in the Theology of Barth and Pannenberg' (dissertation, Princeton, 1970).

Daniel W. Hardy, 'Christian Affirmation and the Structure of Personal Life' in *Belief in Science and in Christian Life: The relevance of Michael Polanyi's thought for Christian Faith and Life*, ed. T. F. Torrance (Edinburgh, 1980), pp.71-90.

Wilfried Härle, Sein und Gnade: Die Ontologie in Karl Barths Kirchlicher Dogmatik (Berlin and New York, 1975).

Herbert Hartwell, The Theology of Karl Barth: An Introduction (London, 1964).

Van A. Harvey, The Historian and the Believer: The Morality of Historical Knowledge and Christian Belief (London, 1967).

George S. Hendry, The Holy Spirit in Christian Theology (London, 1957).

George S. Hendry, 'The Freedom of God in the Theology of Karl Barth', S.J.T., 31 (1978), 229-244.

R. W. Jenson, Alpha and Omega: A study in the Theology of Karl Barth (New York, 1963).

R. W. Jenson, God after God: the God of the Past and the God of the Future, seen in the work of Karl Barth (Indianapolis and New York, 1969).

Brian Johanson, 'Review Article of Karl Barth: Studies of his Theological Method', King's Theological Review, 4 (1981), 37-43.

Eberhard Jüngel, 'Die Möglichkeit theologischer Anthropologie auf dem Grunde der Analogie: Eine Untersuchung zum Analogieverständnis Karl Barths', Evangelische Theologie, 22 (1962), 535-557.

Eberhard Jüngel, 'Karl Barths Lehre von der Taufe', Theologische Studien (1968), 3-55.

Eberhard Jüngel, '...keine Menschenlosigkeit Gottes...: Zur Theologie Karl Barths zwischen Theismus and Atheismus', Evangelische Theologie, 31 (1971), 376-390.

Eberhard Jüngel, 'Die Welt als Möglichkeit und Wirklichkeit: Zum ontologischen Ansatz der Rechtfertigungslehre' in Unterwegs zur Sache: Theologische Bemerkungen, ed. E. Wolf, Beiträge zur evangelischer Theologie, 61 (Munich, 1972), pp.206-233.

Eberhard Jüngel, 'Quae supra nos, nihil ad nos: Eine Kurzformel der Lehre vom verborgenen Gott - im Anschluss an Luther interpretiert', Evangelische Theologie, 32 (1972), 197-240.

Eberhard Jüngel, 'Was ist »das unterscheidend Christliche« ?' in Unterwegs zur Sache: Theologische Bemerkungen, ed. E. Wolf, Beiträge zur evangelischen Theologie, 61 (Munich, 1972), pp.296-299.

Eberhard Jüngel, 'Das Dilemma der natürlichen Theologie und die Wahrheit ihres Problems: Überlegungen für ein Gespräch mit Wolfhart Pannenberg' in Denken im Schatten des Nihilismus: Festschrift für Wilhelm Weischedel zum 70 Geburtstag, ed. A. Schwan (Darmstadt, 1975), pp.419-440.

Eberhard Jüngel, 'Das Verhältnis von »ökonomischer« und »immanenter« Trinität', Zeitschrift für Theologie und Kirche, 72 (1975), 353-364.

Eberhard Jüngel, The Doctrine of the Trinity: God's Being is in Becoming, trans. by Horton Harris, Monograph Supplements to the Scottish Journal of Theology, eds. T. F. Torrance and J. K. S. Reid (Edinburgh and London, 1976).

Eberhard Jüngel, Gott als Geheimnis der Welt: Zur Begründung der Theologie des Gekreuzigten im Streit zwischen Theismus und Atheismus (Tübingen, 1978).

Eberhard Jüngel, Geistesgegenwart: Predigten I/II (München, 1979).

R. T. Kendall, Calvin and English Calvinism to 1649 (Oxford, 1979).

Bertold Klappert, Die Auferweckung des Gekreuzigten: Der Ansatz der Christologie Karl Barths im Zusammenhang der Christologie der Gegenwart (Neukirche, 1971).

Walter Kreck, Die Zukunft des Gekommenen: Grundprobleme der Eschatologie (München, 1961).

Hans Küng, Justification: The Doctrine of Karl Barth and a Catholic Reflection, trans by T. Collins, E. E. Tolk & D. Grandskou (London, 1966).

A. E. McGrath, 'Justification: Barth, Trent and Küng', S.J.T., 34 (1981), 517-529.

John McIntyre, St. Anselm and his critics: a re-interpretation of the Cur Deus Homo (Edinburgh and London, 1954).

John Macquarrie, An Existentialist Theology: A Comparison of Heidegger and Bultmann (London, 1955).

John Macquarrie, Christian Hope (London and Oxford, 1978).

F. W. Marquardt, Theologie und Sozialismus: Das Beispiel Karl Barths (München u. Mainz, 1972).

M. Douglas Meeks, Origins of the Theology of Hope (Philadelphia, 1974).

Hugo Meynell, Grace versus Nature: Studies in Karl Barth's Church Dogmatics (London and Melbourne, 1965).

Jürgen Moltmann, Theology of Hope: On the Ground and the Implications of a Christian Eschatology, trans. by James W. Leitch (London, 1967).

Jürgen Moltmann, The Crucified God: The Cross of Christ as the Foundation and Criticism of Christian Theology, trans. by R. A. Wilson and John Bowden (London, 1974).

Jürgen Moltmann, The Church in the Power of the Spirit: A Contribution to Messianic Ecclesiology, trans. by Margaret Kohl (London, 1977).

Jürgen Moltmann, The Trinity and the Kingdom of God: The Doctrine of God, trans. by Margaret Kohl (London, 1981).

S. M. Ogden, The Reality of God and other essays (London, 1967).

Colm O'Grady, The Church in the Theology of Karl Barth (London, 1968).

H. P. Owen, Concepts of Deity (London, 1971).

Wolfhart Pannenberg, Jesus——God and Man, trans. by Lewis L. Wilkins and Duane A. Priebe (London, 1968).

Wolfhart Pannenberg, 'Time, Eternity, and Judgment' in What is Man? Contemporary Anthropology in Theological Perspective, trans. by D. A. Priebe (Philadelphia, 1970), pp.68-81.

Wolfhart Pannenberg, 'Redemptive Event and History' in Basic Questions in Theology, vol.1, trans. by George H. Kehm (London, 1970), pp.15-80.

Wolfhart Pannenberg, 'Insight and Faith' in Basic Questions in Theology, vol.2, trans. by George H. Kehm (London, 1971), pp.28-45.

Wolfhart Pannenberg, 'What is Truth?' in Basic Questions in Theology, vol.2, trans. by George H. Kehm (London, 1971), pp. 1-27.

Wolfhart Pannenberg, The Apostles' Creed: In the Light of Today's Questions, trans. by Margaret Kohl (London, 1972).

Wolfhart Pannenberg, Theology and the Kingdom of God, Eng. trans. ed. R. J. Neuhaus (Philadelphia, 1975).

Karl Rahner, Theological Investigations, vol.IV, trans. by Kevin Smyth (Baltimore and London, 1966).

Richard H. Roberts, 'Eternity and Time in the Theology of Karl Barth: An essay in Dogmatic and Philosophical Theology' (dissertation, Edinburgh, 1975).

Richard H. Roberts, 'Barth's Doctrine of Time: its nature and implications' in Karl Barth: Studies of his Theological Method, ed. S. W. Sykes (Oxford, 1979), pp.88-146.

Philip J. Rosato, S.J., The Spirit as Lord: The Pneumatology of Karl Barth (Edinburgh, 1981).

Wolfhart Schlichting, Biblische Denkform in der Dogmatik: Die Vorbildlichkeit des biblischen Denkens für die Methode der 'Kirchlichen Dogmatik' Karl Barths (Zürich, 1972).

J. L. Scott, 'The Covenant in the Theology of Karl Barth', S.J.T., 17 (1964), 182-198.

Dorothee Sölle, Christ the Representative: An Essay in Theology after the 'Death of God', trans. by David Lewis (London, 1967).

S. W. Sykes, 'Barth on the centre of theology' in Karl Barth: Studies of his Theological Method, ed. S. W. Sykes (Oxford, 1979), pp.17-54.

John Thompson, 'The Humanity of God in the Theology of Karl Barth', S.J.T., 29 (1976), 249-269.

John Thompson, Christ in Perspective: Christological Perspectives in the Theology of Karl Barth (Edinburgh, 1978).

T. F. Torrance, 'Universalism or Election?' S.J.T., 2 (1949), 310-318.

T. F. Torrance, Karl Barth: An Introduction to his Early Theology 1910-1931 (London, 1962).

T. F. Torrance, Space, Time and Incarnation (Oxford, 1969).

T. F. Torrance, Theological Science (Oxford, 1969).

T. F. Torrance, The Ground and Grammar of Theology (Belfast, 1980).

R. D. Williams, 'Barth on the Triune God' in Karl Barth: Studies of his Theological Method, ed. S. W. Sykes (Oxford, 1979), pp.147-193.

Arthur S. Yates, The Doctrine of Assurance: with special reference to John Wesley (London, 1952).

H. Zahrnt, The Question of God: Protestant Theology in the Twentieth Century, trans. by R. A. Wilson (London, 1969).

Index